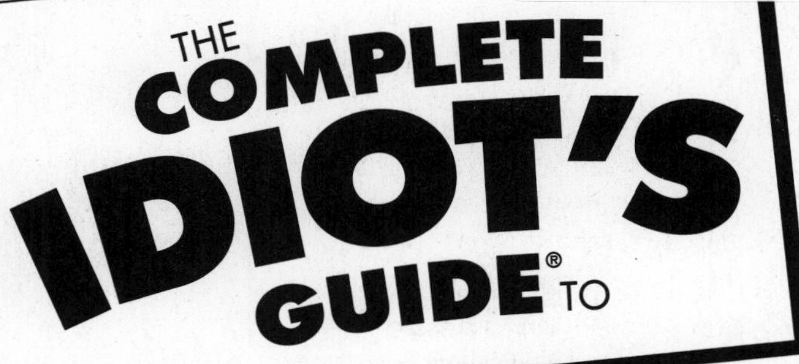

Robert's Rules

Second Edition

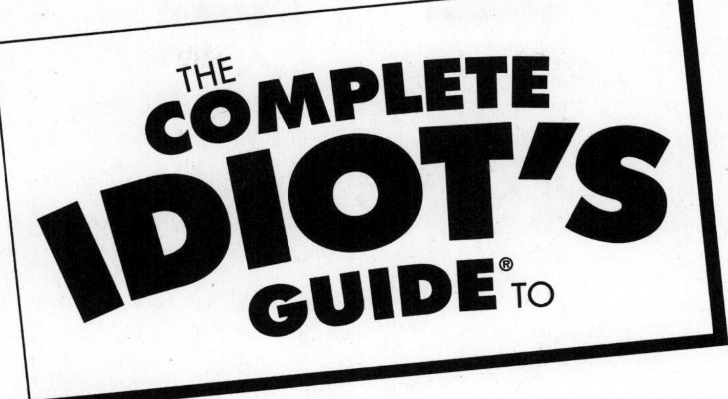

Robert's Rules

Second Edition

by Nancy Sylvester, PRP, CPP-T

A member of Penguin Group (USA) Inc.

ALPHA BOOKS

Published by the Penguin Group

Penguin Group (USA) Inc., 375 Hudson Street, New York, New York 10014, USA

Penguin Group (Canada), 90 Eglinton Avenue East, Suite 700, Toronto, Ontario M4P 2Y3, Canada (a division of Pearson Penguin Canada Inc.)

Penguin Books Ltd., 80 Strand, London WC2R 0RL, England

Penguin Ireland, 25 St. Stephen's Green, Dublin 2, Ireland (a division of Penguin Books Ltd.)

Penguin Group (Australia), 250 Camberwell Road, Camberwell, Victoria 3124, Australia (a division of Pearson Australia Group Pty. Ltd.)

Penguin Books India Pvt. Ltd., 11 Community Centre, Panchsheel Park, New Delhi—110 017, India

Penguin Group (NZ), 67 Apollo Drive, Rosedale, North Shore, Auckland 1311, New Zealand (a division of Pearson New Zealand Ltd.)

Penguin Books (South Africa) (Pty.) Ltd., 24 Sturdee Avenue, Rosebank, Johannesburg 2196, South Africa

Penguin Books Ltd., Registered Offices: 80 Strand, London WC2R 0RL, England

International Standard Book Number: 978-1-61564-034-8
Library of Congress Catalog Card Number: 2009943483

12 11 10 8 7 6 5 4 3 2 1

Interpretation of the printing code: The rightmost number of the first series of numbers is the year of the book's printing; the rightmost number of the second series of numbers is the number of the book's printing. For example, a printing code of 10-1 shows that the first printing occurred in 2010.

Printed in the United States of America

Publisher: *Marie Butler-Knight*
Associate Publisher: *Mike Sanders*
Senior Managing Editor: *Billy Fields*
Executive Editor: *Randy Ladenheim-Gil*
Acquisitions Editor: *Karyn Gerhard*
Development Editor: *Michael Thomas*
Production Editor: *Kayla Dugger*
Copy Editor: *Amy Lepore*
Cover Designer: *Kurt Owens*
Book Designer: *Trina Wurst*
Indexer: *Celia McCoy*
Layout: *Ayanna Lacey*
Proofreader: *John Etchison*

To my family, Jim, Marcy, and Holly, my greatest supporters; my parents, Marge and Leonard Jochim, for raising me in a family in which rules were honored; and my clients, for all you taught me.

Contents at a Glance

Appendixes

Contents

Foreword

Congratulations on your purchase of this book. You've already shown one thing—you're no idiot! *The Complete Idiot's Guide to Robert's Rules, Second Edition*, is the most comprehensive guide available on meeting procedures, running effective meetings, and the world of parliamentarians.

The start of my own interest in parliamentary procedure may sound familiar. Some 20 years ago, I attended a meeting where an important proposal was being considered. I decided to say something and went to a microphone. Before I was called on, another member made a motion, it was seconded, there was a vote, and the whole matter was resolved—all before I had a chance to speak! At that instant, I decided to learn enough about meeting procedure so that would never happen again.

Unfortunately, as I tried to learn about parliamentary procedure, there wasn't a lot to help me. There were rulebooks, like *Robert's Rules of Order*, but most of these were overwhelming. There were books on organizing meetings, but most of these didn't even mention parliamentary procedure or how to make proposals and express views in a meeting. I don't recall *any* book that listed parliamentary organizations or where to go for further study.

Oh, how *The Complete Idiot's Guide to Robert's Rules, Second Edition*, could have helped! This book has it all. You'll find information on parliamentary authorities (like *Robert's Rules*), tips for planning and running effective meetings, differences between board meetings and other kinds of meetings, listings of parliamentary organizations, and much more. If you need it, it's in here.

To get started, just jump right in. Sure, the best idea is to read this book from start to finish, but you might not have that much time before your meeting. Whether you're pretty sure of yourself or a novice, start with Chapter 1, Chapter 2, and Chapter 4. Then, if you're new to parliamentary procedure, you may want to read Part 2. On the other hand, if you will soon have to run a meeting yourself, you may want to jump to Chapter 15 and Chapter 16. Wherever you start, you'll learn valuable tips about effective meetings.

Best of luck as you start your *Robert's Rules* journey. You're likely to find that knowing meeting procedure makes a big difference. Those who know the rules can get their ideas across and often quickly assume leadership positions. If you're already in a leadership role, proper procedure can help turn long, confrontational meetings into short, painless ones. As a result, you should make every effort to learn the essentials of this guide.

Time to get started! As Henry M. Robert (yes, *the* Robert of *Robert's Rules*) once stated:

> It is difficult to find another branch of knowledge where a small amount of study produces such great results in increased efficiency in a country where the people rule, as in parliamentary law.

I couldn't have said it better!

—Jim Slaughter

Jim Slaughter is the most active parliamentary consultant in the country. He is a practicing attorney, Certified Professional Parliamentarian-Teacher, and Professional Registered Parliamentarian. Jim has served as Parliamentarian to hundreds of national and state conventions, including many of the largest trade and professional associations in the country. His articles on procedure have been published in many magazines, including the *American Bar Association Journal*, CAI's *Common Ground*, and ASAE's *Association Management*.

Introduction

Parliamentary procedure is all about helping people run meetings efficiently, effectively, and fairly. It's important stuff for any group that wants to make sure it doesn't violate the rights of its members and that wants to get its business done as quickly and efficiently as possible.

People often mistakenly view parliamentary procedure only as a set of rules. When looked at this way, I can understand why people approach the subject with dread—for those rulebooks are capable of curing the most severe cases of insomnia! But parliamentary procedure is so much more than a set of rules. It is a process for conducting business.

The approach I have taken in this book is to explain that process and the foundation upon which the rules are based. Then, when you find yourself without this book and you need to decide the proper way to handle the situation, you can fall back on that understanding of the process instead of trying to recall some long-forgotten rule.

My goal in writing this book was to take this very technical subject and explain it in plain English so that, at your next meeting, you'll understand what's going on, what you can do, and what you can't do. To that end, I've divided this book into five parts.

You've probably heard the term "parliamentary procedure" before, but do you really know what it's all about? In **Part 1, "What's Parliamentary Procedure All About?"** I'll fill in the background information on this subject. It will help you understand the concepts that *Robert's Rules* are based on so that you can use your judgment instead of memorizing rules.

Motions introduce business to meetings; without them, parliamentary procedure would be meaningless. **Part 2, "Let's Get Moving: The Motion-Making Process,"** will help you move, debate, and vote on motions efficiently and fairly. It is a process that is best understood when broken down into the six easy-to-understand steps.

In **Part 3, "Motions for (Almost) Any Occasion,"** I explain approximately 25 motions. Motions are the heart of parliamentary procedure. They are the process by which a group makes a decision. You need to know about and understand these motions in order to effectively use parliamentary procedure.

Part 4, "Let's Get to Order," helps you prepare for your meeting, say the right things during the meeting, and make sure you handle those all-important elections properly. The information in this part is for all members of the group, but leaders will really love it.

In **Part 5, "Officers, Committees, and Meetings,"** you'll learn all about minutes and hopefully find that they are much easier to prepare than you thought. You will also learn about the responsibilities of officers and committees and the purposes of their respective reports. In addition, you'll find a chapter devoted to conventions and their unique requirements and another chapter introducing you to using parliamentary procedure to run electronic meetings.

The greatest change from the first edition of this book is the appendixes. Since parliamentary procedure has its own language, I have prepared an extensive glossary, Appendix A, for your quick reference. Appendix B is a quick-glance guide to motions. If you have this in front of you at each meeting, you can find the answer to the vast majority of your questions. In Appendix C, you will find a main motion script and a board meeting agenda and script. A script is a guide to what to say when processing a motion, and you will find one for most of the motions in this book on my website, www.nancysylvester.com. I encourage you to print them out and use them during your meetings. Appendix D is full of help on minutes and forms that are included in the minutes, including the steps in preparing and a sample tellers' report. Minutes are not as difficult to do as most people believe, and hopefully this appendix convinces you of that. You will find a tremendous amount of support information for the preceding information and the rest of the book on my website at www.nancysylvester.com.

Sidebars

You'll find the following sidebars scattered throughout the book:

Gavel Gaffes

Follow these warnings to avoid making parliamentary blunders.

Point of Information

In these boxes, I expand on key parliamentary points.

Parliamentary Pearls

These parliamentary tips will help you implement *Robert's Rules.*

def•i•ni•tion

Here you'll find easy-to-understand definitions for those technical terms that plague parliamentary procedure.

Acknowledgments

A special thank you goes to my family: Jim, Marcy, and Holly. They have been incredibly supportive during the time of the writing of this book and throughout my entire career. They have not only allowed me to get lost in writing for days at a time, but each of them has taken on a different yet very active role in helping me prepare this book. Jim, my husband, read each chapter to give me the perspective of a nonparliamentary person reading the book. According to him, he played the role of the token idiot. Jim's favorite statement about *Robert's* is that the rulebook is the greatest cure for insomnia. The good news is that he stayed awake while reading this book. My daughters, Marcy and Holly, each contributed—Marcy's wit and Holly's attention to detail were appreciated. For this second edition, Holly deserves a very special thank you.

Thank you to Dr. Otis J. Aggertt, my college parliamentary procedure professor who got me hooked, and all of the parliamentarians I have had the pleasure to learn from. This book is payback because now I can pass that wonderful knowledge on to others. I also appreciate all of my clients who have helped me learn more about parliamentary procedure than even I sometimes wanted.

Special Thanks to the Technical Reviewer

The Complete Idiot's Guide to Robert's Rules was reviewed by a fellow expert who double-checked the accuracy of what you'll learn here, to help us ensure that this book gives you everything you need to know about the rules of parliamentary procedure. Special thanks are extended to Jim Slaughter, J.D., CPP-T, PRP.

Trademarks

All terms mentioned in this book that are known to be or are suspected of being trademarks or service marks have been appropriately capitalized. Alpha Books and Penguin Group (USA) Inc. cannot attest to the accuracy of this information. Use of a term in this book should not be regarded as affecting the validity of any trademark or service mark.

Part 1

What's Parliamentary Procedure All About?

I like to call parliamentary procedure the rules of the road for meetings. When driving, you need to know whether you can turn right on red, who goes first at a four-way stop, and how fast you can go. In a meeting, you need to know when you can introduce an item of business, who gets to speak first on the issue, and how long each person can speak on it.

This first part is designed to give you an overview of parliamentary procedure. You will finally get an answer to those questions you've been wondering about for a long time: What *is* parliamentary procedure? Who is this Robert guy? And why do I need to follow his rules?

Chapter 1

Robert's Rules 101

In This Chapter

- Parliamentary procedure, defined
- Other parliamentary authorities besides *Robert's*
- How *Robert's Rules* have changed
- Why *Robert's* still rules

Imagine the following scenario: As an active member of your community, you attend a meeting about an issue that is important to you. During the discussion, you want to make a point, but you have no idea how to phrase it or even when it's acceptable to speak up. You try once but are ruled out of order by the chair! Embarrassed, you sit quietly during the rest of the meeting and never share your idea with the rest of the group.

Sound familiar? Unfortunately, a lot of people are scared off by parliamentary procedure when in reality it's meant to allow all members to participate fairly and equally.

So What Is Parliamentary Procedure?

Parliamentary procedure is a system of conducting business when working in a group. (That group is sometimes called a *deliberative assembly.*) Simply stated, it's an organized system that allows a group of people to come together and make a decision. The system is made up of basic principles and rules that determine how the group will proceed through the decision-making process.

def•i•ni•tion

A **deliberative assembly** is a group of people meeting to openly discuss issues and make decisions that then become the decision of the group.

Parliamentary procedure is about helping the group come to a decision; it is not about helping any one individual get his or her way, and it is certainly not intended to prevent members from participating in the group.

Parliamentary procedure also helps the group stay focused on a single issue until the members resolve it. This technique helps groups make better, more logical decisions; they have the advantage of many minds working together using a systematic approach to problem solving.

In many respects, parliamentary procedure is the "rules of the road" for meetings, but I hope you will see that it's not simply a set of rules. Rather, you should think of it as a set of guidelines by which to conduct meetings.

Getting Down to Basics

The following are the foundational concepts upon which parliamentary procedure is based:

- **One thing at a time.** Only one main motion is allowed on the floor at a time, but there is a system to put that motion aside if something more urgent comes up.
- **One person, too.** Only one person may talk at a time.
- **Only one time per meeting.** The same motion, or practically the same motion, cannot be made more than once per session. (The only exception is if a member changes his or her mind.)

- **Enough of us have to be here to decide.** The group determines the minimum number of people (called a quorum) that must be present to make a decision for the whole group.
- **Protected even if absent.** The rights of the members who are absent are protected.
- **Vote requirements are based on members' rights.** The determination of what kind of vote is needed (such as majority, two-thirds, and so on) is based on members' rights. If an action gives rights to the members, it requires a majority vote to pass. If an action takes away rights from members, it requires a two-thirds vote to pass.
- **Silence = consent.** If a member chooses to abstain from voting, that member is giving his or her consent to the decision made by the group.
- **Everybody is equal.** All voting members have equal rights. The majority rules, but the minority has the right to be heard and to attempt to change the minds of the majority.

Make the Rules Meet Your Needs!

Because each group is different, parliamentary procedure is designed to be the basis for the rules, which groups can then adapt to their own needs. So in a deliberative assembly, you have the rules that are determined by your parliamentary authority, and you have the rules that are determined by your particular organization (bylaws, special rules, and so on, which I discuss in Chapter 4).

Other Parliamentary Authorities

What do I mean by parliamentary authority? Parliamentary authority is the set of rules that a group adopts as the rules that will govern it. Although this book is about *Robert's Rules of Order*, it is only one, albeit the most popular, parliamentary authority that a deliberative assembly might choose to use. Other parliamentary authorities include the following.

Parliamentary Pearls

You can find the parliamentary authority for your organization in your bylaws. If the bylaws are written following the format prescribed in *Robert's*, you will find an article titled "Parliamentary Authority." That article should be one of the last articles in the bylaws.

- *The Standard Code of Parliamentary Procedure*, originally by Alice Sturgis, is in its fourth edition. The author's aim was to write a concise book based on common sense and parliamentary principles. She got away from the more technical language used in *Robert's*. Sturgis is most popular in the medical profession. Alice Sturgis is dead, and the American Institute of Parliamentarians authored the current edition.
- *Demeter's Manual of Parliamentary Law and Procedure*, by George Demeter, was first published in 1948 and has been revised a few times. The differences between *Demeter's* and *Robert's* are very minor. *Demeter's* is usually considered to be more user-friendly than *Robert's*.

Gavel Gaffes

Don't let people tell you that *Robert's Rules* is outdated and therefore not needed anymore! Although following correct parliamentary procedure might seem outmoded and overly fussy in today's informal, fast-paced world, it's actually more crucial now than ever. As long as large groups make decisions, we will need parliamentary procedure.

- *Mason's Manual of Legislative Procedure* is used by more than half of all legislative bodies. It was written by Paul Mason and was first published in 1935. The latest revision in 2000 was written by the National Conference of State Legislatures.
- *Cannon's Concise Guide to Rules of Order*, by Hugh Cannon, was published in 1992. Although not used as a parliamentary authority per se, this book is frequently looked to by presiding officers to help simplify *Robert's*.

While these other parliamentary authorities have gained a small following, *Robert's* still rules when it comes to parliamentary procedure.

Robert's Revisions

When people refer to *Robert's Rules*, they are referring to a lot of different books. Since the first edition came out in February 1876, nine subsequent editions—many of them with substantial revisions—have been published. Here's a list of all of the revisions, their dates, and the key changes:

- **First edition, February 1876.** The complete title of this first book was *Pocket Manual of Rules of Order for Deliberative Assemblies.* Author Henry M. Robert had 4,000 copies printed, thinking that would last for at least two years. However, he sold all 4,000 copies in six months!
- **Second edition, July 1876.** Robert added a few pages and quickly got out the second edition because of the surprising success of the book.

Point of Information

Henry Martyn Robert (1837–1923) was a general in the United States Army. Robert began researching the subject of parliamentary procedure after he was elected chairman of a group. There were only a few technical books available on the topic, and he soon became frustrated with the lack of information available. Making matters worse, the books that were available contained conflicting information.

- **Third edition, 1893.** Robert's plan from the very beginning was to get the first book out to the public, receive feedback on it, and once the printing plates were worn out, revise the book, taking the feedback into consideration. The 1893 edition was that revision.
- **Fourth edition, 1915.** Robert himself best explained this edition when he wrote, "The constant inquiries from all sections of the country for information … that is not contained in *Rules of Order* seems to demand a revision and an enlargement of the manual. To meet this want, the work has been thoroughly revised and enlarged, and to avoid confusion with the old *Rules*, is published under the title of *Robert's Rules of Order Revised.*"

- **Fifth edition, 1943.** Henry M. Robert died in 1923, and the 1943 edition of *Robert's Rules of Order Revised* was based on notes that he wrote before his death.
- **Sixth edition, 1951.** This was published as the Seventy-fifth Anniversary Edition.
- **Seventh edition, 1970.** This 594-page revision almost doubled the size of the previous edition and was the first edition with the title *Robert's Rules of Order Newly Revised.* The principles were the same, but in addition to rules it included many examples and explanations of the rules. This revision was written by Sarah Corbin Robert, the wife of Henry's only son, Henry M. Robert Jr., with the assistance of Henry M. Robert III, James W. Cleary, and William J. Evans.
- **Eighth edition, 1981.** The changes in this edition were so minor that they were able to make them within the same pages, sometimes referred to as an in-pagination revision. So if you find something on page 365 of the seventh edition, it will be on page 365 of the eighth edition.
- **Ninth edition, 1990.** *Robert's Rules of Order Newly Revised*, 1990, was a whopping 706 pages long. The authors of this edition made many changes and enhancements, which were described in the preface to the book.
- **Tenth edition, 2000.** This edition (written by Henry M. Robert III, William J. Evans, Daniel H. Honemann, and Thomas J. Balch) maintained the basic rules but clarified and updated them. The specific changes and clarifications were listed in the preface to the book.
- **Eleventh edition, announced for Fall 2011.** This edition will again maintain the basic rules but further clarify and update them. The specific changes and clarifications will be listed on my website (www.nancysylvester.com) as soon as they are available.

Parliamentary Pearls

The object of *Rules of Order* is to assist an assembly to accomplish in the best possible manner the work for which it was designed. To do this it is necessary to restrain the individual somewhat, as the right of an individual, in any community, to do what he pleases, is incompatible with the interests of the whole. Where there is no law, but every man does what is right in his own eyes, there is the least of real liberty.

—Words of wisdom from Henry M. Robert, December 1875

Everybody Loves *Robert's*

Robert did not set out to be the leading authority in parliamentary procedure. He simply envisioned a need for a set of rules that were consistently followed everywhere. That was the beginning of what is today the most recognized authority on parliamentary procedure.

More than five million copies of *Robert's*, in its various editions, have been sold. While it is impossible to verify exactly, approximately 90 percent of the organizations in the United States that follow parliamentary procedure use some form of *Robert's* as their parliamentary authority. Sturgis is the second most popular parliamentary authority, and the other authorities have been adopted by only a small number of organizations.

Because it has been distributed so widely and used by so many people and groups, if you understand *Robert's*, you understand parliamentary procedure.

The Least You Need to Know

- Parliamentary procedure is a system of conducting business when working in a group.
- Parliamentary procedure helps to ensure that the rights of individuals are protected while the will of the group is achieved.
- *Robert's* has undergone many revisions since it was first published in 1876. It is currently in its tenth edition, with an eleventh on its way.
- Other books on parliamentary procedure have been written, but none has surpassed *Robert's* in popularity.

Chapter 2

What *Robert's Rules* Can Do for You and Your Meeting

In This Chapter

- Shorten your meetings
- Protect the minority voice
- Avoid getting sued (or at least from losing if you do get sued!)
- The importance of a quorum
- Kinds of meetings and acceptable levels of formality
- Revised rules for small meetings

Imagine playing a baseball game in which the umpire makes random calls. Or imagine driving in a country where there are no rules of the road. Both situations would result in instant chaos!

The same is true for meetings. Almost any group activity—and meetings fall into this category—must follow a set of rules and guidelines to be successful.

When you walk into a meeting and you know and understand the rules, you are empowered to participate actively. In this chapter, we examine what knowing the rules can do for you and your organization and how you can adapt them to various kinds of meetings.

How *Robert's* Helps You Manage Your Meeting

Whether your group's meetings regularly have 5 or 5,000 attendees, you can hold an orderly meeting. To do so, however, requires adopting parliamentary procedure. Parliamentary procedure gives meetings structure, which aids in meeting management.

Point of Information

The main purposes of parliamentary procedure are …

- To expedite business.
- To ensure legality.
- To protect the rights of the minority.

Keep It Short and Sweet

I've never met anyone who wished that meetings lasted longer. One of the greatest advantages of parliamentary procedure is that, if it is followed properly, it makes for shorter meetings. Over the years, I have observed large groups following parliamentary procedure make major decisions in a relatively short period of time. I have also witnessed smaller groups, not using any formal procedure, take a half a day to make a minor decision.

Gavel Gaffes

Just saying that you are following parliamentary procedure doesn't shorten the meeting. It is the discipline of actually following the procedures that makes the meetings shorter.

As you read the later chapters on processing a motion (Chapters 5 through 9), you will encounter many tools that you can use to keep the meeting short and to the point. For instance, *Robert's* limits the length (10 minutes) and number of times (2) that each member can comment on an issue. In addition, it limits discussion to the specific motion that is on the floor. When people are forced to focus their remarks, it is amazing how much time everyone saves!

Preserve the Rights of the Minority

Although the majority rules in parliamentary procedure, the rights of the minority are protected. For instance, everyone is given the same amount of time to speak on an issue, and the rules strictly prohibit making personal verbal attacks.

It's important to protect the rights of the minority because often the minority point of view, over time and with proper discussion, becomes the majority point of view. This is particularly true when it comes to social issues. For example, when I was a college student, no one ever even thought about the dangers of drinking and driving, and the people who pushed for stricter drinking and driving laws were clearly in the minority. Today, few people oppose strict drinking and driving laws. The minority point of view has turned into the majority point of view.

Gavel Gaffes

Lawsuits over improper use of parliamentary procedures have involved not giving proper notice, improper calling of adjourned meetings, violating a member's right to speak or vote, failing to establish or maintain a quorum, using an improper method of nomination, and on and on.

Defend Yourself Against Lawsuits

As I'm sure you know, we live in a litigious society. People file lawsuits all the time and over almost anything imaginable. (Remember the lady who sued McDonald's because her coffee was too hot?) Just as you can get into legal trouble for not following the rules of the road while driving, you can get into legal trouble for not following the governing documents when you are meeting as a member of a group. The governing documents serve as a contract between and among the members. You can even be 100 percent right and still get slapped with a lawsuit that costs you precious time and money, so it's important that you protect yourself by following the rules that your organization adopts.

There Must Be a Quorum

Since parliamentary procedure is based on each group deciding its own rules, it is the group itself (or a higher authority governing the group, such as the national organization) that decides how many members are necessary to come together to make a decision on behalf of the entire group. In the parliamentary world, we call that number a *quorum.*

> **def•i•ni•tion**
>
> A **quorum** is the number of voting members who must be present in order for business to be legally transacted.

Once a quorum has made a decision, the whole group should accept this decision.

Quorum = Majority

The most frequent quorum requirement is a majority of the members. If your bylaws don't specify how many members constitute a quorum, the quorum is a majority of the entire membership. However, your group can choose any number it wants as the quorum number.

Be careful not to set the quorum number too low. If, for example, you have an organization of 100 members and your quorum is 20 percent, 20 people constitute a quorum. Do you really want 20 people deciding issues on behalf of the entire group? That means that 11 people—a majority of the 20—can commit the organization of 100 people to an action.

Count the Warm Bodies

To determine whether a quorum is present, you count the number of voting members in attendance, not the number of members who vote. In other words, members who choose not to vote on an issue are still counted in the quorum.

For example, let's say that your organization has a membership of 100 and the bylaws indicate the quorum is a majority of the membership, which would be 51 members. At a meeting there is a motion, and the vote is 20 yes, 19 no, and 12 abstentions (meaning that the members are present but not voting). Is there a quorum?

Simply adding the number of yes and no votes together gives a total of 39, so if you only counted votes, there is no quorum. But there are also 12 members who are present but who did not vote, bringing the total number of members present to 51. In this case, there is a quorum, and business can be legally transacted. However, if an hour into the meeting two of the members leave, you no longer have a quorum and must stop conducting business unless you have a rule to the contrary.

What You Can Do Without a Quorum

In the absence of a quorum, the group is severely limited in the kinds of actions it can take. Permissible actions are as follows:

- Set the time for another meeting—using the motion to *Fix the Time to Which to Adjourn* (see Chapter 11).
- End the meeting—using the motion to *Adjourn* (see Chapter 11).
- Take a short break—using the motion to *Recess* (see Chapter 11).
- Take measures to obtain a quorum. In other words, go out and beat the bushes to try to find enough members to have a quorum.

Taking Action Without a Quorum

If the group believes that it must take a particular action, even though a quorum is not present, it can do so, but it is not considered to be an action of the group until it is ratified at the next meeting in which a quorum is present.

For instance, let's say that your group can get some unexpected money if you send in a proposal for a grant by Friday. It is Thursday, your regular meeting, and you don't have a quorum. The members who are in attendance are absolutely certain that the rest of the members would think that applying for the grant money is a great idea.

The treasurer reminds the group of how helpful this money would be. The members present see no downside to proceeding, so they vote on a motion to send in the proposal.

Gavel Gaffes

Don't overuse or abuse taking actions without a quorum and then ratifying those actions at the next meeting. Remember, you are taking the action individually until it is ratified by the group with a quorum present! Save such actions for emergency situations.

At your next meeting, a member must make the motion to *Ratify* the action taken at the previous meeting. If that motion passes, you legitimize the action taken at the meeting without a quorum. If not, the individuals attending the previous meeting are responsible for the action taken without a quorum.

Types of Meetings

Robert's defines a meeting as an assembly of members gathered to conduct business during which there is no separation of the members except for a short *Recess.* A session is a meeting or a series of connected meetings, as in a convention.

If your organization meets regularly (for example, monthly, weekly, and so on), the distinction between meeting and session will probably not matter to you. For example, if you meet each month, your February meeting is a meeting that is also a session. But if you attend a convention, which has a series of connected meetings, the distinction will matter. Each of those meetings held at the convention is just that, a meeting. The collection of all of those meetings at a single convention is referred to as a session. Why does it matter? Sometimes the rules depend on whether you're having a meeting or a session.

Robert's distinguishes between several different kinds of meetings, each serving a particular parliamentary purpose:

- **Regular meeting.** A business meeting of a permanent group that is held at regular intervals (weekly, monthly, quarterly, and so on). Each meeting is a separate session. The meetings are held when prescribed in the bylaws or the standing rules or through a motion of the group that is usually adopted at the beginning of the administrative year.

- **Special meeting.** A meeting called at a specific time for a specific purpose. The time, place, and purpose of the meeting must be included in the information sent to all of the members regarding the meeting—referred to as the call of the meeting. Only business that was specified in the call of the meeting can be transacted at the meeting. A group cannot hold a special meeting unless it's authorized in the bylaws. Special meetings are usually held for emergency purposes, things that were not, nor could be, planned for in advance.
- **Annual meeting.** A meeting held yearly, usually for the purpose of electing officers and receiving the annual reports of current officers. The annual meeting is usually specified in the bylaws.
- **Adjourned meeting.** A meeting that is a continuation of a previous meeting. It occurs when the work wasn't completed at a regular or special meeting, and there was a motion to continue the meeting at a different time (called a motion to *Fix the Time to Which to Adjourn*, discussed in Chapter 11). The original meeting and the adjourned meeting make up a single session. Because it is a continuation of a previous meeting, special notice of the meeting doesn't need to be sent out to the membership. The adjourned meeting begins where the meeting it is continuing left off.

Point of Information

An organization's board of directors can be known by several different names, including board of governors, board of managers, executive board, or board of trustees. Whatever they're called, they still need to follow the rules.

- **Mass meeting.** An open meeting of a group of people with a common interest but not formally organized. If you wanted to form a new organization or a local chapter of a national organization, you would begin with a mass meeting. Before that meeting you would send out an announcement to anyone who either meets specific qualifications or has an interest in a particular subject. That formation meeting is an example of a mass meeting.

- **Board of directors meeting.** A meeting of a specified group of members who make decisions on behalf of the organization. The membership, authority, and limitations of this group are specified in the bylaws. Meetings of the board are usually only open to members of the board and the board's invitees.
- **Convention.** An assembly of delegates usually chosen for one session. The participants frequently attend as representatives of a local, state, or regional association. The convention participants come together to make decisions on behalf of the entire organization. Because conventions are unique in several ways, I discuss them in detail in Chapter 21.
- **Committee meeting.** A meeting of a group of members who have been elected or appointed to carry out a task. They have only the power given to them by the body that created them (members, board, president, bylaws).
- **Executive session.** A meeting or a portion of a meeting in which the proceedings are secret and the only attendees are members and invited guests. All or part of any of the other meetings in this list may be held in executive session. Deliberations of an executive session are secret, and all attendees are honor bound to maintain confidentiality. Meetings of boards of directors are usually held in executive session. Some bodies are limited in when they can go into executive session. They are limited by state laws, frequently referred to as the open meetings act or sunshine laws. Those laws only apply to public bodies. Therefore, most nonprofit entities have no requirements regarding when they can go into executive session or what they can discuss or decide in executive session.

Level of *Robert's* to Use

One of the reasons that some people don't like parliamentary procedure is that they think it must be all or nothing—they believe that you have to use all of it or you should ignore it completely.

Even Henry M. Robert recognized that it's important to adapt his rules to meet the needs of the group. Keep in mind, however, that the rules are intended to protect the rights of the members. If your adaptation of the rules infringes upon any members' rights (not just those members who agree with you), the adaptation is unacceptable.

Point of Information

If you are ever in a meeting and can't remember the parliamentary rule that applies, ask yourself the following three questions:

- What is the fairest thing to do in this situation? Be sure to consider what is fairest to all, not just to you.
- What is the most logical answer to this problem? *Robert's* is a very logical system, so the most logical answer is probably the correct one.
- What is the most efficient way of doing this? If you can get there in two steps, don't take three!

Formal vs. Informal

How formal should your meeting be? Only you and your organization can answer that question. You have to look at what you are doing presently and how effective it is.

The size of the group plays a large part in determining how formal it needs to be. As a general rule, the larger the group, the greater the amount of formality there should be. A meeting of 10 committee members can be conducted very casually. (See the next section for revised rules for small meetings.) A meeting of 100 at the same level of informality could be highly ineffective. A meeting of 1,000 at the same level of informality could be an out-and-out disaster.

Gavel Gaffes

Not all meetings should be conducted with the same level of formality. Three things you might consider in determining the level of formality for your group are …

- The size of the group.
- The purpose of the meeting.
- The cost in time and money of the meeting.

The meeting's purpose should also be taken into account when determining how formal or informal to make it. If you are getting together with some committee members simply to discuss an issue, an informal approach might be your best bet. If you have very difficult and controversial issues to resolve, a more formal format might help keep the group focused on the issues.

How much time and money you want to spend are other factors that you should consider when establishing your level of formality. If members live just a few miles apart and get together on a regular basis, informality may be the answer. But if members must travel long distances, must pay for lodging and other travel-related expenses, and have a limited amount of time to spend together, the more formal format would probably be the more time- and money-saving approach.

Parliamentary Pearls

Henry M. Robert gives great advice to the presiding officer about adapting the meeting:

Use your judgment; the assembly may be of such a nature through its ignorance of parliamentary usages and peaceable disposition, that a strict enforcement of the rules, instead of assisting, would greatly hinder business; but in large assemblies, where there is much work to be done, and especially where there is liability to trouble, the only safe course is to require a strict observance of the rules.

No More Than a Dozen: Rules for Small Boards and Committees

Henry M. Robert realized that you need different rules for a board or committee of 5 versus a convention of 5,000. Therefore, he established less stringent rules when there is a meeting of a board or a committee with no more than 12 members present. Those rules include the following:

- It's not necessary to rise in order to make a motion or when seeking recognition by the chair.
- There is no limit on the number of times a person may speak.

- The presiding officer does not have to leave the chair when making a motion or when participating in debate.
- Motions to close or limit debate are not allowed.
- Motions do not need to be seconded.

The following rules apply only to committees:

- A person can *Reconsider* a motion, regardless of when the motion was made.
- Anyone can *Reconsider* a motion who did not vote on the losing side. (A member who was not present can move to *Reconsider*, as can a member who abstained.)
- If the motion to *Reconsider* is made at a later meeting, it requires a two-thirds vote without notice, or a majority vote if all committee members who voted with the prevailing side are present or have been notified.

The Least You Need to Know

- *Robert's* is all about protecting the rights of the minority, ensuring legality, and expediting business.
- Various meetings serve different parliamentary purposes. All of them should follow parliamentary procedure, however.
- It is essential to establish a quorum before any meaningful business is conducted.
- The level of formality you use at your meeting depends on how many people are involved, the purpose of the meeting, and how much time and money is available.
- *Robert's* provides less stringent rules for meetings with 12 or fewer members.

Chapter 3

Who's Who?

In This Chapter

- The power of the bylaws
- The various leadership roles in an organization
- The position of executive director
- Where professional parliamentarians fit in

Leadership is always an important aspect of an organization's success. This chapter reviews each of the leadership positions of an organization. However, it's not the title that gives someone power—a person holding a leadership position only has the power that is given to the position in the bylaws, which are the primary rules governing an organization (for more on bylaws, see Chapter 4).

When you take on a leadership role in your organization, you should always review the governing documents to see what roles, duties, and responsibilities are outlined there. You are responsible for performing those duties, whether or not the person who held the office before you did.

The President: Facilitator, Not Dictator

The roles of the president vary according to the organization and, as with everyone else's duties, should be clearly spelled out in the bylaws. Some of the common duties of the president are as follows:

- Act as the *presiding officer* at all meetings. (See Chapter 16 for tips on presiding at meetings.)
- Serve as the official representative of the organization.
- Report at each meeting and prepare an annual report. (See Chapter 20 for more on reports.)
- Sign documents on behalf of the organization.
- Make position appointments as specified in the bylaws.
- Serve as ex officio member of committees as specified in the bylaws. Ex officio means a person is a member by nature of the office held. (While we're on the topic of ex officio members, it's worth pointing out that many people believe that an ex officio member doesn't have the right to vote. Not so! An ex officio member has all of the rights of membership unless the bylaws say otherwise.)
- Work with the secretary to prepare the agenda for meetings. (See Chapter 15 for information on the agenda.)

def•i•ni•tion

The **presiding officer** is the person—often the president—who is in charge of the meeting. The term is interchangeable with the terms *chair* and *chairman*. (Some organizations opt for the more gender neutral *chairperson*.) When addressing the presiding officer, *Robert's* recommends using the following: Mister Chairman or Madam Chairman.

Most people find that presiding at meetings, including board and general membership meetings, is the most challenging part of the president's job. While presiding, the chair has many responsibilities, some of which include …

- Calling the meeting to order on time.
- Announcing the business before the assembly in the order prescribed in the agenda.

- Determining the presence of a quorum.
- Recognizing members who are entitled to the floor.
- Processing all motions.
- Expediting business.
- Ruling on any points of order (motions made by members when they feel that the rules are not being followed).
- Conducting the meeting in a fair and equitable manner.

Because the president is presiding over the meeting, he or she should maintain an aura of neutrality and refrain from making any motions. In addition, the president should vacate the chair if he or she wishes to debate on any motions. (In Chapter 8, I explain the process for vacating the chair; in Chapter 16, I offer many more tips for presiding at a meeting.)

Parliamentary Pearls

Henry M. Robert gave some wonderful advice to the presiding officer: "Know all about parliamentary law, but do not try to show off your knowledge. Never be technical, or more strict than is absolutely necessary for the good of the meeting."

The President-Elect: Lady/Gentleman in Waiting

Some organizations choose to have an office of the president-elect. When this is the case, the organization doesn't elect a president. Instead the election is for president-elect, who serves one term as president-elect and then automatically becomes president the following term. If the organization has the position of immediate past president, the president automatically becomes immediate past president after his or her term as president is over. Thus, it's possible to have one election for up to three terms, one in each of the three offices.

As with any other position, the office of president-elect does not exist unless it is specified in the bylaws. Organizations' bylaws usually specify that the president-elect is to preside in the absence of the president and to fill a vacancy in the office of president.

The Pros and Cons of Having a President-Elect

When someone knows one full term ahead of time that he or she will be the next president of the organization, the transition is usually much smoother. The president-elect can give careful thought to his or her appointments and will have plenty of time for training and mentoring. If the organization has a heavy travel schedule for the president, the year advance notice makes scheduling much easier.

Some of the advantages are also disadvantages. For example, when you know one year ahead of time that you will be the next president, you just might start doing that job a little bit too early. Also, if members aren't getting their way with the current president, they might begin working on the next president. If that occurs, it unfairly erodes some of the president's effectiveness.

Because the move to president from president-elect is automatic, if the person does not rise to the occasion as president-elect and it becomes clear that he or she will not be a good president, you are stuck with him or her. The only way to have that person not become president is to remove him or her from office, which is usually not a pretty sight.

An organization should give serious consideration to the decision of whether or not to have a president-elect. If you choose to have a president-elect and that position succeeds the president in case of a vacancy in the office of president, some of the responsibilities that are listed in the section for vice president later in this chapter apply to the president-elect.

The President-Elect and the Bylaws

If you have a president-elect or are thinking about having one, be sure to review the bylaws. The bylaws must provide for a president-elect and the function of the office, especially with respect to vacancies.

- **Vacancy in the office of president.** Make sure the bylaws indicate that the vacancy is filled by the president-elect, not the vice president. Also examine how the bylaws indicate the organization will handle the situation in which the president's office is vacated and the president-elect fills the vacancy. Remember, the president-elect was already elected to serve as president during the next term. If that person serves as president for a part of this term, does the organization want to cut short the time as president or lengthen it? Those are the only two choices. If the bylaws don't indicate otherwise, the president-elect will fill the unexpired term of the president and then be finished. If the bylaws indicate that the president-elect fills the vacancy in the office of president and then serves the term for which elected, then the president-elect serves more than one term as president. The choice belongs to the organization when it writes the bylaws.

- **Vacancy in the office of president-elect.** Remembering that the president-elect will someday, without further election, become the president, you should construct the bylaws to prohibit election of the president-elect by the board rather than the membership. A vacancy in the office of president-elect should not be filled by a smaller body than the body that originally elected the president-elect. Frequently bylaws indicate that the office of president-elect will either not be filled or the duties will be assigned to someone and then the membership will elect a president during the next election.
- **Vacancy in the offices of president and president-elect.** Should that unusual circumstance arise, the bylaws should have it covered. Again, organizations usually like to have their president elected by the membership instead of appointed by the board, and to have that happen it must be in the bylaws.

The Vice President: Second, Third, or Fourth in Command

If there is no president-elect and only one vice president, the position of vice president is straightforward—the vice president presides when the president is absent or must vacate the chair and fills a vacancy in the office of president. Once we add a president-elect or more than one vice president to the mix, things get a bit more complicated. For example, if your organization has a position of president-elect and the bylaws *do not* specify that the president-elect presides when the president is absent and fills a vacancy in the office of president, the vice president performs those tasks. If the bylaws *do* specify that the president-elect fulfills those duties, obviously the president-elect, *not* the vice president, does them. That's why some organizations that have a president-elect don't have any vice presidents—the positions are somewhat redundant. You have to read your bylaws to know what applies in your organization's situation.

From this point on in the discussion of vice president, we will assume that there is no position of president-elect.

The main job of the vice president is to be familiar with the president's duties so that, if the president becomes unable to serve, the vice president is prepared to step in and take over. Many organizations assign other duties to the vice president such as oversight of specific committees. I encourage people to think of the vice president as a support system for the president.

Sometimes there is more than one vice president. In that situation, the vice presidents should be numbered first vice president, second vice president, third vice president, and so on. When there are multiple vice presidents and the positions are not numbered, it creates uncertainty. When they are numbered and there is a vacancy in the office of president, the first vice president becomes president, the second vice president becomes first vice president, and so on.

Gavel Gaffes

One of the main duties of the office of vice president is to be prepared to take over for the president should he or she become unable to fulfill the duties of president. Therefore, it is inappropriate to accept the position of vice president if you are not willing to become the president should there be a vacancy in the office of president.

Should the vice president be unwilling to perform the duties of the president, the only choice the vice president has is to resign.

When the Veep Fills In for the President

When presiding at a meeting in the absence of the president, the vice president should refer to himself or herself as the "chair" or the "presiding officer," not as the "vice president" and certainly not as the "president."

When the vice president assumes the authority of the president only for a particular meeting, his or her authority is limited. For example, if the bylaws require that the president appoint all committees, when the vice president presides over a meeting for the president and a committee needs to be appointed, the vice president cannot appoint the committee members. The vice president should only assume those duties that are prescribed in the bylaws, which usually means conducting the meeting. In addition, if the bylaws indicate that the president is an ex officio member of all committees, the vice president does not attend those meetings for the president.

Parliamentary Pearls

A vice president should always be prepared to take over for the president. Some ways of doing that include discussing with the president the agenda before each meeting; having an agenda, the bylaws, and the parliamentary authority for all meetings; and arriving at the meeting early enough to be prepared for the start of the meeting. If a vice president prepares in this manner and then an emergency delays the president, attendees won't have to sit around wasting time waiting for the president. The vice president can start the meeting on time. You would be surprised how popular this can make a vice president!

The Secretary: More Than Minutes

People often overlook the importance of the office of secretary, but they shouldn't. The secretary is the official record keeper of the organization. This position goes far beyond keeping the minutes—it includes keeping an accurate list of members, the roll call list, the governing documents, delegate information, committee membership, and so much more. This position is usually an elected position.

Although the most common name for this office is secretary, it might also be called clerk, recording secretary, recorder, or scribe. In large organizations that have a full staff, this position, or sometimes simply the work of this position, is done by a staff member. Some of these same large organizations have the executive director serve as corporate secretary and have no elected secretary.

Point of Information

Some organizations choose to split the secretary position into two positions: recording secretary and corresponding secretary. When that is done, the bylaws should specify the responsibilities of each position. Usually the recording secretary takes the minutes and the corresponding secretary sends out notices of meetings and handles the general correspondence of the organization.

As we review the position of secretary, it is helpful to examine it from the perspective of duties and responsibilities before, during, and after the meeting.

Before the meeting:

- Work with the president to prepare the agenda.
- Distribute to the members before the meeting the packet of materials needed for the meeting, including the agenda. (See Chapter 15 for more on preparing an agenda.)
- Send out the call of the meeting (the official notice of a meeting given to all members of the organization).
- Before the annual meeting, prepare an annual report.

During the meeting:

- In the absence of the president and vice president, the secretary calls the meeting to order and immediately conducts the election for the chairman pro tem (the temporary chairman).
- Have access to the minutes book.
- Have access to all of the governing documents of the organization.
- Have a list of the current membership as well as the current committees and committee members.
- Have ballots in case of a ballot vote.
- Maintain the official list of members and the official attendance list, if there is one.
- Keep notes of what occurred at the meeting.
- Sit near the president and serve as a resource to the president.

After the meeting:

- If any governing documents were amended at the meeting, the secretary should make the changes in the governing documents and distribute new copies to the appropriate parties.
- Maintain the file of committee reports.
- Prepare the minutes from the meeting.
- Distribute the minutes to the members.
- Give each committee any information that has been referred to them.
- Notify officers, delegates, and committee members of their election or appointment.

The Treasurer: The Buck Stops Here

The size and kind of organization have a large bearing on the duties of the treasurer, and as with all of the other offices, these should be spelled out in the bylaws. Basically, the treasurer is the custodian of the funds of the organization. This office is usually an elected position.

The treasurer receives all incoming money and disburses that money according to instructions from the organization. In large organizations it is the treasurer's job to oversee the income and expenditure of funds, but the actual tasks are performed by staff members. In that situation, it is the treasurer's job to make sure funds are handled correctly.

In addition, the treasurer is usually involved in preparing the organization's budget, making sure that the books are audited, and filling out appropriate tax forms. Once the board or the members have adopted the budget, it is the treasurer's responsibility to make sure that the organization spends within the established budget.

Parliamentary Pearls

If the treasurer handles large sums of money, he or she should be bonded. Bonding is a form of insurance that protects the organization in case of financial loss. The bonding should be paid for by the organization, not the person serving as treasurer.

The treasurer needs to keep accurate records and report regularly to the membership. For more on the treasurer's reports, the audit, and the budget, see Chapter 20.

The Executive Director: Working Behind the Scenes

While not an official member of the leadership team of the organization, the executive director is a very important leader nonetheless. The executive director is a salaried position in charge of the association headquarters and staff. The executive director is usually appointed by the board or the executive committee. The bylaws should reflect who makes that appointment. Just like other positions, the bylaws should specify the responsibilities of the executive director and to whom the executive director reports.

The position has many names. Years ago, the position was most frequently referred to as executive secretary. Now you will see it referred to as the chief executive officer (CEO), the chief operating officer (COO), or even the president (in which case the title "chairman of the board" is given to the position usually referred to as president).

The responsibilities of the executive director vary according to the size and needs of the organization. In many organizations, the position is a full-time job with a full staff reporting to it. In some smaller organizations, the position of executive director is part time, and the organization has no additional staff.

Besides the fact that the executive director is salaried, as opposed to volunteer, the executive director is also usually involved in the leadership of the organization for longer than most other leaders. One executive director will usually be in that position throughout many administrations.

The advantage of that longevity is that the executive director becomes the consistent force behind the organization. The disadvantage, at least for the executive director, is that each term he or she reports to a different board. It requires a fair bit of flexibility.

Your organization's bylaws should specify who is in charge of hiring and firing the executive director. It is then the executive director's responsibility to hire and fire the remainder of the staff.

There Are Professional Parliamentarians!?!

When I tell people that I'm a professional parliamentarian, they look at me like I just told them I have some strange, incurable disease. After I assure them that being a parliamentarian is not a disease, I proceed to explain the profession. Just in case you didn't know there are such creatures as professional parliamentarians out there, let me explain my profession to you.

What Is One?

A professional parliamentarian is an expert in parliamentary procedure who is hired by a person or an organization to give advice on matters of parliamentary law and procedure. A professional parliamentarian is qualified to assist the organization or the individual in the application of parliamentary procedure, thus improving the effectiveness of their meetings.

A professional parliamentarian can help ensure that your convention, membership meeting, board meeting, or stockholder meeting is conducted smoothly and efficiently. As a consultant, the professional parliamentarian can advise the presiding officer, the organization, and the individual members on the application of parliamentary procedure for the orderly conduct of the business of the association. Since the professional parliamentarian is not a member of the association, the appearance of bias is not an issue.

Just like other professionals, parliamentarians belong to one or more professional organizations and are bound by a code of ethics. They come to your organization as objective experts, thus assisting the group in a way that no member of the organization can.

Parliamentary Designations

Behind the name of a professional parliamentarian you will see some letters. Those letters indicate the level of professional designation that person holds. There are two national organizations, and each has multiple designations.

The National Association of Parliamentarians (NAP) has two levels of parliamentary proficiency and thus two levels of designations, as follows:

- *RP* stands for Registered Parliamentarian.
- A *PRP* is a Professional Registered Parliamentarian.

The American Institute of Parliamentarians (AIP) has three levels of designations:

- A *CP* is a Certified Parliamentarian.
- A *CPP* is a Certified Professional Parliamentarian.
- A *CP-T* or *CPP-T* is a designated Teacher of Parliamentary Procedure.

For a complete explanation of these designations and a list of the services a parliamentarian can perform, go to my website: www.nancysylvester.com.

The Role of a Parliamentarian

Professional parliamentarians should be impartial advisors. They should avoid getting into the issues being debated and instead focus on the procedure of the debate. Because the rules are the same no matter which "side" you are on, good parliamentarians are able to advise both sides on an issue.

In addition, because professional parliamentarians are focusing on the parliamentary procedure, attendees are free to focus on the issues.

Gavel Gaffes

Don't ask about the ruling of the parliamentarian! The parliamentarian does not rule. The parliamentarian is an advisor and therefore makes no final decisions. The parliamentarian may give an interpretation of a rule, an opinion on a rule, or even be asked to cite a rule, but never rules!

The only person who can rule is the chair of the meeting. If you disagree with the ruling of the chair, then you have an avenue to deal with that disagreement, called the motion to *Appeal from the Decision of the Chair.* Notice there is no motion to *Appeal* from the decision of the parliamentarian. That is because the parliamentarian does not make decisions.

What a Professional Parliamentarian Can Do for You

A parliamentarian assists the organization before, during, and after meetings. A parliamentarian also may be of assistance to the organization throughout the entire year, not just at convention time.

The parliamentarian's role is mainly to give advice on parliamentary procedure to the president, officers, committees, and members. The parliamentarian should be an integral part of the presiding team.

When and How to Hire a Professional

When should you consider hiring a professional parliamentarian? You may not need to hire a parliamentarian if yours is a small group getting together for social or professional reasons. But once the group is large or the problems you are facing are difficult, then it may be time to call on a professional. One clear red flag is when members are feeling that their rights are being infringed on. Another clear red flag is when the minority appears to be running the show.

There are many different approaches to hiring a professional parliamentarian. Some organizations hire a parliamentarian who is located in or near the convention city and hire a different parliamentarian each year. Other organizations hire the same parliamentarian year after year, and that parliamentarian travels to the convention site each time.

There are both advantages and disadvantages to each of these approaches. The one-time stand is frequently cheaper for the organization because the organization doesn't have to pay travel expenses. The long-term relationship is in many ways advantageous to the organization because the parliamentarian knows the organization and understands how it works. Every organization has its own personality, and many times it takes a while to understand the personality of the group.

Looking for a Professional

Both national parliamentarian organizations—the National Association of Parliamentarians (NAP) and the American Institute of Parliamentarians (AIP)—will refer you to professional parliamentarians in your area free of charge.

Point of Information

National Association of Parliamentarians
213 South Main Street
Independence, MO 64050-3850
Tel: 1-888-NAP-2929 or 816-833-3892
www.parliamentarians.org

American Institute of Parliamentarians
PO Box 2173
Wilmington, DE 19899-2173
Tel: 1-888-664-0428 or 302-762-1811
www.AIPparl.org

If you're considering hiring a parliamentarian, be sure that the person you select has skills and talents that match the needs of your organization. If, once you've finished reading this book, you'd like to learn more about parliamentary procedure, contact the NAP or AIP for more information on its training courses. You can even learn about parliamentary procedure through online or correspondence courses offered through these national organizations.

The Least You Need to Know

- Be sure to read the bylaws of the organization after taking an office—you need to know what you are expected to do.
- The president should use his or her powers to facilitate, not to dictate.
- The president-elect and the vice president should always be prepared to step into the position of president, either temporarily or permanently.
- The secretary is not just a minute taker, but the keeper of the records of the organization.
- The executive director is often the stabilizing force in the whirlwinds of position changes.
- A professional parliamentarian can help you keep your meeting running smoothly.

Chapter 4

The Law's the Law

In This Chapter

- The order of governing documents
- Which state's statutes to follow
- The typical order of bylaws
- How to change an organization's bylaws

How do you think a judge would react if you tried to avoid paying a ticket for driving 70 mph in a school zone by pleading ignorance of the speed limit? Any judge worthy of his or her black robe would probably inform you that it's your responsibility to know the rules of the road if you are going to drive on them and then order you to pay your ticket. Just as ignorance is no excuse for violating traffic laws, it's not an acceptable excuse for violating your organization's "rules of the road" either.

This chapter examines the different rules that govern your organization. In the parliamentary world, all these laws and rules are collectively referred to as governing documents.

The Hierarchy of Governing Documents

Any number of laws and documents govern an organization, but certain ones take priority over others. For instance, your organization's bylaws can't be in violation of federal or state laws, and the governing documents of a parent organization trump the constitution of any branch of that organization.

Generally, the hierarchy of governing documents looks like this:

- Federal laws
- State statutes
- Articles of incorporation
- Governing documents of the parent organization
- The organization's constitution
- Bylaws
- Special rules of order
- Parliamentary authority
- Standing rules
- Policies and procedures

Federal Laws and State Statutes

Most of the time people don't give much thought to the federal and state laws that affect their organizations. Whether you think about them or not, however, you are still responsible for knowing them.

Federal Laws

Federal tax laws govern many of the procedures of nonprofits, unions, and many other organizations. For instance, federal Internal Revenue Code has specific requirements for an organization to be chartered as a charitable (tax-exempt) organization. The tax code where this exemption is found is IRC 501(c). Not-for-profit organizations must apply for and receive from the IRS a "tax-exempt determination letter" that will state under which IRS 501(c) code section the organization qualifies. For example, nonprofit voluntary health and welfare organizations are identified as 501(c)-3 organizations, trade organizations are 501(c)-6, and social clubs are 501(c)-7.

State Statutes

In addition, each state has laws that govern not-for-profit and for-profit organizations as well as governmental bodies and community associations. If you are on a board of a local business, you will be governed by the for-profit statutes; if you are on a board of, say, your local United Way chapter, you would be governed by the not-for-profit statutes.

Your organization is required to follow the statutes of the state in which your organization is incorporated—even if your meetings aren't always held in that state. The state of incorporation can be found in the articles of incorporation and is often mentioned in the bylaws.

Parliamentary Pearls

You can find state statutes that govern organizations on the Internet (all statutes are available online) and through the office of the attorney general or the secretary of state in the state of incorporation. Always check to make sure that all such statutes are up-to-date.

Because each state's laws vary, it is important that your attorney be familiar with the state statutes that affect your organization. Check with the governing state body (such as the attorney general's office or secretary of state's office) to determine what filing or audit requirements exist since the state requirements can be different than the requirements of the IRS.

Governing Documents of the Parent Organization

Some groups are local branches of a state, national, or international organization. In these cases, the very existence of the local organization is authorized in the governing documents of what is referred to as the *parent organization.* In these situations, the local organization exists at the will of the national organization.

def•i•ni•tion

A national organization that has in its bylaws a system to charter local, state, or regional associations is referred to as the **parent organization.**

Just like in real life, the parent can tell the child what to do and what not to do. Because bylaws of the parent organization are a higher body of authority for the local organization than its own bylaws, the bylaws of the local organization can't conflict with the bylaws of the parent organization.

This gets to be a touchy situation. The bylaws of the local organization can't conflict with the bylaws of the parent organization (unless the parent organization's bylaws specifically allow them to), but they don't have to mirror the bylaws of the parent organization, either. Although each situation is unique, the following examples will help illustrate this point:

- **Membership qualifications.** Membership qualifications at the local level cannot conflict with the membership qualifications specified in the national bylaws, unless the national bylaws specifically allow them to.

  Let's say that the national bylaws of the Association of Complete Idiots (ACI) require that all members be complete idiots. There is nothing in ACI's national bylaws that give local associations the right to have members who are not complete idiots. Because local organizations are limited by national bylaws, the local association's bylaws can't require that its members be dummies or dunces; it can only require that they be complete idiots.

- **Officers.** The set of officers at the local level does not have to mirror the officers at the national level. For example, if there is a president-elect at the national level, you do not have to also have a president-elect at the local level. That is, unless the parent organization's bylaws specify the set of officers at the local level.

The parent organization's bylaws can affect all levels of your rules. It's important that you become familiar with them.

Point of Information

Different states have different names for the articles of incorporation. In some states they are referred to as articles of organization; other states refer to them as a corporate charter.

Articles of Incorporation

The articles of incorporation must conform to state and federal laws. The articles are the legal instrument required to incorporate the organization. An organization usually hires a lawyer to write its articles of incorporation. They must be filed with the state of incorporation.

Incorporation may be necessary or advisable for an organization to own property, enter into a contract, hire employees, and so on. An attorney can advise an organization on whether or not it should become incorporated. The need for incorporation depends on the state of incorporation and the activities of the organization.

The articles of incorporation are the highest legal document of a particular organization. In other words, you can't have items in your bylaws, constitution, or policies that contradict the articles of incorporation. Usually this document is very skimpy and contains only a few rules, but they are the law of the land, so to speak, for your group. If, for example, you want to change the name of your organization, you probably have to change your articles of incorporation because the name of your organization is usually contained in that document.

The articles of incorporation should include a method for amending them.

Constitution

For most of the last century, parliamentary authorities have recommended not to have both a constitution and bylaws but to combine them into a single document. The main reason for combining the constitution and bylaws is ease—it's easier for members to look up information when there is only one document to refer to.

Some organizations believe that having two separate documents is best for their situation, for whatever reason. In addition, old habits die hard—if an organization has always had both a constitution and bylaws, and no one wants to change them, that's fine.

If you choose to have a constitution for your organization, make sure it doesn't contain any rules that are procedural in nature. The constitution is where you define the primary characteristics of the organization, not its policies. Make sure this document contains only the highest level of rules, in the form of articles, as follows:

- **Name.** The full name of the organization, properly punctuated, should be included here.
- **Objective.** A concise statement of the objective of the organization.
- **Members.** The classes of members, qualifications of membership, the method of becoming a member, and the duties, rights, and obligations of members.
- **Officers.** The officer titles, terms, the nomination and election process, duties that are different from those stated in *Robert's*, and the method of filling vacancies.
- **Meetings.** Information on regular, annual, and special meetings as well as how meetings are called, the quorum for a meeting, and any information on changing the meeting in case of emergency.
- **Method of amendment.** How the constitution can be changed, who can change it, what kind of vote and notice is required, and so on.

Bylaws

Bylaws are rules that, for the most part, cannot be suspended (unless the bylaws themselves provide for a method of suspending them, which is somewhat self-defeating). Your organization's bylaws should include all of the rules the group considers to be so important that they cannot be changed at the whim of the members present at a single meeting and cannot be suspended.

The rights and responsibilities of members when they meet as a group and of individuals as members of the organization should be included in the bylaws. This is a basic concept of bylaws. It helps to think of the bylaws as a contract between the members and the organization. If a responsibility is not spelled out in the bylaws, members cannot be held to that responsibility.

For instance, suppose that the Association of Complete Idiots has been having some legal problems lately, and the legal fees have put a huge strain on the finances of the organization. At a meeting of the membership, a motion is adopted to assess all members $50. If ACI's bylaws do not authorize an assessment of the membership, this motion is out of order. (A motion is out of order when it violates the rules of the organization.) It is out of order because it is putting a responsibility on the members that is not authorized in the bylaws.

Parliamentary Pearls

If you are considering joining an organization, my advice is to first read the bylaws. You can tell a lot about an organization by reading its bylaws. The areas that I find particularly insightful are the membership article, the meetings article, and the article on the board of directors. These articles give you a lot of information regarding membership rights and where the power of the organization is housed.

Construction of the Bylaws

Bylaws are usually divided into articles, and information within the articles is divided into sections. Some bylaws use headings within the sections. In organizations that have combined the constitution and bylaws into one document, the generally accepted articles of the bylaws are as follows:

- **Article I: Name.** The full name of the organization, properly punctuated, should be included here.
- **Article II: Object.** A concise statement of the objective of the organization.
- **Article III: Members.** The classes of members; qualifications of membership; the method of becoming a member; and the duties, rights, and obligations of members.

- **Article IV: Officers.** The officer titles, terms, the nomination and election process, duties that are different from those stated in *Robert's*, and the method of filling vacancies.
- **Article V: Meetings.** Information on regular, annual, and special meetings as well as how meetings are called, the quorum for a meeting, and any information on changing the meeting in case of emergency.
- **Article VI: Executive Board.** The composition, powers, and rules of the board.
- **Article VII: Committees.** The names of the standing committees as well as their composition, manner of selection, and duties. Also, the requirements and composition for special committees.
- **Article VIII: Parliamentary Authority.** The parliamentary manual that the organization will use as the basis for the rules for conducting business and the rights of the members.
- **Article IX: Amendments.** How the bylaws can be changed, who can change them, what kind of vote and notice is required, and so on.

Additional articles might include …

- Dues and fees.
- Finance.
- Nominations and elections.
- State, local, or regional bodies authorized to exist.
- Dissolution, if incorporated.

Format for Bylaws

Articles of the bylaws are usually organized using roman numerals. Sections are usually organized using numbers. Subsections are usually organized using letters of the alphabet, as illustrated in the following example.

> **Bylaws of the American Association of Fun-Loving People**
>
> **ARTICLE III**
>
> **Members**
>
> Section 1. Eligibility. Any person with a degree in Fun-Loving shall be eligible for membership, provided that such person shall be proposed by one member and seconded by another member of the Association. A proposal for membership, signed by the two endorsers, shall be sent to the Association's headquarters. A person shall be declared a member of the Association upon:
>
> A. payment of the initiation fee;
>
> B. payment of annual dues for the first year; and
>
> C. proof of degree in Fun-Loving.

Bylaw Advice

When writing or changing bylaws, keep the following tips in mind:

- **Avoid administrivia.** By administrivia I mean administrative details. The bylaws are not the place for bureaucratic minutiae. That's not to say that organizations don't have their fair share of administrivia. It's just that it belongs in the rules, which we'll get to later in the chapter (see the section "More Rules!").
- **Write in plain English.** Any member should be able to pick up a copy of the bylaws, read them, and (for the most part) understand what they say. Therefore, keep the language of the bylaws simple and straightforward. This is not the place to impress your friends with your use of big words and long sentences.
- **Keep them amendable.** You might as well provide for some way to *Amend* your bylaws because I guarantee you're going to want to change them at some point in the future. In addition, if you include items in your bylaws that are required by a federal or state law or by the parent organization, identify them as such so that members know what can and can't be amended—or at least not amended without first amending the governing document of the higher authority.

Parliamentary Pearls

A helpful way to identify what is governed by other laws is to add "in accordance with the requirements of the statute under which XXX is incorporated" or to simply include a statement similar to the following: "(as stated in the *Illinois Not-For-Profit Corporate Act*)."

- **Avoid dates.** Very seldom should you include dates in the bylaws. The bylaws become effective once they are adopted. If you don't want them to become effective upon adoption, all you have to do is add a *proviso* to them. If, for example, you *Amend* your bylaws to eliminate the position of assistant treasurer but you currently have someone in that position whom you want to be able to finish out his or her term, you can use a proviso. The proviso might be as simple as stating that the bylaw amendment to eliminate the position of assistant treasurer shall not take effect until the end of the current term, and then you would indicate the end date of the current term.

def•i•ni•tion

A **proviso** is a provision on when the new bylaws change will take effect. It is not a part of the bylaws. Provisos can be put on a separate sheet of paper or in a footnote and then be removed after they are no longer in effect.

- **Watch the little words.** Sometimes it is the littlest words that have the biggest impact. Don't write *may*—which means that it is optional—or *should*—which means "ought to" but not necessarily "will"—when you mean *must*, *shall*, or *will*. Take the following example: "A local association shall provide for primary and affiliate members and may include provisional members …." This statement *requires* the local association to have two classes of members: primary and affiliate. It also *allows* the local association to choose whether or not to have a third class of members called provisional members.

- **Give freedom; avoid taking it away.** Bylaws shouldn't put unnecessary restrictions on the organization. Instead, the bylaws should be an empowering document. Restrict only those things that are necessary to restrict, such as duties of the members. Beyond that, allow for flexibility within the bylaws.

- **Specify a parliamentary authority.** Your bylaws should include an article that identifies the parliamentary authority for your organization, such as the current edition of *Robert's Rules of Order Newly Revised.* If a parliamentary authority is established in the bylaws, your bylaws don't need to include rules for every situation. Instead, if a particular situation isn't covered in the bylaws, the parliamentary authority will be your source for how to handle it.

Adopting the Bylaws

Once bylaws are written, they must be distributed to the membership, which must then vote on whether to accept them. The adoption of the original bylaws requires a majority vote.

Changing Bylaws

Once bylaws are adopted, there are basically two ways to change them: by amendment or by revision. Either method usually requires previous notice and a two-thirds vote. The following table indicates what kind of vote is necessary for various changes.

Methods of Changing Bylaws

Method	Frequency	Vote Needed	Purpose
Adopt	Once	Majority	Create the org
Amend	Most frequent	Usually two-thirds with notice	Fix a problem
Revise	Seldom	Same as *Amend*	Complete rewrite

Amending Bylaws

If you only want to make one or a couple of changes, the proper way to change the bylaws is to *Amend* them. This usually requires advance notice (so that they can't be changed at the whim of the attendees of a specific meeting) and a two-thirds vote. The bylaws should provide for changing them, so refer to the specific bylaws to find out how to *Amend* them.

When notifying membership of plans to change a specific amendment, the following format comes in handy:

Proposed Bylaw Amendments

Proposed Amendment #1:

Amend Article V, Section 1 by striking "an assistant treasurer."

Current Wording	Proposed Wording
The elected officers shall be a president, a vice president, a secretary, a treasurer, ~~an assistant treasurer,~~ and three directors-at-large.	The elected officers shall be a president, a vice president, a secretary, a treasurer, and three directors-at-large.

When your organization wants to make a change that requires amendment of the bylaws in several places, you might want to tie them all together into a single amendment. If, for example, you are proposing to change a name that occurs in six different places in the bylaws, you could label the change "Proposed Amendment #1" and then letter the individual instances of the name change a, b, c, and so on. You can then vote on the changes *in gross* and have only one vote because if it is to be changed in one place, it needs to be changed in them all.

def•i•ni•tion

When you are dealing with several related amendments, it is common practice to vote on them all at one time, referred to as **in gross**. It makes sense to vote on them all at once because if one was adopted and another one was not, then you would have created an inconsistency in the bylaws.

Scope of Notice

Scope of notice is a concept in parliamentary procedure that is designed to prevent game playing. Essentially, requiring that an amendment be limited to its scope of notice prevents people from making changes beyond what was indicated in the notice sent out in advance of the meeting.

Imagine that a member gives notice of an amendment to increase the dues of the organization from $10 to $12. At the next meeting, a member moves to *Amend* the bylaws, and it is seconded, restated by the chair, and opened for discussion. (The motion-making process will be described in detail in Chapters 5 and 6.) Sam thinks that the organization should increase the dues even more. He looks around and notices that most of the people who would object to a big dues increase are not in attendance at the meeting. Sam believes that with the combination of members present, a higher dues amount would pass. Sam moves to *Amend* the amendment by striking $12 and inserting $20.

Because changes to the bylaws require previous notice and because it would be unfair to give notice of a specific change and then *Amend* it to a higher amount, Sam's proposed amendment is out of order. It is out of order because it exceeds the scope of notice. In this situation, the scope of notice is $10 (the current amount) to $12 (the proposed amount). An amendment that is more than $12 or less than $10 is out of order. Only amendments between $10.01 and $11.99 would be in order.

Revising the Bylaws

Sometimes the proposed changes to the bylaws are so significant that amendments would have to be made throughout the document. If this is the case, it is appropriate to throw out the old bylaws and completely rewrite a new set of bylaws. That is called a revision of the bylaws.

A bylaw revision is similar to a bylaw amendment in that, to pass, it needs the same vote requirements as an amendment, which is usually previous notice and a two-thirds vote. If the revised bylaws are adopted, the revision replaces the current bylaws. The revision is considered *seriatim*, which means it is considered section by section and voted on at the end of consideration of the entire document.

def•i•ni•tion

Seriatim means considering a motion section by section or paragraph by paragraph, amending as you go, and voting on the entire document at the end.

Because notice is given that the entire document is to be substituted for the current bylaws, the concept of scope of notice does not apply to revision. You are starting with a clean slate, and it is as if you were adopting the bylaws for the first time, so any changes are acceptable.

More Rules!

There are a few other rules that you should be familiar with. They include special rules of order, standing rules, and policies and procedures.

Special Rules of Order

The rules contained in the parliamentary authority are called the rules of order. Sometimes organizations feel a need to have additional rules of order, called special rules of order, that differ from the parliamentary authority. However, most organizations don't find the need to have special rules of order.

Standing Rules

Standing rules govern the administration of the organization as opposed to rules regarding parliamentary procedure. If you want to include some unusual duties of officers, this would be the place to do so.

When you attend a convention, rules are adopted at the beginning of the convention. These are usually called convention standing rules.

Policies and Procedures

Some organizations have additional detailed policies and procedures regarding the administration of the organization. These organizations sometimes choose to combine all of their policies and procedures together in a single document. That document may be referred to as the organization's Policies and Procedures.

The Least You Need to Know

- Ignorance is not bliss—know the rules before you act.
- An organization's articles of incorporation and bylaws cannot violate federal and state statutes governing the organization.
- Bylaws should include all of the rules that the group considers to be so important that they cannot be changed at the whim of the members present at a single meeting and cannot be suspended.
- Amendments to bylaws usually require previous notice and a two-thirds vote to pass.

Part 2

Let's Get Moving: The Motion-Making Process

For a group to take an action, take a stand, spend money, or do almost anything else, it must first pass a motion. This part of the book is the how-to guide for taking your idea and turning it into a group action. Follow the six simple steps to processing a motion that I describe in the next few chapters, and you will be ready to get what you want done.

Chapter 5

Getting Into the Motion

In This Chapter

- Processing motions: the first three steps
- Making and seconding a motion
- Putting the motion in writing
- Owning the motion and why it matters

Before a group can do anything or even take a stand on an issue, someone must make a motion. A motion states specifically what the maker of that motion wants the organization to do. Think of a motion as the ultimate action plan: In order to get anything done in the group, you need to start with a motion.

Kinds of Motions

There are two kinds of *motions*—main motions and secondary motions:

- **Main motions** bring business before the assembly. They can be further subdivided into two categories:

a. **Original main motions** bring before the assembly a new subject, sometimes in the form of a resolution, upon which action by the assembly is desired.

b. **Incidental main motions** are incidental to, or related to, the business of the assembly or its past or future action.

- **Secondary motions** are any motions that are made while a main motion is pending. They can be further divided into three different classes:

   a. **Privileged motions** don't relate to the main motion or pending business but relate directly to the members and the organization. They are matters of such urgency that, without debate, they can interrupt the consideration of anything else.

   b. **Subsidiary motions** aid the assembly in treating or disposing of a main motion. They are in order only from the time the main motion has been stated by the chair until the chair begins to take a vote on that main motion.

   c. **Incidental motions** relate to matters that are incidental to the conduct of the meeting rather than directly to the main motion. They may be offered at any time when they are needed.

def•i•ni•tion

A **motion** is a proposal on which a group takes a specific action or stand.

Point of Information

"The motion" is sometimes referred to as "the question." Both mean basically the same thing.

I'll discuss each kind of motion in detail in Part 3 of this book. For now, it's important to simply keep in mind that there are different kinds of motions and that they have different rules.

It's Time to Get in Motion!

To make any kind of motion, a person must be a voting member of the body that is meeting. That is, the person needs to be a member of the immediate group—not a larger constituency. For instance, even though I'm a citizen of the United States of America, I am not a member of the U.S. Senate. That means I can't go to the Senate chambers, grab the microphone, and make a motion.

The motion process involves the following six steps:

1. A member makes a motion.
2. Another member seconds the motion.
3. The chair states the motion, formally placing it before the assembly.
4. The members debate the motion.
5. The chair puts the question (in this context, "question" means the same thing as "motion") to a vote.
6. The chair announces the results of the vote.

In this chapter, I'll walk you through the first three steps. We'll cover the second three steps in Chapter 6.

Step 1: Making a Motion

To make a motion, you need to seek recognition from the chair, which you typically do by raising your hand. After the chair recognizes you, you are free to make your motion. Although a lot of people say "I make a motion to …," it's far simpler to use three short words: "I move that …."

Be Precise

Make sure that the motion states exactly what you want the organization to believe or do. The following two motions might seem similar, but they aren't:

- "I move that we form a committee to investigate the purchase of a computer."
- "I move that we form a committee to purchase a computer."

Only three words are different, but it makes a big difference. The committee in the first motion is only authorized to investigate whether to purchase a computer. The committee in the second motion is authorized to purchase the computer.

Be specific in stating the motion. For example, let's say you make the following motion:

> "I move that we host a party Thursday night to celebrate Sam's birthday."

You're envisioning everyone going over to someone's house, someone else baking a cake, and everyone bringing their own beverages and snacks. After your motion has passed, Janice offers to set up the party, and everyone agrees. On Thursday night you go to Janice's house for the party and discover that she hired a caterer and ordered a fancy birthday cake from the local bakery. Whereas the party that you had in mind was simple and at no cost to the organization, the party that Janice had in mind cost the organization big bucks. Clearly, the wording of your motion wasn't clear enough. The confusion could have been avoided had you worded the motion as follows:

> "I move that we host a party Thursday night to celebrate Sam's birthday. The party should be at a member's house, and everyone should bring food so there is no cost to the organization."

Only Make Motions That You Agree With

Although it's not a requirement of *Robert's* to do so, members should try to phrase their motions in such a way that they agree with them. This is particularly important since the member who makes the motion is restricted from speaking against his or her motion during debate (although that person can vote against the motion).

The maker of the motion gets first right to speak on it. Again, logic and fairness come into play. The person who made the motion should get first chance to "sell" his or her idea to the other members.

Gavel Gaffes

If, in order to make a motion, you have to be a voting member of the body that is meeting and you should agree with it, how can you get away with voting against it? The purpose of debate is to try to change members' minds, even the mind of the maker of the motion. It is unlikely, but possible, that during the debate the maker of the motion could see the light and now want to vote against his or her own motion. That's the democratic process in action!

Make Positive Motions

Use positive words to express a negative thought. Otherwise, members will need to vote "yes" on an issue that they disagree with, which can become very confusing. Consider the following two motions:

- "I move that we not support the national dues increase."
- "I move that we oppose the national dues increase."

Although they mean the same thing, the second motion is much easier to understand.

Put Your Motion in Writing

Even though the presiding officer has the right to ask for a motion in writing, most organizations don't require written motions. However, there are good reasons for you to put your motions in writing.

Most important, members are far less likely to forget or become confused about the meaning of a motion if it is written down. In other words, it ensures that what you say is what you get. Otherwise you get the secretary's interpretation of what you said, and that might not always be on target.

In this day and age of advanced technology, why not have the motion written down in a PowerPoint presentation and displayed on a screen? This way everyone can see it, and if it is to

Parliamentary Pearls

The longer your motion is, the more crucial it is that you present it in writing.

be amended, you can do so in front of everyone so that the new wording is clear. If you do this, use the strikeout feature for words that are struck out and colored font for the words added.

If you're in a more formal setting or in front of a large group, it's particularly important to write your motion down. It not only helps you to say exactly what you mean to say, it also can be passed on to the meeting chair and can even be used in the preparation of the minutes. That way, everyone is in agreement as to the exact wording of your motion and its intent.

Putting the motion in writing can be remarkably simple. You almost always have a pencil and paper with you in a meeting. If not, the person sitting next to you probably does. Write it down and read it over to make sure it says exactly what you want to say. Then, when you are recognized by the chair, read the motion straight from your paper.

Your group could even put blank paper and pencils around the room so that members who don't bring pen and paper can write down their motions. For larger groups, I recommend that you get "no carbon required" (NCR) paper, which makes copies as you write on it. The person making the motion can keep the bottom copy and can pass the other copies to the presiding officer, the secretary for the minutes, and so on. That way, everyone who needs it will have a copy of the exact wording of the motion in front of them throughout the processing of the motion.

Avoid Saying "So Move"

A frequent faux pas in making a motion is saying "so move." These two lovely words usually dance out of someone's mouth after there has been discussion on an issue at a meeting. It seems like shorthand. But unless the statement made right before "so move" was called out is extremely clear, it can cause confusion. I once observed a meeting where an issue was discussed, a member stated a solution, and another member said "so move." Everyone thought that the issue was settled until the secretary asked for the exact wording of the motion. It took the group over 20 minutes to agree on the wording! Had she not asked for the wording, different people would have left the meeting with different ideas of what the motion they had agreed upon really said.

Although there are all kinds of situations where professionals can use it, here's a good rule: Don't use "so move" unless it is a motion to approve the minutes, *Recess*, or *Adjourn*. The motion must be absolutely clear to everyone in the room before you use those two little words.

Step 2: Seconding the Motion

Once someone has made a motion, another voting member must second it. To second a motion is to publicly agree that the motion should be considered. The purpose of this step is to make sure that at least two members want to discuss this issue before the group spends time on it.

But I Don't Agree!

Unlike the maker of the motion, who should agree with the motion before making it, the person who seconds the motion doesn't have to agree with it—he or she must only believe that the issue should be discussed and decided upon. The person seconding the motion might even be against the motion but be in agreement that the organization should take a stand or make a decision on the issue.

An example might be helpful: Let's say there has been a lot of discussion in your group about painting the headquarters building green. You think it is a bad idea, but you are tired of hearing about it. In a meeting, a member named Steve makes the motion to paint the building green. You may choose to second the motion, even though you are against it, simply so the group can finally decide on this issue and put it to bed!

Seconding a motion does not give you any special rights, like the right to speak before other members on the motion. It simply gives you the assurance that the members are going to make a decision on this motion.

No Second Needed

Particularly urgent or important motions, such as the motion to raise a *Question of Privilege* (which is explained in Chapter 11), don't need a second. Motions that don't require a second are as follows.

- ***Question of Privilege.*** This is used to bring an urgent request or a main motion relating to the rights of either the assembly or an individual up for immediate consideration. It may interrupt business (see Chapter 11).
- ***Call for the Orders of the Day.*** By the use of this motion, a single member can require the assembly to follow the order of business or agenda, or to take up a special order that is scheduled to come up, unless two thirds of the assembly wish to do otherwise (see Chapter 11).
- ***Point of Order.*** If a member feels that the rules are not being followed, he or she can use this motion to ask the chair to follow the rules. It requires the chair to make a ruling and enforce the rules (see Chapter 13).
- ***Objection to Consideration.*** The purpose of this motion is to prevent the assembly from considering the question/motion because a member deems the question irrelevant, unprofitable, or contentious (see Chapter 13).
- ***Division of the Assembly.*** The effect of this motion is to require a standing vote (not a counted vote). A single member can demand this if he or she feels the vote is too close to declare or unrepresentative. This motion can only be used if the voice vote or the show of hands vote is too close to declare (see Chapter 13).
- ***Parliamentary Inquiry.*** This is a question directed to the presiding officer concerning parliamentary law or the organization's rules as they apply to the business at hand (see Chapter 13).
- ***Point of Information.*** This is a nonparliamentary question about the business at hand (see Chapter 13).

Parliamentary Pearls

The practice of seconding a motion ensures that more than one person in the group is remotely interested in the issue. If no one seconds a motion, you go on to the next agenda item, having saved the time of the participants.

In addition, it's common practice today to not require a second on a motion when it comes from a committee. That's because the purpose of a second is to make sure that at least two people are interested in the issue before it is brought before the assembly, and in order for a committee to make a motion to a superior body, the committee must have voted on it. Therefore, at least two members are in favor of the motion, so a second is not needed.

No Second, No Debate!

Since Step 2 of processing a motion is that a voting member seconds the motion, if no member is willing to second the motion, the process ends at that point. In other words, if there is no second, then the motion dies for a lack of a second. The group can then proceed to the next item on the agenda.

Step 3: The Chair States the Motion

Step 3 in the processing of a motion is that the presiding officer states the motion, formally placing it before the assembly. At first blush this step doesn't sound very important or even necessary, but it's an essential step. It ensures that everyone understands the motion that's before the assembly.

At this point in the process, the presiding officer will be very pleased if the maker of the motion has submitted the motion in writing. All the presiding officer has to do is to read the motion from his or her copy, thereby increasing the likelihood that it will be stated accurately. In situations where the presiding officer doesn't have a written copy of the motion, he or she can do one of the following:

- Read the motion from the notes taken when the motion was made by the member.
- Ask the secretary to restate the motion.
- Ask the member who made the motion to restate it.

Gavel Gaffes

When the presiding officer doesn't restate the motion or have someone else restate it, the usual consequence is that the discussion wanders all over the place instead of staying focused on the particular motion under consideration.

Proper restatement of the motion by the presiding officer helps make sure everyone has heard the motion exactly as it was proposed. Those who were daydreaming when the motion was first made will get a second chance to hear it. Proper restatement also helps keep everyone on target as to the exact wording of the motion to be debated.

Ownership of the Motion

At the completion of Step 3 in the processing of a motion, the *ownership of the motion* is transferred from the individual who made the motion to the whole group. It might be helpful to envision that, at the end of Step 3, the presiding officer goes over to the member who made the motion, takes the motion from that individual, and gives it to the entire group. Once the motion belongs to the group, it's the group's to do with as it pleases.

def•i•ni•tion

Ownership of a motion is a concept that refers to whose property the motion is at a given time and, therefore, who had a right to make any changes to it. In the six steps of the motion process, the maker of the motion owns the motion up until the completion of Step 3. After Step 3, the ownership of the motion is transferred to the assembly.

If you own something, you can change it. But if you don't own something and you want to change it, you have to go to the owner and ask his or her permission to change it. If you want to take it home with you, you have to ask his or her permission. This simple concept applies to motions as well. So if you understand who the owner of the motion is during each of the six steps of processing the motion, you then understand whose permission you must get to change it.

To fully understand the concept of ownership of the motion, let's return to Steve's motion to paint the building green. After Steve made the motion (Step 1), someone else seconded it (Step 2), and then the presiding officer repeated it (Step 3). As the members are discussing it (Step 4, which we'll cover in Chapter 6), Tom speaks up and says that he wants to strike "green" from the motion and replace it with "blue." In other words, Tom wants to *Amend* the motion.

Because the motion is owned by the group, Tom must get the permission of the members in attendance at the meeting to change it. He would do so by making the motion to *Amend* by striking "green" and inserting "blue." After another member seconds Tom's amendment, the members would then talk about Tom's proposed change and decide, through a majority vote, whether they want the motion changed. Even if Steve disagrees with the amendment, there's nothing he can do about it except speak and vote against it. If the majority passes the amendment to the motion, Steve must accept the change—he cannot "take his ball and go home." He must live with the decision made by the current owners of the motion.

When could Steve by himself have made a change to the motion? After he made the motion and it was seconded but before the presiding officer restated the motion—in other words, between Steps 2 and 3. Let's go back in time to the moment when Steve makes the motion to paint the building green and the presiding officer calls for a second. Right after someone seconds it, Tom informs Steve that the organization would have to buy green paint but that they currently have enough blue paint on hand to paint the building. Jill, the treasurer, also tells Steve that there is not enough money in the budget to pay for the green paint. At that time, Steve could change his motion from painting the building green to painting the building blue, and he would not have to get anyone else's permission.

Point of Information

Before the completion of Step 3 in the processing of a motion, the motion is owned by the maker. After Step 3 it is owned by the assembly. If you can remember that, you can answer many questions without memorizing rules.

Withdrawing a Motion

Continuing with our painting theme, let's say that Joan makes a motion to paint the building brown. The motion is seconded and restated by the chair. During debate of the motion, it is pointed out that there are too many other brown buildings, that brown is the color of an opponent organization, that brown paint costs too much, and that there isn't really enough money in the treasury to buy any paint. Joan wishes she had never made the motion in the first place.

Can Joan *Withdraw* her motion at this time? The concept of ownership of a motion indicates that the motion no longer belongs to Joan. Therefore, Joan may not *Withdraw* her motion without the permission of the owners of the motion. Since the motion is now owned by the members who are present, the presiding officer must ask them for permission to allow Joan to *Withdraw* her motion. If any one member of the group objects, the presiding officer must put it to a vote on whether to allow Joan to *Withdraw* her motion.

Don't Memorize, Understand!

As you can see from these examples, understanding the concept of ownership of a motion makes it very easy to understand what can be done by whom. It beats memorizing rules! When you want to change a motion in some way, ask yourself, "Who owns the motion at this specific time?" You will know whose permission you must get.

This chapter covered the first three steps of making a motion. Chapter 6 picks up where this chapter leaves off and covers the final three steps in processing a motion.

The Least You Need to Know

- You must be a member of the body that is meeting in order to make or second a motion.
- Whenever possible, state your motion in the affirmative.
- Putting your motion in writing and giving a copy to the chair ensures that the motion is restated exactly as you want it to be.
- After the presiding officer states the motion, the ownership of the motion is transferred from the member who made the motion to the people assembled.

Chapter 6

Getting Out of the Motion

In This Chapter

- The motion process: the second three steps
- What can happen during debate
- Amending the motion
- Taking a vote
- Announcing the results of the vote
- Making your vote count

Once the presiding officer puts a motion before the members (Step 3 in the motion-making process), the members must process that motion, which essentially means that they must make a decision on the motion. At this point, it's up to the members to debate the issue and vote on it, and it's up to the presiding officer to ensure that the vote is properly counted and announced. If you have found yourself confused at meetings, it is probably at this point. Understanding all that can happen during the debate step will help you feel more comfortable during your next meeting.

Step 4: Members Debate the Motion

Step 4 is potentially the longest and most complicated of all the steps in the motion process. It is at this point that the motion is considered *pending*, meaning that it has been stated by the presiding officer and hasn't yet been disposed of either permanently or temporarily. This is a critical time for a motion—many things can happen, and you must be prepared.

def•i•ni•tion

A motion is considered **pending** when it has been stated by the presiding officer but has not yet been disposed of either permanently or temporarily (during Step 4).

Not everyone in the group will see the problem and possible solutions the same way. (That is the beauty of the group process!) Therefore, in the group decision-making process, it's often the case that members spend a lot of time discussing, negotiating, and compromising before they are ready to take a vote. Step 4 is when all of this occurs.

Now's the Time to Fix It

While a motion is pending, members can *Amend* it, *Postpone* it, put it aside, send it to a committee, and so on. All of the actions that take place while the main motion is pending are secondary motions. (We will discuss secondary motions in detail in Chapters 11 through 13.)

If the group members are dissatisfied with a motion before them and decide they want to change it, they must *Amend* the motion before voting on it. To help you understand the amendment process, let's continue the example of the motion to paint the building that we started in the preceding chapter; this example will help you see why you must first *Amend* the motion before you decide to vote on it.

The "Paint the Building Green" Example ... Again

Let's return to our painting example from Chapter 5. Steve's motion to paint the building green has been seconded, restated by the presiding officer, and the group is debating it. You have done extensive research on the resale value of buildings as affected by the building's color. Your research indicates that a green building loses 10 percent of its resale value over a building that is freshly painted another color. You have also found that a building that is not freshly painted loses only 5 percent of its resale value. A fair bit of money hangs on what color you paint the building, so it only makes sense that you should debate the issue and, if necessary, *Amend* it before voting on it. Let's look at the options:

- If you don't paint the building, it will lose 5 percent of its resale value, so your $100,000 building would be worth $95,000.
- If you paint it white, it would maintain its current resale value or even gain in value, making it worth $100,000 or more.
- If you paint the building green, it could lose 10 percent of its value, making it worth $90,000.

Based on this information, you decide that you will vote "no" on Steve's motion to paint the building green. However, if you could first *Amend* the motion to strike "green" and insert "white," you would vote "aye" on the motion.

No matter how logical it may seem to do it the other way around, if there are amendments to be made to the motion, those amendments must be made while the motion is *on the floor*. If you wait until after the motion is voted on, it is too late to change it. (Okay, you can change it later [see Chapter 14] but not without jumping through a bunch of hoops. It is much easier to change it now.)

Because debate is such an essential component of the parliamentary process, let's devote a few more pages to it before we move on to the vote, which is Step 5 in the motion-making process.

def•i•ni•tion

When a motion is pending, it is considered to be **on the floor.** These terms are interchangeable. Saying that the motion is on the floor is symbolic of having the motion before the members so that they can discuss and fix it.

Talk, Talk, Talk: Debate

One of the greatest time-savers of parliamentary procedure is that debate is limited to the specific motion that is being considered. If this principle is followed, the debate portion of the motion process not only will stay focused, but it will also usually take far less time than it otherwise would. In addition, only the specific aspects covered in the motion are open to debate, not the whole subject.

If the motion on the floor is for the organization to paint the building green, the debate should focus on discussing the advantages and disadvantages of painting the building green. The debate should not be allowed to wander off to other aspects of the building, such as whether or not the building needs a new roof or gutters. Nor should the debate be allowed to go into a general discussion of whether the building should be sold or kept for at least a few more years. Or that if someone cut the grass on a regular basis, fewer neighbors would complain about its appearance. As you've likely figured out by now, the examples could go on and on, as could the debate if it isn't focused.

As you'll discover in Chapter 7, more than one motion may be pending at any one time. However, the debate must be limited to the *immediately pending* motion, which is the last pending motion stated by the chair. You can't discuss other pending motions until they become the immediately pending motion. (Don't worry. If you're confused, this concept will make a lot more sense after you read Chapter 7.)

def•i•ni•tion

A motion is considered to be **immediately pending** when several motions are pending and it is the motion that was last stated by the chair and will be first to be disposed of.

Stay on Target

If a member gets off the subject or starts talking about an aspect of the subject that isn't covered in the motion, it is important for the presiding officer to bring the focus back to the specific motion, even if that means interrupting the speaker. A kind way of doing this is to say, "The motion before you is to paint the building green. Please confine your remarks to a discussion of painting the building green." You might even add, "If you want to discuss the possibility of a new roof on the building, you could make a motion regarding the roof after we have voted on the current motion to paint the building green. Is there any further discussion on the motion to paint the building green?"

Point of Information

If the members begin to stray from the subject matter, as frequently happens, a nice way for the chair to bring them back on task is to ask, "Is there any further discussion on the motion to …?" This is a helpful way to remind the members of exactly what they are, or should be, discussing.

If the member continues to discuss an issue that isn't directly related to the specific motion that is pending, the presiding officer should interrupt the member and indicate that the comments are out of order. This is difficult to do because most people don't like interrupting someone to, in essence, ask them to stop talking. But an important part of the job of the presiding officer is to keep the discussion on track. If the presiding officer doesn't keep the discussion focused, it might take far longer than it should to process the motion.

Parliamentary Pearls

The most effective presiding officers are those who are willing to speak up, interrupt the wandering speaker, and make sure the discussion stays focused on the specific motion on the floor.

Don't Forget Your Manners

In addition, don't …

- Discuss the personalities of the people involved.
- Question the motives of other members.
- Make any derogatory remarks, including name calling, about other members.

By keeping the debate focused on the motion rather than on the people involved, the meeting will go much more quickly, and everyone will be able to voice his or her opinion without fear of a personal verbal attack by other members.

Gavel Gaffes

During debate, avoid calling another member by his or her name, especially when there is a lot of controversy. While it may seem impersonal, this technique keeps the focus on the issue, not the person who said it.

Robert's suggests that you refer to another person by the office he or she holds or by when he or she spoke to the assembly. Some examples include the following:

- The previous speaker
- The bylaws committee chairman
- The treasurer
- The member who made the motion

What About Nonmembers?

In a meeting of members, all members are treated equally; therefore, they all have the right to speak. But guests at the meeting do not have the same rights as members. A person who is not a member of the body that is meeting does not have the right to speak unless the members give that nonmember permission to speak.

Point of Information

The following phrases can be of assistance to the presiding officer in concluding Step 4:

- Is there any further discussion?
- Are you ready for the question?
- Is there any further discussion on … (here briefly state the exact subject of the motion)?
- Are you ready to vote?
- Are there any other new points that need to be made before we vote on the motion?

Time to Wrap Up Debate

The presiding officer doesn't have the authority to put an end to debate when members still want to discuss the issue. (Only the members, by the use of the *Previous Question* motion, can stop debate when members want to speak. That motion is discussed in Chapter 12.) But when it is clear that the members are finished discussing the motion, the presiding officer doesn't have to wait for a member to request that debate ends. The presiding officer can simply conclude the debate and move on to Step 5. It could be stated as simply as, "Seeing no members seeking recognition, debate is closed."

Step 5: Putting the Motion to a Vote

Once all members have had a chance to debate the issue, it's time for the fifth step in processing the motion: the vote. To begin, the presiding officer should restate the motion to remind members of the exact issue they will be voting on. With the motion regarding painting the building, the presiding officer would say, "We will now vote on the motion to paint the building green."

Don't Forget the "No" Vote

After telling the members what motion they are voting on, the presiding officer then gives direction on what method of voting will be used. (See Chapter 9 for an explanation of the methods of voting.) In addition to explaining the voting process, the presiding officer should tell members how to express the vote. For example, on a voice vote, the presiding officer might say "All those in favor say *aye*. All those opposed say *no*."

Even when it's obvious how the vote will turn out, the presiding officer should call for votes in favor of and votes against the motion. An exception to this is with courtesy resolutions. An example of a courtesy resolution is the resolution at the end of the convention that thanks everyone who worked on the convention.

The Declaration Is Up to the Chair

It is the responsibility of the presiding officer to determine whether the motion passed or failed and then to announce that determination to the members.

Vote Again, if Necessary

The presiding officer should never declare which side prevailed in a vote unless he or she is absolutely positive which side won. If there is the least bit of doubt, the presiding officer has the right to have the vote taken in a different manner so that the results are clear before the decision is made. For example, if there is a voice vote and the presiding officer is unclear as to the outcome of the vote, he or she may simply say, "The chair is unclear as to the outcome of the vote, so we will have a standing vote." If the outcome still isn't clear, then the presiding officer might call for a counted vote. (Again, I cover voting methods in detail in Chapter 9.)

Point of Information

The presiding officer can help to ensure that everyone is comfortable with the decision of the voting results by observing the members during the vote. Look for pockets of members who vote on the side that does not prevail. If, for example, there is a large group of people sitting together who vote in favor of the motion and the motion fails, it might appear to the people in that group that more members voted in favor of the motion than really did. Therefore, conducting the vote using a different method that will provide a clearer picture of the true outcome may be advisable. Redoing the vote in this situation is not done so that the presiding officer is sure of the results but rather so that the members are comfortable with the announcement. In Chapter 13, we will cover *Division of the Question,* which is how a member can clarify a vote if the presiding officer does not.

Step 6: Complete Announcement

The sixth and final step in processing a motion is the complete announcement of the results of the vote. This announcement should include the following four elements:

- **Which side has the vote.** The first part of the announcement indicates which side has the necessary votes and is thus the prevailing side. It might be stated as, "The affirmative has it" or "The negative has it." The exact wording of this portion would be adapted to the kind of vote that is taken. In a counted vote, the presiding officer should first give the count before announcing the prevailing side. Thus, it might sound like this: "There are 10 votes in favor of the motion and 7 votes against the motion; the affirmative has it."

- **Whether the motion passed or failed.** Simply state either "The motion is adopted" or "The motion is lost." If you question the necessity of this part, imagine the lack of clarity where the vote was nine in favor and five opposed, and a two-thirds vote was required.
- **The effect of the vote.** If the motion was to purchase a computer and it passed, this part might sound like, "And we will be purchasing a computer." If the motion was an amendment to the bylaws, this statement can be very simple. It might be, "Our bylaws have been amended" or "Our bylaws have not been amended and will remain as they currently read."
- **The next step.** Where applicable, announce the next item of business. When one remembers that the role of the presiding officer is to facilitate the process, it is logical that when the group concludes one item of business, the facilitator tells the members where they are going next. The presiding officer might simply say, "The next business in order will be the report of the finance committee." Or in a series of proposed amendments to the bylaws, "The next business in order is Proposed Bylaw Amendment 3."

Complete announcement of a vote has an additional effect that is difficult to quantify. In the case of highly controversial motions, a complete announcement of the results of the vote appears to have a very positive effect on the membership in attendance at the meeting. It is almost as if it helps bring closure to the issue, allowing members to put the issue behind them and move on to the next item of business.

The Least You Need to Know

- While a motion is pending, members should make sure that it is worded to their satisfaction, amending it as needed.
- When debating a motion, all members should focus their remarks on the issue and avoid personal attacks and straying off topic.

- The presiding officer should restate the motion before putting it to a vote.
- The four steps of the complete announcement of the vote lend closure to an issue and prepare the group to move on to the next item of business.

Chapter 7

The Ladder of Motions: a.k.a. Precedence of Motions

In This Chapter

- Climbing up and down the ladder of motions
- Timing of particular motions
- Why your motion might be out of order
- Knowing which motion is immediately pending

Suppose you're sitting in on your first meeting in which parliamentary procedure is followed. After the chair calls the meeting to order and establishes the presence of a quorum, and after the minutes are approved, a member makes a motion. The motion is quickly seconded, the chair states it, and it is being discussed. Makes sense so far.

Then another member makes another motion and that motion is allowed by the chair. That second motion is seconded, is restated by the chair, and is being discussed. Your head is beginning to spin when suddenly a third member makes a third motion. That motion is ruled out of order by the chair—much to your relief! But then another member makes a motion, and that motion is allowed by the chair. At this stage in the process, you are probably wondering if there is a dartboard somewhere that the chair is using to decide on the rulings because it makes about that much sense.

A concept in parliamentary procedure helps this scenario make sense. It is called the *precedence of motions*, and if you understand the concept, you will know when motions are allowable (also called in order) and when they are out of order.

The Concept of Precedence

Let's set the groundwork for explaining the concept of precedence of motions by reemphasizing three ideas that I covered in previous chapters.

- Only one main motion is allowed on the floor at a time, but many secondary motions can be on the floor at the same time.
- The term *pending* refers to Step 4 in the motion-making process. It is the period after the motion has been restated by the presiding officer (Step 3) and before the presiding officer puts the motion to a vote (Step 5).
- As the term *immediately pending* suggests, many different motions can be pending at the same time. The immediately pending motion is, of the motions that are pending, the motion that was the last one made.

def•i•ni•tion

Precedence of motions is a list of specific motions that indicates the priority of motions. When a motion on the list is pending, any motion above it on the list is in order, and any motion below it on the list is out of order.

In *Robert's*, the precedence of motions contains the following 13 motions:

- *Fix the Time to Which to Adjourn*
- *Adjourn*
- *Recess*

- *Raise a Question of Privilege*
- *Call for the Orders of the Day*
- *Lay on the Table*
- *Previous Question*
- *Limit* or *Extend Limits of Debate*
- *Postpone to a Certain Time* (sometimes called *Postpone Definitely*)
- *Commit* or *Refer to a Committee*
- *Amend*
- *Postpone Indefinitely*
- *MAIN MOTION*

Gavel Gaffes

The term *precedence* is usually pronounced *PRESS-i-dens*. However, in the world of parliamentary procedure, it is pronounced *pre-SEED-ens*.

The motion to *Amend*, as will be further explained in Chapter 13, has two forms. A primary amendment is an amendment that changes the main motion, and a secondary amendment is an amendment that changes the primary amendment. Therefore, when I list the motions included in the precedence of motions, I prefer to separate out *Amend* and make it a list of 14 motions, as follows:

1. *Fix the Time to Which to Adjourn*
2. *Adjourn*
3. *Recess*
4. *Raise a Question of Privilege*
5. *Call for the Orders of the Day*
6. *Lay on the Table*
7. *Previous Question*
8. *Limit* or *Extend Limits of Debate*
9. *Postpone to a Certain Time (Definitely)*

Point of Information

A secondary amendment is not just the second amendment. It differs from the primary amendment in that it amends the primary amendment instead of the main motion.

10. *Commit* or *Refer to a Committee*
11. Secondary amendment—*Amend* an amendment
12. Primary amendment—*Amend* a main motion or resolution
13. *Postpone Indefinitely*
14. *MAIN MOTION*

When any one of these motions on the list is the immediately pending motion, any motion above it on the list can be made at that time, and any motion below it on this list cannot be made at that time. It is truly that simple. If you have this list in front of you at a meeting, you can easily check which motions can be made when.

The Vote and the Ladder

To understand how the votes are taken on the various motions in the precedence list, it would be helpful to walk through a scenario in which several motions are pending. In this sample situation, you need to assume that after each motion is made, it is seconded, is restated by the presiding officer, and is being discussed before another motion is made.

Higher on the List Is Okay, Lower Is Out of Order

If a main motion is pending (that is, it's been made, seconded, and restated by the chair and is being discussed by the members), it is the immediately pending motion and is #14 on the precedence of motions list.

While discussing that main motion, a member moves to *Amend* the main motion. That proposed amendment is in order because it is #12 on the list, and 12 is higher than 14. (I told you the concept was easy!)

While discussing the amendment, another member moves to make a secondary amendment—in other words, to *Amend* the amendment. Secondary amendments are #11 on the list of precedence, so the motion is in order because 11 is higher on the list than 12.

While discussing the amendment to the amendment, another member moves to *Postpone* the motion to the next meeting (*Postpone to a Certain Time*, also called *Postpone Definitely*). The amendment to the amendment is the immediately pending question and is #11 on the precedence of motions list. The motion to *Postpone* to the next meeting is #9, *Postpone to a Certain Time*, and is above #11 on the list. Therefore, the motion is in order.

While discussing whether or not we should *Postpone* this motion to the next meeting, another member moves that this motion be *Referred to a Committee*. That motion to *Refer* (#10) is below the immediately pending motion (#9, *Postpone to a Certain Time*) and is therefore out of order.

Needed: An Organized Method of Getting Out of This

Now stay with me because things are about to get interesting. What you have now, besides potential confusion, are four different motions that are all pending, as follows:

> #14: *MAIN MOTION*
>
> #12: Primary amendment
>
> #11: Secondary amendment
>
> #9: *Postpone to a Certain Time*

What you need now is an organized method of getting out of this mess. That organized method does exist. Close your eyes, take a deep breath, and visualize a ladder.

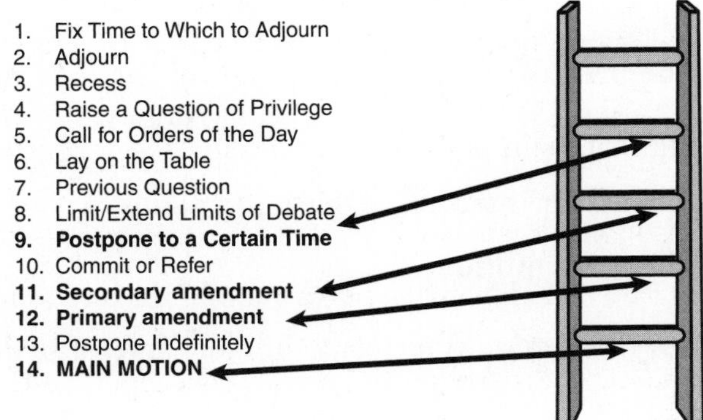

The precedence of motions, with the pending motions in bold. You work your way out of the sequence of pending motions by stepping down the ladder, voting on each immediately pending motion as you go.

Every motion that is pending is a step up a rung of the ladder. When it is time to vote on the motion, you must come down the ladder in reverse order of the steps you took up the ladder.

If we follow the ladder visually, the bottom rung of the ladder is #14, the main motion; the second rung is #12, the primary amendment; the third rung is #11, the secondary amendment; and the top rung is #9, *Postpone to a Certain Time.* We are up four rungs on the ladder and are ready to come down. We must now vote on those four motions in reverse order of how they were made. In other words, the last motion made is the first one voted on and so on.

Vote in Reverse Order

Let's follow these steps in order:

1. **Vote on the motion to *Postpone to a Certain Time.*** If this motion passes, the main motion and the amendments that are pending will be *Postponed* with it until the next meeting. At the next meeting, under the agenda item of unfinished business, you will have three motions still pending. If the motion to *Postpone to a Certain Time* fails, you'll move on to the next motion down the ladder, which is the secondary amendment.
2. **Vote on the secondary amendment.** If the secondary amendment passes, the primary amendment is now adjusted to reflect this change. If not, you move on to the primary amendment as it was originally stated.
3. **Vote on the primary amendment.** If the vote on the primary amendment passes, the main motion on the floor is the main motion as amended. If the primary amendment fails, the main motion on the floor is the original main motion.
4. **Vote on the main motion.**

If you skip any of these steps, you violate the rules and thus fall off the ladder!

There is, of course, an exception to the ladder voting rule. That exception is motion #13 on the precedence of motion, which is the motion to *Postpone Indefinitely.* As you will learn in Chapter 13, the purpose of the motion to *Postpone Indefinitely* is to kill the motion that is pending.

Since the sole purpose of passing the motion to *Postpone Indefinitely* is to kill the motion, if it passes, the main motion is thus killed, and there does not need to be a vote on the main motion. Thus, if there is an affirmative vote on the motion to *Postpone Indefinitely*, you do not come down the final rung of the ladder, and you do not vote on the main motion.

How to Apply It

A specific example may help in the application of the precedence of motions:

- Member A makes the motion: "I move that we purchase a computer."

  The motion is seconded, is restated by the chair, and is being discussed by the members. This is a main motion (#14 on the ladder of precedence).

- Member B thinks we should put a price limit on that computer or the person responsible for purchasing the computer will buy all kinds of extras that are not needed.

  Member B says: "I move to *Amend* the motion by adding the words 'not to exceed $2,000.'"

  The motion made by Member B is a primary amendment—an amendment to the main motion (#12 on the ladder of precedence). It is in order. The presiding officer gets a second on Member B's amendment, restates the amendment, and opens the amendment to debate.

- Member C thinks that Member B is cheap or hasn't bought a decent computer in a while and doesn't realize the cost of a computer that meets the needs of the organization. Member C says: "I move to *Amend* the amendment by striking '$2,000' and inserting '$4,000.'"

  The motion made by Member C is a secondary amendment (#11 on the ladder of precedence). It is in order. The presiding officer gets a second on Member C's amendment, restates the amendment, and opens the amendment to debate.

- Member D thinks that we need to know more than we currently do about the cost of a computer.

  Member D says: "I move to *Postpone* this motion until our meeting next month." The motion made by Member D is a motion to *Postpone to a Certain Time* (#9 on the ladder of precedence). It is in order. The presiding officer gets a second on Member D's motion, restates the motion, and opens it for debate.

- Member E believes that the Finance Committee should decide what price range of computer to buy and have a recommendation for the group at the next meeting.

  Member E says: "I move that we *Refer* this to the Finance Committee and direct them to have a recommendation for us at next month's meeting."

  The motion made by Member E is *Commit* or *Refer* (#10 on the ladder of precedence). *Commit* or *Refer* is below *Postpone to a Certain Time* on the precedence of motions and therefore must be ruled out of order.

We now have four motions on the floor, and we still haven't decided whether to purchase the computer. The members appear to be ready to make a decision. We will now proceed down the ladder, voting on each of the motions in reverse order.

Motion from Member D

The immediately pending motion is the motion made by Member D to *Postpone to a Certain Time.* Therefore, discussion on that motion is concluded, and the presiding officer calls for a vote on the motion. If the motion passes, all of the pending motions (the main motion, primary amendment, and secondary amendment) are *Postponed* to the next meeting. The motion fails. What next?

Motion from Member C

Now the immediately pending motion is the motion made by Member C, the secondary amendment, to strike "$2,000" and insert "$4,000."

The members discuss that motion and vote yes. The amendment is amended. What next?

If you guessed that the next step in the process is to vote on whether to purchase a computer, you just fell off the ladder!

Motion from Member B

The immediately pending motion is the motion made by Member B, the primary amendment. That amendment is now amended so that the motion we will be voting on is "to *Amend* the motion by adding 'not to exceed $4,000.'" The members discuss the motion and vote yes. The main motion is amended. What next?

Motion from Member A

Now the immediately pending motion is the motion made by Member A, the main motion. That motion now reads: "I move that we purchase a computer, not to exceed $4,000." The motion is discussed, and the vote is yes. Finally we have decided to purchase a computer, and we have also decided to put a price restriction on the computer that we are going to purchase.

If you keep the ladder in mind and always ask, "What is the immediately pending motion?" it makes it much easier to make a decision.

Parliamentary Pearls

If you are chairing a meeting that gets this complicated, remember that your role is to facilitate the meeting. If a member makes a motion that is out of order at this time, when you get to the place on the ladder that it is in order, call on that member and let them know they could make their motion now, and it won't be out of order. This is the fastest way to be the hero!

Proceed with Caution

The concept of precedence of motions is critical in properly processing a motion.

It is easy to skip steps, so proceed with caution. For instance, when there is a primary amendment and a secondary amendment and the secondary amendment passes, it is very easy to forget to go back down the ladder and process the primary amendment as amended. Many times it appears that if the secondary amendment passes, the primary amendment becomes unnecessary. That is not the case.

To demonstrate this point, let's go back to the computer-purchase motion we just processed. The primary amendment and the secondary amendment were both dealing with money, but they had very different purposes. The purpose of the primary amendment was to add a price limit to the computer we were going to purchase. The purpose of the secondary amendment was solely to determine what that price limit would be.

Another way to demonstrate this is to point out that a member may favor the secondary amendment and oppose the primary amendment. If you, as a member, believe that the person buying the computer is a real tightwad and incredibly knowledgeable about computers, you may not want to put a price limit on the computer. Therefore, you would be against the primary amendment. But if the group is going to insist on putting a price limit on the purchase of the computer, you believe it should be as high as possible. Therefore, you would be in favor of the secondary amendment.

You Can Go Back Up the Ladder

The voting ladder in the precedence of motions is not a one-way ladder. You can move up and down it and then up and down again before finally processing the main motion and getting off the ladder.

Let's go back to our example of the computer purchase. When the members voted down #9, the motion to *Postpone to a Certain Time*, the motion that was immediately pending then was #11, the secondary amendment. If Member E still wanted to make the motion to *Commit* or *Refer*, #10, that motion would now be in order. It was out of order when #9 was immediately pending, but it is now in order when #11 is immediately pending. So, although a motion may be out of order at one time, the same motion may be in order when a different motion is immediately pending.

The Least You Need to Know

- The immediately pending motion is the motion that was last stated by the chair.
- The precedence of motions indicates which motions precede other motions during debate.
- Motions that don't follow the precedence of motions should be called out of order.
- Don't skip steps on the ladder of motions!

Chapter 8

Let's Talk About It: Debate

In This Chapter

- The rules of debate
- What you can and can't debate
- Debate etiquette
- Making your debate effective

A critical part of the democratic process is for members to gather, discuss an issue, and make a decision. As a general rule, better decisions are made when the group has had an open discussion on the issue. Compromise and collaboration are more likely to occur in an environment of free and open discussion. Fortunately, *Robert's* provides you with the tools you need to create such an environment.

In this chapter, we will not only look at the rules you should follow to encourage free and open discussion, but how to debate politely and how to make your debate effective.

Rules of Debate

Robert's includes the following *debate* rules that can assist us in discussing motions in a very fair, well-mannered fashion:

- You need a motion before you can debate. An issue is not debatable until a motion has been made, seconded, and restated by the presiding officer.
- Only one person should speak at a time. The presiding officer calls on only one member at a time, and therefore only one member should be speaking at a time.
- Debate is limited to the motion immediately pending. (Exception: Because the purpose of the motion to *Postpone Indefinitely* is to kill the main motion, that motion has relaxed debate rules, and the debate can cover the merit of the motion it is trying to kill.) See Chapter 7 for a discussion of the precedence of motions.

> **def•i•ni•tion**
>
> **Debate** is the discussion regarding a motion that occurs after the presiding officer has restated the motion and before he or she has put it to a vote.

If a main motion is on the floor and so is an amendment to that motion, the discussion must be limited to the amendment. After the amendment is voted on, the discussion will then be limited only to the main motion as amended, if amended.

- The maker of the motion, if he or she chooses to, has the right to be the first speaker on the motion.
- The maker of the motion is prohibited from speaking against the motion.

Limits on the Chair

The role of the presiding officer during the time of debate is critical. It is the presiding officer's responsibility to ensure that debate is conducted in a fair and appropriate manner. If debate rules are not being followed, the presiding officer should initiate corrective action. An effective presiding officer doesn't wait for a member to point out a problem.

Because the presiding officer is a member of the group, he or she should not have to give up the right to debate. However, the chair shouldn't be an active participant in the very debate that he or she is in charge of facilitating. So, although the presiding officer has the right to debate, that right should be used very sparingly.

Leave the Chair!

When the presiding officer feels that it is important for him or her to speak on an issue, which should be very seldom, he or she must vacate the chair (sometimes called "relinquish the chair") before speaking.

The presiding officer relinquishes the chair to the member who would normally take his or her place if he or she were not there. So if the bylaws indicate that the vice president would take over if the president were not there, the president should relinquish the chair to the vice president.

> **Point of Information**
>
> The presiding officer may exercise his or her membership right and speak on a motion only after relinquishing the chair.

However, if the vice president has spoken on the motion, the chair should not be turned over to the vice president. If there are other vice presidents who have not spoken, they should assume the chair. If not, the presiding officer should get permission from the members to appoint another person who is judged to be objective on the issue.

Once the presiding officer has relinquished the chair, he or she should not resume presiding until that particular motion is disposed of.

Exceptions

As with so many rules in parliamentary procedure, there are two exceptions to this rule. The presiding officer does not leave the chair when discussing the motion to *Appeal from the Decision of the Chair.* Actually, as we will learn in Chapter 13, the presiding officer has more debate rights with the motion to *Appeal from the Decision of the Chair* than members of the assembly have. The second exception is when the presiding officer wishes to speak in a small committee or board. Of course, you remember that from the discussion of small committees and boards that we had in Chapter 2.

When the Chair Is Up for Election

Many people believe that if the presiding officer is up for election or reelection to a position, the presiding officer should relinquish the chair during that election. Not so! The presiding officer can preside over his or her own election. If, though, there is a motion that is specific to the presiding officer, such as a motion to censure the presiding officer, then the presiding officer should relinquish the chair just as he or she would if he or she wished to speak on a motion.

Questions Through the Chair

While debating an issue, it is not unusual for members to have questions. The proper method of handling those questions is to address them to the presiding officer. If the presiding officer knows the answer and wishes to answer the question, he or she may do so. Otherwise, the presiding officer may choose to direct the question to a member or a person in attendance who knows the answer.

Let's return to the motion from Chapter 7 to purchase a computer. When discussing what kind of computer to purchase, a member asks whether anyone knows which of the brands is rated highest on technical support. If the presiding officer knows the answer, he or she may simply answer the question. If the presiding officer knows that John knows the answer, the presiding officer could simply ask John whether he would answer the question. If the chair does not know whether anyone knows the answer, he or she may simply ask if anyone in the group knows the answer to the question.

Parliamentary Pearls

Whenever possible, presiding officers should direct the question to someone else rather than answer the question themselves. By directing another person to answer the question, the presiding officer is sharing the limelight and giving members an opportunity to develop their leadership skills. In addition, if the issue is controversial, members may perceive any answer from the presiding officer as prejudicial. Thus, not answering questions increases the chances of being perceived as objective.

You Can't Debate Everything!

Although debate is a basic component of parliamentary procedure, there are times when the need to move on and make a decision outweighs the need to allow for debate to occur. Thus, the following motions are *undebatable:*

- *Fix the Time to Which to Adjourn*
- *Adjourn*
- *Recess*
- *Raise a Question of Privilege*
- *Call for the Orders of the Day*
- *Lay on the Table*
- *Previous Question*
- *Limit* or *Extend Limits of Debate*

def•i•ni•tion

A motion is **undebatable** when there is no debate allowed on that motion. In essence, Step 4 in the processing of a motion (see the section "Step 4: Members Debate the Motion" in Chapter 6) is skipped.

Note, however, that main motions are debatable. When one of the preceding motions is secondary to the main motion, it is usually not debatable.

When a motion is undebatable, the presiding officer may recognize a member who wants to ask a question that, when answered, will aid the members in transacting business. However, the presiding officer should make sure that the question or brief suggestion is not debated but simply helps clarify the motion on the floor.

Speaking Order

When a motion is pending, the general rule is that the first person to seek recognition of the presiding officer should be assigned the floor. Again, there are exceptions to this general rule. The times when the floor should be assigned to a person other than the first person seeking the floor are as follows:

- If the member who made the motion has not yet spoken on the motion, he or she can be recognized as the speaker even if he or she wasn't the first person to seek recognition.
- Anyone who has not spoken gets recognized before anyone who has.
- In cases where the chair knows the opinions of the persons seeking the floor, the assignment should alternate between those favoring and those opposing the motion. There are many ways the presiding officer can determine the side of the speaker. One easy method is to simply ask. After a member speaks against the motion, the presiding officer may simply say, "Are there any members who would like to speak in favor of the motion?" A method that works well in large groups is to have two microphones, one marked affirmative and the other marked negative. Members who want to speak line up at the appropriate microphone, and the presiding officer simply alternates between the two microphones.

Parliamentary Pearls

Alternating between members speaking in the affirmative on a motion and members speaking in the negative on the motion is sometimes a very effective way of controlling the length of debate on an issue. Let's say the presiding officer asks whether anyone wants to speak in favor of the motion. Many hands go up, and the presiding officer calls on the first member to seek recognition. After that member speaks, the presiding officer asks whether anyone wants to speak against the motion, and no hands go up. When the presiding officer asks if anyone wants to speak in favor of the motion, most of the time fewer or no hands go up because it is obvious that the motion is going to pass even without further affirmative comments.

Speaking Time

To save time, no member may speak more than two times on any one motion in any one day, and each of those speeches is limited to 10 minutes. This rule may be the best-kept secret of parliamentary procedure! The basis of this rule is that, in the democratic process, everyone should be able to participate in the debate. If one member dominates the debate, that reduces the rights of the other members.

In conventions, because of the large number of people in attendance, the time limit is usually reduced to somewhere between two and five minutes. In small groups, there is no limit to the number of times a member may speak.

Debate Manners

Manners for debating a motion aren't much different than the manners that are appropriate in all aspects of our life.

In a group of people, it is considered mannerly to speak one at a time, not all at once. Therefore, in debate, if a member wants to speak, that member should seek recognition. How you seek recognition is usually set by the norms of the group. In most meetings, seeking recognition is usually as simple as raising your hand and waiting for the presiding officer to call on you. This is probably the most appropriate method for most situations.

Here are some other rules of parliamentary etiquette:

- **Only speak when called on.** Whatever method your group uses to seek the floor, a member should not speak until called on by the presiding officer.
- **Direct all comments to the chair.** Avoid directing comments to another member.
- **Don't be disruptive.** Side conversations are not allowed. Neither is walking around the room in a manner that is disruptive

> **Gavel Gaffes**
>
> Comments must be directed to the issue of the motion, not the personality of the members. Discussion should be refuting the facts, not making accusations against other members.

to the meeting. That doesn't mean you can't get up and go to the restroom during a meeting, just don't be disruptive about it. If the member is disruptive, the presiding officer should call the member to order.

- **You can make corrections.** If you hear information that you know is inaccurate, you have the right to call attention to the inaccuracy and to have the accurate information shared with the group. Of course, this must be done politely.
- **The chair can interrupt you.** While you shouldn't interrupt another speaker, if the presiding officer interrupts you while you are speaking, you should stop and listen to the presiding officer. There are situations in which the presiding officer has the right to interrupt a speaker, and you should assume that it is one of those situations and allow the interruption.

Point of Information

If you have already spoken on the motion, be aware of other members who have not spoken yet and attempt to help the presiding officer by inviting them to speak before you. For example, if you are in line at a microphone to speak a second time on a particular motion, allow anyone who is behind you in line who has not yet spoken on the motion to step ahead of you in line. Since you do not have the right to speak before them, this action sets a cooperative tone among the members and is clearly seen as helpful to the presiding officer.

Debate Effectively!

We have all seen times when the right words spoken by the right person at the right time have swayed the whole group. Those times serve as a reminder of the power of debate. If you have strong feelings on the issue, put forth the extra effort to make your debate effective. I've included some tips to help you hone your debating skills.

Which Side?

It is a good idea to begin your debate by telling the members which side you are speaking on. You might say something like, "Madam Chairman, I rise to speak in favor of the motion." Then, no matter how unclear the rest of your comments are, the members know which side of the motion you favor.

Organize Your Thoughts

The fact that the rules only allow you to speak two times on any motion in any one day should make it clear to you that you need to organize and write down your thoughts. Also, remember that you cannot speak a second time until everyone who wants to speak has had the opportunity to speak the first time. You need to make sure that, when you do speak, your thoughts are well planned and cover the major points you want to make.

In addition, pay close attention to your delivery. Speak clearly and slowly, project your voice, and say it like you mean it.

Organize your thoughts into two or three main points and communicate them during your debate time. Avoid going down a long list of reasons you favor or oppose the motion—the longer the list, the less likely people will remember it. Keep focused on the major reasons why you have taken your stand.

At the end of your debate speech, you should restate which side you favor and summarize the main reasons you expressed during your debate. It might sound something like this: "I have spoken against this motion because, as I just explained, the cost of this program is too high, and the potential harm of this program to our organization outweighs any possible advantage. Therefore, I urge you to vote against this motion."

As you can see from this example, the summary can reinforce the points you have made and leave the other members with a clear vision of where you stand on the issue and why you stand there.

The Least You Need to Know

- The presiding officer should appear neutral on the issues being debated at all times; when the chair feels that it is essential to speak up on an issue, she or he should first relinquish the chair.
- Use proper manners at all times when debating.

- The order of assignment of the floor is there to make sure every side gets its points heard.
- Think before you speak during a debate.

Chapter 9

Voting: The Democratic Way

In This Chapter

- Ways to conduct the vote
- The power of general consent
- What different votes mean
- Why you normally can't vote by proxy

One of the most valuable aspects of living in a democratic society is being able to vote. A vote is a formal expression of will, opinion, or choice by members of an assembly in regard to a matter submitted to it.

Methods of Voting

Parliamentary procedure allows for numerous methods of voting on a motion. Some are somewhat obscure and are used infrequently or only when specified in the bylaws, so we are going to leave those for the technical books. In this chapter, we'll focus on the six methods of voting that are commonly used and would be helpful for you to understand.

Everybody Agrees—General Consent

General consent and *unanimous consent* are interchangeable terms. Voting by general consent involves the presiding officer saying "If there is no objection to [states the issue under consideration] …" Then, if there is no objection, you can skip all six steps of the motion-making process. This method should only be used when the motion is of little importance or when there appears to be no opposition to the motion.

General consent has some very valuable uses. Sometimes it is so obvious that the group is in agreement that it would be a waste of time to go through the six steps of processing a motion. For example, when there is no more business on the agenda and everybody is packing up their things, that would be a perfect time for the presiding officer to say, "If there is no objection, the meeting is adjourned." [pause] "Hearing no objection, we are adjourned."

> **def•i•ni•tion**
>
> **Unanimous consent** is interchangeable with **general consent** and is a method of voting without taking a formal vote. The presiding officer asks if there are any objections, and if none is expressed, the motion is considered passed.

> **Gavel Gaffes**
>
> Don't let the term "unanimous consent" mislead you. *Robert's* includes the following explanation of general consent, indicating that "it does not necessarily imply that every member is in favor of the proposed action; it may only mean that the opposition, feeling that it is useless to oppose or discuss the matter, simply acquiesces."

It takes only one member to object to force a more formal voting method. If a member objects, the chair has to state the motion and put it to a vote. Since it takes only one person to object, no membership rights are being violated by using unanimous consent.

Probably the best example of when to use general consent is in the approval of the minutes of the meeting. Assuming that the minutes have been printed and distributed to the members in advance of the meeting, the presiding officer might simply say, "You have received the minutes. Are there any corrections to the minutes? [pause] "Hearing none, if there is no objection, the minutes are approved as printed."

Viva Voce—Voice Vote

The most commonly used method of voting is the voice vote. It is used effectively when there is little controversy and the outcome appears obvious. However, it should be avoided when a two-thirds vote is required because it is difficult to determine a two-thirds vote by voice.

For example, a call for a voice vote might sound like this: "Those in favor of the motion, say *aye*. [pause] Those opposed say *no*."

After the presiding officer conducts the voice vote, the chair declares the motion to have passed (or lost). Members have the right to question the results of the vote and can request to have the vote clarified by having an uncounted rising vote. All you have to do is call out "*Division of the Assembly*." The *Division of the Assembly* motion requires the presiding officer to call for another vote, this time using an uncounted rising vote—sometimes called a standing vote (discussed later in this chapter). Unlike most other motions, a member can simply call out for a *Division of the Assembly*—it doesn't need a second, and it is not a debatable motion. (*Division of the Assembly* is discussed further in Chapter 13.)

Parliamentary Pearls

When serving as presiding officer, it is advisable to use the words "If there is no objection, …" any time you are not putting an issue to a formal vote. These simple words can protect you from future criticism.

Gavel Gaffes

People sometimes mistakenly believe that the motion *Division of the Assembly* requires a counted vote. It only requires an uncounted rising vote because, in very large groups, a counted vote can take a very long time. If it required a counted vote, members in large groups could use it to delay business or, as we say in the parliamentary world, for dilatory purposes.

Show Me the Hand—Show of Hands Vote

The show of hands voting method is typically used in small groups because it usually only works when everyone can see everyone else. The wording of this method of voting could be as simple as "Those in favor of the motion, please raise your hand. [pause] Those opposed, please raise your hand." Make sure to pause between asking for those in favor and those against so that those voting in favor of the motion have a chance to put their hands down before those voting against it raise theirs.

Stand and Maybe Count Off—Rising Vote

A rising vote sounds just like its name: members cast their vote by standing up. The presiding officer might call for a rising vote by saying something like this: "Those in favor of the motion, please stand. [pause] Please be seated. Those opposed to the motion, please stand. [pause] Please be seated."

As noted previously, the rising vote should be used when a member makes a motion for the *Division of the Assembly* after a voice vote. This method is also effective when the vote requirement is greater than a majority because it's much easier to determine if the two-thirds vote was obtained.

If a member isn't satisfied with the call on a rising vote, the member may move to have the vote counted. The motion to have a counted vote needs a majority to pass. But if there is any doubt, it's smarter for the presiding officer to simply go immediately to a counted vote when requested. The time a counted vote takes is well worth the time spent counting if the members are at all in question of the results of the vote.

An efficient method of counting the vote is referred to as "serpentine" because it follows a winding pattern similar to that of a snake. When the members who are voting in favor of the motion are standing, the chair requests that they remain standing and count off. Starting with the first row at one of the ends, the people standing count off and sit down. So the person on the right end of the first row counts 1 and sits down, the next person standing in that row counts 2 and sits down, and so on until everyone in that row has counted and is seated. Since the first row went from right to left, the second row will count off from left to right.

Thus, the first person in the second row continues with the next number, counts, and is then seated. This continues, one row at a time, until every member who stood to vote in the affirmative has counted off and is seated. You now know the number of votes in the affirmative. Next, the presiding officer asks those voting no on the motion to stand and remain standing until they have counted off. The serpentine counting is done again on the no votes. This method is quick, especially after the group has done it one time and gets the feel of it.

Gavel Gaffes

The Americans with Disabilities Act has influenced voting. It is not at all unusual for an organization to have replaced a rising vote with a vote using a voting card. Each voting member is given a voting card. Instead of rising, the presiding officer directs the members to raise their voting card. It has the same effect as a rising vote, but it is easier on people who find standing up and sitting down difficult.

Write It Down—Ballot Vote

When secrecy is desired, groups can vote by ballot—usually paper ballots. Ballots are usually used for elections or any time the pressure of the group might keep people from voting what they really believe.

The usual wording for the ballot vote is "Please mark your ballot." That comment is usually followed by instructions on folding the ballots and where to deposit them.

Call the Roll—Roll Call Vote

The roll call vote is the exact opposite of a ballot vote. The purpose of the ballot vote is to conceal each member's vote. In a roll call vote, the purpose is to make how each member voted official as part of the record.

The roll call vote should only be used in situations in which the members are answerable to a constituency. You will most frequently see it used in governmental bodies. For instance, the U.S. Senate and House of Representatives vote by roll call so that they remain accountable to the American people.

The presiding officer states the motion and then calls for a vote by asking the secretary (or clerk) to call the roll. It is usual practice to call the roll in alphabetical order, except that the presiding officer's name is called last. However, some organizations have designed a method to ensure that the same members do not have to vote first every time. Instead of always beginning with the first name in the alphabet, some groups rotate how they call roll. Each time there is a vote, they start with the next name on the alphabetical list.

When a person's name is called, that person answers "aye," "no," "present" (abstain), or "pass." If a member calls out *pass* when his or her name is called, that person may vote before the results are announced. I bet you can already imagine how some people in politics use the "pass" to avoid revealing their vote too early in the game!

The roll should be entered in the minutes as a part of the record of that meeting.

Here are the words to use for each of the voting methods:

- **General or unanimous consent:** "If there is no objection …."
- **Voice vote:** "All those in favor, say *aye*. [pause] All those opposed, say *no*."

  (If the chair is in doubt of the results of a voice vote, he or she should state, "The chair is in doubt, and therefore a rising (or counted) vote will be taken." Then proceed with a rising or counted vote.)
- **Show of hands vote:** "All those in favor of the motion, please raise your hand. [pause] Please lower your hands. Those opposed to the motion, please raise your hand. [pause] Please lower your hands."
- **Rising vote:** "Those in favor of the motion, please stand. [pause] Please be seated. Those opposed to the motion, please stand. [pause] Please be seated."
- **Rising counted vote:** "Those in favor of the motion, please stand and remain standing until counted. [pause] Please be seated. Those opposed to the motion, please stand and remain standing until counted. [pause] Please be seated."

- **Ballot vote:** "Please mark your ballots clearly, fold them one time, and hand them directly to a teller."
- **Roll call vote:** "The secretary will now call the roll."

Electronic Voting via Wireless Keypads

Audience participation technology, frequently referred to as wireless keypads, can help make meetings more effective because they allow for extremely quick and accurate voting tabulation.

Let's first understand how it works. Each voting member gets a wireless keypad that looks much like a simple remote control for a television. When the presiding officer instructs the members to vote, the instructions sound something like this: "If you want to vote *aye*, please press 1; if you want to vote *no*, please press 2. Vote now. [Pause for approximately 30 seconds while the members vote.] Voting is now closed. May we see the results?" Then the technician who works with the audience participation technology flashes on the screen either the number of votes in the affirmative and the negative, the percentage of votes in each, and/or a graph that visually shows the votes.

I have many clients who have been using electronic voting for a number of years, and I have been able to observe this marvelous use of technology at work. There are some distinct advantages of using it, and there is only one disadvantage—cost. The advantages include time savings, accuracy, more effective meetings, and the opportunity to collect demographic information.

Time Savings, Big Time

No matter how large the group, voting using wireless keypads, from the time the chair starts the vote until the time the chair announces the results, usually takes approximately one minute. Counting a vote manually can take a long time. While the serpentine method, described earlier in this chapter, helps reduce the time, it usually takes much longer than a minute. One of the organizations I work with (that, by the way, is very efficient at counting votes) used the wireless keypads for two days of their three-day convention. During the two days with the wireless keypads they took 46 votes, each taking approximately one minute. The third day, each of the numerous votes taken averaged seven minutes in length. It doesn't take a mathematical genius to figure out that wireless keypad voting saves time, big time!

In some delegate bodies, delegates carry various numbers of votes, based on the size of their constituency. In those situations, a manually counted vote is even more time-consuming. With wireless keypad voting, their number of votes is put into the system before the meeting begins, and the processing of those votes still takes approximately a minute.

If you use electronic keypad voting, I advise you to include their use in your meeting rules.

Accuracy

We all know the problems with human error in the counting process when using the traditional methods of vote counting. The confidence in the accuracy of wireless keypad voting has been displayed to me many times. Over my numerous years as a professional parliamentarian, I have seen many close votes, whether they are tie votes or votes with one or two vote differences. In almost every situation where the votes were counted by human beings, when there was a close vote, someone in the assembly asked for a recount. In every situation where wireless keypads were used and there was a close vote, no one ever asked for a recount. The participants were confident with the count.

More Effective Meeting

The time spent counting votes manually is very distracting to the attendees. The meeting's flow is interrupted, and frequently members get frustrated with the process. With electronic keypad voting, members can spend more of their valuable time staying focused on the issues instead of the process.

Opportunity to Collect Demographic Information

Frequently, when using wireless keypad voting, the organization uses the keypads to gather demographic information on their attendees.

They ask questions regarding gender, age, education, work settings, and so on. It is a valuable information-gathering tool for the organization.

Absentee and Proxy Voting

It is a fundamental principle of parliamentary law that only the members physically present at a legally called meeting can vote. Therefore, the only way that an organization can allow for either absentee voting (voting prior to a meeting) or proxy voting (sending a representative to the meeting to vote for you) is if it is specifically permitted in the bylaws or required by state statute. However, it is recommended that neither absentee nor proxy voting be allowed because they violate the principles of parliamentary procedure. Because one member carries the votes of another member in addition to his own, proxy voting is also in violation of the parliamentary principle of one member, one vote. With proxy voting, a member may have numerous votes.

Meaning of Vote

Although an organization is free to specify in its bylaws the number of votes necessary for adoption of a motion (two-thirds, three-fifths, three-fourths, nine-tenths, and so on), the majority vote and the two-thirds vote are the most common. Let's look at each in turn.

Majority Vote

A majority vote is "more than half" of the votes cast. So if 20 votes are cast, you need at least 11 votes. If 19 votes are cast, you need at least 10 votes.

If a vote ends in a tie, a majority was not attained. That's because a majority means more than half, and a tie vote is not more than half. If the vote is tied and a majority vote is needed, the vote fails. We are well aware that a 13 to 14 vote fails. But a 13 to 13 vote also fails. It just doesn't fail by quite as much!

Two-Thirds Vote

A two-thirds vote simply means that there must be at least twice as many votes in favor of the motion as there are against it.

Figuring out a two-thirds vote is much easier than most people think. Most of the time people take the votes in favor and add them to the votes against, divide that number by 3, and multiply that number by 2. Let's use an example to help you understand that process. Let's say 20 people voted aye and 10 people voted no. The aye votes plus the no votes equals 30. Thirty divided by 3 is 10. Ten times 2 is 20. Therefore, a two-thirds vote of 30 votes is 20.

There's another easy way to determine a two-thirds vote, and you don't need to be a math whiz to do it. You take the number of no votes, multiply that number by 2, and the result is the number of aye votes that are required for a two-thirds vote. Let's use the same example here again. If the vote was 20 in favor and 10 against, and a two-thirds vote was needed, then the motion passed—10 (the number of no votes) times 2 is 20 and there were 20 votes in favor, so the motion passed.

Gavel Gaffes

When calling for the vote, you will often hear the presiding officer ask for abstentions. It would sound like: "Those in favor, say *aye*. Those opposed, say *no*. Abstentions?"

The presiding officer does not need to call for abstentions. An abstention is a member's way of not voting. When you don't vote aye or no, you have abstained.

In a ballot vote, a member abstains by not turning in a ballot or by turning in a blank ballot. The blank ballot is not counted as a vote.

A Percentage of What?

People sometimes try to figure out how many votes are needed for a majority or two-thirds vote before the actual vote is cast. However, in voting, if the rules don't say otherwise, "majority" is more than half of the votes cast, and "two-thirds" is two thirds of the votes cast. So you have no way of knowing in advance how many votes will be required to pass a motion. In an unrealistic—yet possible—scenario, there may be

20 members present and yet 16 of those 20 members abstain from voting. In this case, only three votes would constitute a majority.

There are, however, many other bases for votes. These include a majority or two thirds of the membership and a majority or two thirds of the members present. Let's look at how the various bases for voting play out in a situation in which there are:

1,000 members in the organization

100 members present

90 members vote

Vote	Majority	Two-Thirds
Of the members present	51	67
Of the entire membership	501	667
Of the members present and voting	46	60

Remember, in voting, the default basis is a majority of the votes cast or two thirds of the votes cast. If the bylaws only say "majority," it is a majority of the votes cast. If they only say "two thirds," it is two thirds of the votes cast.

Point of Information

Abstentions can have different effects, depending on the basis of the vote:

- Of the members present and voting: no effect whatsoever
- Of the entire membership: the same effect as a no vote since you are a member and are not voting aye
- Of the members present: the same effect as a no vote since you are present and are not voting aye

You want to make sure that, when you abstain, the vote requirement allows you to truly take a neutral stand on the issue—otherwise, your abstention is really a no vote.

Meaning and Use of Plurality Vote

A plurality vote requires that one candidate or proposition receive more votes than the others. A plurality vote is particularly nice when there are more than two candidates running for an office. When there are three or more candidates slated for the same office, it's difficult to get a majority vote, but most of the time one of those candidates will get more votes than the other two candidates. Thus, that candidate has a plurality.

> **Parliamentary Pearls**
>
> The advantage of the plurality vote over a majority vote is that it takes less time. Unless there is a tie vote, a plurality elects on the first ballot.
>
> The advantage of the majority vote over a plurality vote is that more than half of the members support (voted for) the decision or the candidate elected.

Plurality vote can only be used for an election when it is specifically stated in the bylaws that the member shall be elected by plurality. Otherwise, the election is by majority vote. With three or more candidates, it can take a lot of ballots to get to a majority vote.

The Chair's Vote

It's important that the chair maintain an appearance of objectivity. At the same time, the presiding officer should not lose his or her voting rights simply because he or she became the presiding officer. This is particularly important in bodies in which the chair was elected by a constituency. Toward this end, the chair is allowed to vote when his or her vote will affect the results of the vote or if the vote is by ballot. People often mistakenly believe that this rule means that the chair can vote only to break a tie. Numerical examples will help here.

Vote Required	Aye Votes	No Votes	Presiding Officer Vote: Aye vote	Presiding Officer Vote: No vote
Majority	13	13	Affects results	Doesn't affect results
Majority	14	13	Doesn't affect results	Affects results

Vote Required	Aye Votes	No Votes	Presiding Officer Vote: Aye vote	Presiding Officer Vote: No vote
Two-thirds	9	5	Affects results	Doesn't affect results
Two-thirds	10	5	Doesn't affect results	Affects results

The chair can also vote in a roll call vote, but the name of the chair should be called last.

The Least You Need to Know

- There are many ways to conduct a vote; be sure to use the one most appropriate for the situation.
- It only takes one member's objection during a vote by unanimous consent to force a formal vote.
- By default, a majority vote means a majority of the votes cast by members present and voting; however, the bylaws can also specify a majority of members or a majority of members present.
- The chair can only vote if the vote is by ballot, by roll call with name called last, or if his or her vote will change the outcome.

Part 3

Motions for (Almost) Any Occasion

There's a motion for almost any situation imaginable. Want to take a bathroom break? Move to *Recess.* Want to ask a question about parliamentary procedure? Make a *Parliamentary Inquiry.* Don't trust the presiding officer's vote count? Call out "*Division.*" Want to change a pending motion? Move to *Amend* it.

I could go on and on … and I will!

In this part, I explain approximately 25 motions that can help you move your ideas forward. Understanding the motions is crucial to being able to appropriately use them in the next meeting you attend.

Chapter 10

Main Motions

In This Chapter

- Understanding main motions
- How secondary motions perfect main motions
- How to say what you mean in a motion
- How to phrase a resolution
- Giving notice to minimize game playing

In Chapter 7, you learned that a main motion is the lowest-ranking motion on the precedence of motions ladder. It is the motion that all of the other motions in the precedence list can be applied to—they can be made while it is pending. In this chapter, we're going to explore main motions in more detail. While we're at it, we'll explore the difference between main motions and resolutions and secondary motions.

The Bottom Rung: Main Motions

Main motions are debatable, amendable, and can have all kinds of things happen to them. Not only can all of the other 13 motions on the motion ladder be applied to a main motion, but so can many secondary motions. (The variety of secondary motions are discussed in Chapters 11 through 13.) As a general rule, a main motion needs a majority vote to pass. As usual there are exceptions, but we'll deal with those later.

Because main motions serve as the bottom rung of the precedence of motions ladder, they take precedence over nothing, which means that a main motion cannot be made while any other motion is pending. That means that only one main motion is allowed on the floor at a time.

Point of Information

If a member made the motion that the association "purchase a copy of *The Complete Idiot's Guide to Robert's Rules* for each member of the board of directors," that motion would be a main motion. Another member could not now move to "purchase a computer for the association" while the first motion is pending because the computer motion is also a main motion. It would be too confusing to decide on the book and the computer at the same time. But while the motion to buy the book was on the floor, it would be in order to *Amend* it by striking "of the board of directors" so that, if amended, the motion would then read "purchase a copy of *The Complete Idiot's Guide to Robert's Rules* for each member."

It's All About Relationships: Main and Secondary Motions

The content of the motion isn't what determines whether it's a main motion or a secondary motion. Rather, it is a motion's relationship to other motions that establishes the type of motion it is.

If a motion is made while another motion is pending and it is ruled to be in order, it is by its very nature a secondary motion. If a motion is made while no other motions are pending and it is ruled to be in order, it is a main motion. I know this is confusing, so stay with me.

On the motion ladder, you will find the motion to *Recess*, which introduces an intermission, or break, during a meeting. Say we are in a meeting and have been debating a motion for more than an hour, and it looks like it still has a way to go. You notice that you aren't the only member squirming in your chair—almost everyone else is, too. During the debate, you get recognized by the chair and say, "I move that we take a 10-minute *Recess*." Your motion passes, and you are the hit of the meeting! That was an example of a secondary motion, the motion to *Recess*.

Go back to that same meeting. Discussion on the controversial motion ends after $1\frac{1}{2}$ hours of nonstop debating, the vote is taken, and the motion passes. The next item of business is as controversial as the one that you just wrapped up. You get recognized by the chair and say, "I move that we take a 10-minute *Recess*." This time, the motion to *Recess* is not a secondary motion because no other motion is pending—remember, we already voted on the controversial motion. The motion to *Recess* can still be processed, but it is now processed as a main motion, not a secondary one. The secondary and main motions to *Recess* are processed much the same except that since this motion is a main motion, when you come back from *Recess* there is no motion pending.

Parliamentary Pearls

When someone makes a main motion that amends an existing document, like the bylaws, keep in mind that in a parliamentary sense it is a main motion, not an amendment. For example: "I move that we *Amend* our bylaws, Article III, Section 2 by striking the words 'temporary member' and inserting 'affiliate member.'" Even though this motion is amending something that is already in existence, it is a main motion, not an amendment. If you keep in mind that it is a main motion, then you will be able to follow the process better (or lead the process should you be chairing the meeting).

Resolution vs. Motion

Many people try to look for an elaborate difference between resolutions and motions. There isn't one. The difference is all about format. A resolution is essentially an elaborate, formally written motion. *Robert's* tells us that a resolution is used when the motion is of great importance or is very long.

A resolution includes the reasons for the motion as well as the actual action that the group is proposing. Resolutions have two parts, as follows:

- **Part 1: The preamble.** The preamble lists the reasons for adoption. Each reason is given its own paragraph and usually begins with the word "Whereas."
- **Part 2: The resolving clauses.** This is the action part where you identify the specific action or position you want the group to take. Each of these clauses, or paragraphs, begins with "Resolved, That."

The following is a sample resolution:

> Whereas, the American Association of Fun-Loving People (AAFLP) must choose a fun city for its 2016 convention;
>
> Whereas, the city of Ain't-It-Fun, North Dakota, was rated as the Funfest City of the Year; and
>
> Whereas, the Fun-Fun-Fun Hotel is available during our convention dates and at a rate that should make it even more fun; therefore, be it
>
> *Resolved,* That the 2016 Annual Convention of the American Association of Fun-Loving People be held in Ain't-It-Fun, North Dakota, at the Fun-Fun-Fun Hotel, on April 1 and 2, 2016; and
>
> *Resolved,* That the attendees at the 2016 Annual Convention have a fun time.

Some groups use the resolution format for all of their motions. Other groups never use the resolution format. I discourage the resolution format because I believe that it makes an easy process (writing a motion) unnecessarily difficult.

A resolution includes the reasons along with the action. Frequently the reasons for a particular action vary from one person to the next. The result is that sometimes groups spend significant time amending the reasons when the focus should be on the action the motion is proposing. The only part of the resolution that really matters is the action portion, the resolve clause. I have observed many groups making a sport of amending both the whereas clauses and the resolve clause. The same energy spent on a motion would have greater benefits.

Point of Information

The following are points for processing a resolution:

- The words that a member uses in moving a resolution are as follows: "I move the adoption of the following resolution …."
- Since the resolving clauses are the important part of the resolution, they are open first to discussion and amendments. After debate on the resolving clauses is concluded, the whereas clauses are open for debate and amendment.

Giving Notice of Motions

In Chapter 4, I introduced an example in which an organization wanted to change its dues from $10 to $12. Because that involved amending the organization's bylaws, I noted that it required previous notice, which is essentially informing the membership of the proposed change in advance of the meeting. Previous notice is usually required before a main motion can be made at a meeting when you are proposing to change something that has been adopted previously, such as amending the bylaws. The example you will see most often is a motion to *Amend* the bylaws. Almost always, the bylaws indicate that in order to *Amend* the bylaws the members must receive the proposed amendment at the previous meeting or in advance of the current meeting.

The notice requirement serves an important purpose by preventing people from taking advantage of certain situations. For example, let's say that at last month's meeting the bylaws were amended to increase the dues from $5 to $7, but it only passed by two votes. At this month's meeting, three of the people who voted in favor of the dues increase are not present, and everyone who voted against it is present. Without the rule requiring previous notice, one of those members could move to *Amend* the bylaws and reduce the dues back to the $5. You can see the potential problem with the bylaws being amended back and forth at each meeting, depending on who is in attendance. Not a healthy situation for an organization!

Summary of the Rules for a Main Motion

- Needs a second
- Is debatable
- Is amendable
- Needs a majority vote

A script (cheat sheet) for a main motion can be found in Appendix C and on my website, www.nancysylvester.com.

The Least You Need to Know

- There can be only one main motion on the floor at a time; many secondary motions can be on the floor.
- A resolution is essentially a very formal motion.
- Depending on the circumstances, the same motion, such as the motion to *Recess*, can be either a main motion or a secondary motion.
- Notice: sometimes you have to give notice before the meeting in order to bring up a motion.

Chapter 11

Privileged Motions

In This Chapter

- Understanding privileged motions
- How to make sure the meeting doesn't last forever
- How to work bathroom breaks into your meetings
- How to handle emergencies

Privileged motions are a class of motions that are important enough to warrant interrupting all other motions. Because they are by their very nature urgent issues, debate on them is not allowed. Their content does not relate to the main motion or to pending business but rather to the members and the organization. Hence, the name *privileged.*

The privileged motions are usually secondary motions, meaning that they are made when a main motion is already on the floor. For instance, if your group is debating the main motion to purchase a computer and you have to go to the bathroom and can't wait until the debate on the computer is over, you can move for a 10-minute *Recess.*

The Five Privileged Motions

The following five motions are in the class of privileged motions:

- ***Fix the Time to Which to Adjourn.*** This sets the time for another meeting to continue business of the session. Adoption of this motion does not adjourn the present meeting or set the time for its adjournment.
- ***Adjourn.*** A motion to close the meeting.
- ***Recess.*** A short interruption that does not close the meeting. After the *Recess*, business resumes at exactly the point where it was interrupted.
- ***Questions of Privilege.*** To bring an urgent request or a main motion relating to the rights of either the assembly or an individual up for immediate consideration.
- ***Call for the Orders of the Day.*** By the use of this motion, a single member can require the assembly to follow the order of business or agenda, or to take up a special order that is scheduled to come up, unless two thirds of the assembly wish to do otherwise.

Privileged motions have special privileges only when they are offered as secondary motions. When they are main motions, they are treated like any other main motion and must follow the rules for a main motion.

Since this is not a rulebook (that's *Robert's* job), I will not include all of the specific rules for each of the privileged motions discussed. For the rules, please refer to *Robert's Rules of Order Newly Revised.*

Point of Information

Privileged motions are unique in that they don't relate to the specific motion that is pending.

Explain, please!

If the main motion is to purchase a computer and you move to *Amend* that motion by adding "at a cost not to exceed $3,000," the amendment relates to that specific main motion. But if, while you were discussing the computer main motion, a member moved that you *Recess* for 10 minutes, the *Recess* motion is not related to the motion to purchase a computer. The *Recess* motion could be made just as it was stated, no matter what the main motion was.

Fix the Time to Which to Adjourn

The motion to *Fix the Time to Which to Adjourn* does not adjourn the current meeting—it just sounds like it does! All this motion does is set up the time and sometimes the place for the continuation of the present meeting. This motion makes the next meeting a continuation of the present meeting, not a new meeting with a new agenda.

The time you fix for the next meeting must be before the next regularly scheduled meeting of the group. So if the group meets on the first Tuesday of the month and the motion to *Fix the Time to Which to Adjourn* is made at the February meeting, the continued meeting must be held before the first Tuesday in March.

Sample Scenarios

You aren't going to use this motion a lot, but it's great to know that it's available if you do need it. Let's look at a couple of situations when it might be used:

- You are in the middle of discussion on a heated issue that must be decided before next week, and you don't meet again until next month. Your time for meeting is up, and you have to get out of the building you're meeting in because it's closing. With this motion, you can continue this meeting later tonight at another location, tomorrow night, or anytime before the decision is needed next week.
- It is Tuesday. The decision on an important issue must be made by Friday. You need some more information to make the decision, but your rules require that you must give four days' notice to have a special meeting. Because this motion calls for a continuation of the current meeting, you don't need the four days' notice. So you could use this motion to continue the meeting on Wednesday or Thursday evening.

Rules for the Motion to *Fix the Time to Which to Adjourn*

- Needs a second
- Is not debatable
- Is amendable but the amendment is not debatable
- Needs a majority vote

A script (cheat sheet) for a motion to *Fix the Time to Which to Adjourn* can be found on my website, www.nancysylvester.com.

Adjourn

The motion to *Adjourn*, which is used to close a meeting, is probably the most popular of all motions. If the business on the agenda has been concluded, the presiding officer may ask if there is any other business to come before the group. If there is none, then the presiding officer may simply say, "Since there is no other business, the meeting is adjourned."

The motion to *Adjourn* is very high in the motion ladder. That's because if a majority of the attendees at a meeting want to conclude the meeting, the minority should not be able to keep them against their will.

Point of Information

Because the motion to *Adjourn* is a privileged motion, it isn't debatable. However, a member may inform the assembly of an urgent matter that needs to be taken up before adjournment. For example, as the presiding officer begins to *Adjourn* the meeting, a member raises his hand to be recognized. The presiding officer calls on him, and the member says, "The location of the meeting next week has been changed to the Woodward Technology Center, Room 141." The announcement in this example is appropriate because it is clearly business requiring attention before adjournment. Similar comments or even questions may be made during any privileged motion as long as such comments do not debate the motion itself.

Taking Care of (Unfinished) Business

In organizations that have regular meetings more than quarterly, the business on the agenda that is not covered before the adjournment is automatically placed on the agenda for the next meeting under unfinished business. So if we had three things on the agenda under new business and only completed items one and two, the third item would automatically go on the agenda for the next meeting under unfinished business.

Rules for the Motion to *Adjourn*

- Needs a second
- Is not debatable
- Is not amendable
- Needs a majority vote

A script (cheat sheet) for a motion to *Adjourn* can be found on my website, www.nancysylvester.com.

Recess

A *Recess* is a brief intermission taken by the assembly. It can be used for getting refreshments, using the restroom, grabbing a meal, or just giving people a chance to stand up, move around, and clear their heads. This is the second most popular motion, second only to *Adjourn*.

Gavel Gaffes

If the *Recess* is for a later time (such as at 3 this afternoon), it is not a privileged motion and can't be made when another motion is pending.

Recess Can Be Amended

The motion to *Recess* is the third motion from the top of the ladder of motions. The motion to *Amend* is the third motion from the bottom. According to the precedence of motions, the *Recess* motion should not be able to be amended. But in this case, an amendment can be "applied" to the motion to *Recess*, but it is limited to amending the length of time of the *Recess*. This concept also applies to the previously discussed motion to *Fix the Time to Which to Adjourn*.

Parliamentary Pearls

Legislative bodies—such as the U.S. Congress or a state's House of Representatives—use the term "recess" differently than the term is commonly used in parliamentary procedure. They use it to indicate a period when they are not in session for days or weeks at a time.

For example, a member moves that we *Recess* for 10 minutes. The lines at the restroom will not allow for everyone to get back in 10 minutes, so you move to *Amend* the motion to strike 10 minutes and insert 20 minutes. That amendment is allowed, but because the *Recess* motion is not debatable, the amendment to it is not debatable.

Recess Without a Motion

If the agenda for the meeting has a *Recess* scheduled and the time for that *Recess* arrives, the presiding officer can call for that *Recess* without having to wait for a motion.

Recess vs. *Adjourn* at a Convention

Because a convention is a series of meetings that make up one session (as we learned in Chapter 5), people many times confuse the use of *Recess* and *Adjourn* at a convention.

def•i•ni•tion

Adjourn **sine die** (pronounced *SIGN-ee DYE-ee*) means to "*Adjourn* without day." You would most likely hear this term used at a convention. It is the adjournment at the end of the regular session of a convention. The last meeting of the convention is said to *Adjourn* sine die.

Instead of giving a very detailed description of the difference, let's keep it simple. If the break is for a meal or for a few hours, the motion used should be *Recess.* If the break is overnight or for a full day, then the motion used should be *Adjourn.* If it is the last meeting of the convention, then it should be *Adjourn sine die.*

Rules for the Motion to *Recess*

- Needs a second
- Is not debatable
- Is amendable (only as to the length of the *Recess* and that amendment is not debatable)
- Needs a majority vote

A script (cheat sheet) for a motion to *Recess* can be found on my website, www.nancysylvester.com.

Questions of Privilege

Questions of Privilege are used when there is a matter, affecting either the entire assembly or an individual in the assembly, that is so urgent that it must interrupt business and be taken care of right away. Sometimes it is a question that can simply be addressed by the presiding officer. Other times it must be made into a motion that is acted on by the group.

During a meeting in which a guest speaker is speaking, if a member raises a *Question of Privilege* indicating that the people in the back of the room cannot hear the speaker, the presiding officer could ask the speaker to speak louder or have the microphone system fixed and no motion would be needed. If, though, the member asks that the group move the entire meeting to the room next door where the acoustics are better—and it's obvious that not everyone wants to move—then the presiding officer would want to turn that request into a motion and have it voted on.

The presiding officer must determine whether the question is of such urgency that it warrants interrupting the speaker. If a member is interrupted, as soon as the *Question of Privilege* is resolved, the presiding officer should go back to the member who was interrupted and allow him or her to pick up where he or she left off.

Questions of Privilege fall into two general categories: *Questions of Privilege* affecting the assembly and questions of personal privilege, with priority given to those affecting the assembly. Let's look at each in turn.

Questions of Privilege Affecting the Assembly

This version of the question is used when there is a problem, affecting all or part of the assembly, that needs immediate attention. It usually has to do with comfort issues (heating, lighting, ventilation, and so on). It can also refer to noise issues or other disturbances that prevent the members from hearing what is going on at the meeting.

Questions of Personal Privilege

A question of personal privilege applies to a single member and is a rare occurrence in the parliamentary world. Keep in mind that it must be so urgent that it can interrupt a speaker or debate on the motion.

For example, during a meeting, if a member receives notification that a child is sick at home and believes the child needs his or her immediate attention, that member may state, "Madam Chairman, I rise to a point of personal privilege." After recognition from the chair, the member would then request permission to be excused from the meeting.

Point of Information

Sometimes the issue before the assembly is so sensitive or private that it should be discussed only in front of members—for example, the discipline of a member or the review and pay of staff members.

While the motion is pending, a member may rise to a *Question of Privilege* and "move that we immediately go into executive session." If that motion passes, the nonmembers are asked to leave, and the meeting proceeds.

It is important to remember that when meeting in executive session, everything that is discussed is confidential. Members may not share with anyone outside of the meeting what was discussed. If they do so, they may be subject to discipline.

Rules for a *Question of Privilege*

- Can interrupt the speaker, if deemed appropriate to do so
- Is ruled on by the chair

A script (cheat sheet) for a *Question of Privilege* can be found on my website, www.nancysylvester.com.

Rules for a *Question of Privilege* Motion

- Can interrupt the speaker, if deemed appropriate to do so
- Needs a second
- Is not debatable on whether or not to admit the question, but once the motion has been made and is pending, it is debatable
- Is amendable
- Needs a majority vote

A script (cheat sheet) for a *Question of Privilege* motion can be found on my website, www.nancysylvester.com.

Call for the Orders of the Day

The *Call for the Orders of the Day* is used when the agenda or program is not being followed or if an item was set to be taken up at a certain time and that time has passed. This motion requires the presiding officer to follow the established agenda.

One Is Enough

It takes only one member to *Call for the Orders of the Day.* It does not need a second and is not voted on. It is really more like a demand than a call.

When you think about the circumstances behind this motion, you understand why only one person is needed for the call. The agenda has been set, and the presiding officer does not have the right to deviate from the agenda without permission of the membership. If the presiding officer is deviating from the agenda, it should not take a majority vote to get him or her back on the established track.

Must We?

Sometimes when a group is not following the established agenda, it isn't because the presiding officer is failing to keep things on track. Sometimes it's because the group willingly went off track and wants to stay there. So what if that is the case and a member *Calls for the Orders of the Day?* Well, the group can decide whether it wants to go back to the agenda. Because not following the agenda is a change from what the group had decided earlier, the motion requires a two-thirds vote. After the *Call for the Orders of the Day*, a member may make a motion to extend the time for the issue that is on the floor, or the presiding officer may sense the group does not want to move on and may put it to a vote. In either case, it will take a two-thirds vote.

What's Next?

What happens to the issue on the floor when a member *Calls for the Orders of the Day* if the assembly decides to follow the set agenda? After the assembly has completed the orders of the day that were called up, the business that was interrupted by the *Call for the Orders of the Day* is taken up right where it was interrupted.

If a member *Calls for the Orders of the Day* and the assembly votes to continue with the issue it was dealing with, that same member or any other member cannot *Call for the Orders of the Day* again until the current issue has been dealt with. Otherwise, it would be a delay tactic.

Rules for a *Call for the Orders of the Day*

- Can interrupt the speaker.
- If the orders are going to be followed, it takes only one member to make this motion, and no vote is needed.
- If the group is going to deviate from the established agenda, a vote is needed. It takes two thirds in the negative to deviate from the established agenda.

A script (cheat sheet) for a *Call for the Orders of the Day* can be found on my website, www.nancysylvester.com.

The Least You Need to Know

- While you won't use *Fix the Time to Which to Adjourn* very often, it can be a lifesaver.
- Privileged motions can be main or secondary motions, depending on what's on the floor.
- Urgent matters can be processed urgently if done correctly.
- One person can get the meeting back on track!

Chapter 12

Subsidiary Motions

In This Chapter

- Setting aside a motion temporarily or permanently
- Limiting or extending limits on debate
- Referring issues to committees
- Amending amendments

Subsidiary motions aid the assembly in treating or disposing of a main motion. They are in order only from the time the main motion has been stated by the chair until the chair begins to take a vote on that main motion. These motions help you get the main motion into its best form before you have to vote on it.

You may want to change the main motion (*Amend* it), send it back to a committee to do more research on it (*Commit* or *Refer*), put off the decision until the next meeting (*Postpone to a Certain Time*), or you may just want to kill it (*Postpone Indefinitely*).

The Seven Subsidiary Motions

The following seven motions are in the class called subsidiary motions:

- ***Lay on the Table.*** This motion places in the care of the secretary the pending question and everything adhering to it. If a group meets quarterly or more frequently, the question laid on the table remains there until taken off or until the end of the next regular session. If a group meets less often than quarterly, such as at an annual convention, the motion cannot be postponed beyond the current session. This motion should not be used to kill a motion.
- ***Previous Question.*** The effect of this motion is to immediately stop debate and any amendments and to move immediately to a vote on the motion. It must be seconded, no debate is allowed, and a two-thirds vote is needed to close debate.
- ***Limit* or *Extend Limits of Debate.*** This motion can reduce or increase the number and length of speeches permitted or can limit the length of debate on a specific question.
- ***Postpone to a Certain Time* (also called *Postpone Definitely*).** If the body needs more time to make a decision or if there is a more convenient time for consideration of this question, this motion may be the answer. If a group meets quarterly or more frequently, the postponement cannot be beyond the next session. If a group meets less than quarterly, such as at an annual convention, the motion cannot be postponed beyond the current session.
- ***Commit* or *Refer.*** This motion sends the main motion to a smaller group (a committee) for further examination and refinement before the body votes on it. It can also send the main motion to the committee with the full authority to act on the motion.
- ***Amend.*** This motion is used to modify the pending motion before it is voted on.
- ***Postpone Indefinitely.*** This motion, in effect, kills the main motion for the duration of the session without the group having to take a vote on the motion.

Since this is not a rulebook (that's *Robert's* job), I will not be including all of the specific rules for each of the motions discussed. For the rules, please refer to *Robert's Rules of Order Newly Revised.*

Lay on the Table

The object of this motion is to allow the group to set aside the pending motion in order to attend to more urgent business. The pending motion is laid aside in such a way that the members can bring it back up at will, which is easier than introducing a new motion.

How long it stays on the table (set aside) depends on how often the group meets. If you meet at least one time a quarter (four times a year), the motion laid on the table remains there until taken off or until the end of the next regular session. If you meet less than quarterly, the motion cannot be postponed beyond the current session.

Abused and Confused

This motion clearly wins the award for the most overused and abused of all of the motions. All too often, it is improperly used to kill a motion without the benefit of discussion. It is also improperly used to postpone a motion to the next meeting.

It is frequently confused with and used in place of two other motions: *Postpone Indefinitely* and *Postpone to a Certain Time* (definitely). The following table of the three motions should help clarify the proper use of each:

Motion	Debatable	Position on Ladder	Purpose
Lay on the Table	No	6	Temporarily set aside
Postpone Indefinitely	Yes	13	Kill
Postpone to a Certain Time	Yes	9	Put off to a specific time

With this table in mind, let's look at why it matters when you confuse the motions.

Whereas the motion to *Lay on the Table* is frequently used to kill a motion, that is not its proper use—it is intended to be used to temporarily set aside a motion. If you want to kill a main motion, you should use the motion to *Postpone Indefinitely.* Why? *Lay on the Table* is not debatable and is very high on the motion ladder. Therefore, you can't talk about it or *Amend* it before you vote on it. Those are two things you would want to do before you kill an idea; if you don't, you run the risk of violating the rights of the members.

The motion to *Lay on the Table* is also frequently improperly used to put a motion off to the next meeting. If you want to table something to a time specified, the proper motion is to *Postpone to a Certain Time.* The difference? *Lay on the Table* is not debatable, is not amendable (so you can't set a time and date for when to address it again), is high on the motion ladder, and when you do bring it back up, it needs a motion (the motion to *Take from the Table*) to accomplish that. *Postpone to a Certain Time* is debatable, is not as high on the motion ladder, and automatically comes up at the next meeting as an item of unfinished business.

So you see, using the appropriate motion protects the rights of the members, who should at least be allowed to discuss a motion before it is killed (*Postpone Indefinitely*) or before it is put off to the next meeting (*Postpone to a Certain Time*).

Proper Use

Now that you've seen the improper use of the motion to *Lay on the Table,* what is its proper use? This motion is designed for unexpected urgent situations. It is also designed for setting something aside when you do not know when it will be time to bring it back again.

Point of Information

When a motion is *Laid on the Table,* all motions that are currently adhering to it go with it to the table and come back with it off the table. For example, the motion to purchase a computer was made, someone moved to *Amend* that motion, and the amendment was being discussed at the time of the emergency. If the motion was tabled at that time, when it comes back from the table you have the motion to purchase a computer plus the amendment to deal with.

An Example Would Be Very Helpful About Now!

Your group is meeting at 6 tonight and has invited a guest to speak at 7. That gives you an hour to attend to your other business before the guest is scheduled to arrive. However, at 6:30, while the group is in the midst of debating a controversial motion, the guest speaker shows up—she's a half-hour early, and you haven't finished your business! Now what do you do? If you continue the discussion, you will have a heated debate in front of her, which isn't appropriate. But this is an issue that really needs to be addressed, and you don't know when the guest will leave after her speech, so you are not sure whether you can continue the debate tonight or at the next meeting. This is a perfect time to use the motion to *Lay on the Table*. If, after her presentation, she leaves and you have time to complete the debate and vote, a member can move to *Take it from the Table*. If not, you can wait until the next meeting and *Take it from the Table* at that time.

Gavel Gaffes

The scripts found on my website (www.nancysylvester.com) for the motions in this chapter are only applicable when the subsidiary motion is a secondary motion. When it is a main motion (no other motion is on the floor), you should use the script for a main motion (also found in Appendix C).

How Do You Control This Motion?

After the member makes the motion to *Lay on the Table*, the presiding officer should ask the member who made the motion, "For what purpose does the member seek to lay the motion on the table?" If it is a proper use of the motion, the chair should then proceed to process it. If it is an improper use of the motion, the chair should rule the motion out of order. In addition, the chair should tell the member what motion to use to achieve the desired end. For example, if the member wants to kill the motion without actually taking a vote on it, the chair should guide him or her to make the motion to *Postpone Indefinitely*.

Rules for the Motion to *Lay on the Table*

- Needs a second
- Is not debatable
- Is not amendable
- Needs a majority vote

A script (cheat sheet) for a motion to *Lay on the Table* can be found on my website, www.nancysylvester.com.

Previous Question

The *Previous Question* motion is used to stop debate on a motion and any subsidiary motions except the higher-ranking motion to *Lay on the Table*. The motion must be seconded, no debate is allowed, and a two-thirds vote is needed. If the motion passes, it requires an immediate vote on the pending motion. The proper statement of this motion is "I move the *Previous Question*."

This is the second-most overused and abused of all of the motions. It is abused by people who don't understand that it is a motion that needs a two-thirds vote. They try to call it out, as a command, and intimidate the presiding officer into stopping debate without a vote. It is also frequently called by other names, such as "close debate," "call for the question," "call the question," or "question." Whatever name it is called by, it should be treated as a *Previous Question* motion.

Gavel Gaffes

Usually someone with a Godlike voice calls out from the back of the room: "Question." Then, as if God came down and whispered, "They can't talk about this anymore," in the presiding officer's ear, he or she jumps up and says, "The question has been called. We will now vote."

It doesn't make sense that one person can tell the rest of us that we have to stop discussing an issue and move to the vote. That should be your cue that calling it out without a vote is not proper parliamentary procedure.

On This or All Pending Questions?

If there are multiple motions on the floor (pending), the *Previous Question* motion must be qualified. You must indicate when making this motion whether it is referring only to the motion that is immediately pending or to all of the pending motions. However, the *Previous Question* motion must always include the immediately pending motion. Let's say that there are four motions on the floor, as follows:

1. Main motion: "I move that we purchase a computer."
2. Primary amendment: "I move that we *Amend* the motion by adding 'not to exceed $2,000.'"
3. Secondary amendment: "I move to *Amend* the amendment by striking '$2,000' and inserting '$4,000.'"
4. *Refer* to committee: "I move to *Refer* this motion to the finance committee."

While the group is discussing the motion to *Refer* (#4), someone could "move the *Previous Question*" (which would only apply to #4), or he or she could "move the *Previous Question* on this and all pending questions" (which would apply to all four pending motions). If the *Previous Question* motion applies to all four motions and passes, the presiding officer would first call for a vote on #4, *Refer.* If that motion fails, then immediately, with no further discussion, the vote would be taken on #3, then #2, then #1. If the vote on #4, *Refer*, passes, the discussion stops and the motion, along with the two amendments, is referred to the committee. After the committee has considered it, it comes back to the meeting with the primary and secondary amendment still in place, waiting to be voted on.

In this example, the *Previous Question* motion could have been made to apply to the motion to *Refer* and the two amendments without having included the main motion. If that had happened, the vote would have been taken on #4. If that motion failed, then immediately, with no further discussion, the vote would have been taken on #3 and #2. Because the *Previous Question* motion didn't apply to the main motion, discussion would have been allowed before a vote is taken on it.

Rules for the *Previous Question* Motion

- Needs a second
- Is not debatable
- Is not amendable
- Needs a two-thirds vote

A script (cheat sheet) for a *Previous Question* motion can be found on my website, www.nancysylvester.com.

Unique form: "I move the *Previous Question* on this and all pending motions."

Effect: Go immediately to the vote on this motion and then immediately to the vote on each of the pending motions.

Limit or *Extend Limits of Debate*

This motion can reduce or increase the number and length of speeches permitted or can limit the length of debate on a specific motion. *Robert's* gives each member the right to speak twice on any one motion in any one day, and each of those speeches can be 10 minutes long. Sometimes, however, it is determined that members need more or less time to debate an issue, and that's when the motion to *Limit* or *Extend Limits of Debate* comes in handy.

This motion can apply to the total amount of time that the group spends on any one motion, to the amount of time of each speech on the motion, or to both.

Parliamentary Pearls

Here are some possible forms of this motion:

- "I move that the debate on the pending motion be limited to 20 minutes."
- "I move that debate on the pending motion be closed at 8 P.M., and we immediately proceed to the vote."
- "I move that each speaker on this motion be limited to three minutes per speech."

The Limit on the Limit

This motion applies only to the limit on debate of the pending motions and subsequent subsidiary motions, unless otherwise specified. It also is applicable only to the session in which it was adopted.

Rules for the Motion to *Limit* or *Extend Limits of Debate*

- Needs a second
- Is not debatable
- Is amendable, but the amendment is not debatable
- Needs a two-thirds vote

A script (cheat sheet) for a motion to *Limit* or *Extend Limits of Debate* can be found on my website, www.nancysylvester.com.

Postpone to a Certain Time (Postpone Definitely)

Sometimes you just don't have the information you need to make a decision, you are not ready to make that decision for other reasons, or the right people are not present for the decision to be made. Under any of these circumstances, this motion, to *Postpone to a Certain Time*, is for you.

Postponed to When?

For groups that meet at least quarterly, the postponement is limited to the remainder of the current session and up until the close of the next regularly scheduled session. That would include a special meeting called before the next regular meeting. If there is more than a quarterly time interval between your meetings (such as a annual convention), you can only postpone it until sometime before the end of the current session.

Point of Information

When a motion has been postponed to the next meeting, it automatically comes up under unfinished business at the next meeting.

Once you have postponed something to a certain time, you cannot take it up before that time unless you *Reconsider* the motion to postpone it or *Suspend the Rules* to allow for it to be taken up earlier.

Don't Try to Make It Something It Isn't!

Just as with the motion to *Lay on the Table*, you cannot move to postpone something to a time that would in effect kill it, thus really making the motion to *Postpone Indefinitely*.

For example, your organization has been asked to send a representative to a special function on March 15. The current meeting is on March 3, and your next meeting isn't until March 17. At the current meeting, it would be out of order to postpone the motion to the next meeting. The motion would be out of order because the next meeting is after the function, so postponing it until that time would have the effect of killing it. If you really want to kill it, you need to make the motion to *Postpone Indefinitely*.

Postpone Ahead of Time?

If a matter is prescribed in the bylaws to occur at a certain meeting (such as election of officers at the November meeting), you cannot, in advance, postpone it to a later time. But when the time arrives, you can then move to postpone it. To meet the bylaws requirement, you would have to set up a meeting that would continue the current meeting and then postpone it to that meeting.

Rules for the Motion to *Postpone to a Certain Time*

- Needs a second
- Is debatable
- Is amendable
- Needs a majority vote

A script (cheat sheet) for a motion to *Postpone to a Certain Time* can be found on my website, www.nancysylvester.com.

Commit or *Refer*

This motion sends the main motion to a smaller group (a committee) for further examination and refinement before the body votes on it. Be sure to be specific—what committee, the size of the committee, and so on.

This motion can have as much or as little detail as you choose. You can simply *Refer* the motion to a committee, or the motion can tell what committee, when it will report, and what its authority is. Whenever any of these details are added, that part of the motion is amendable.

Check the Bylaws

You can't just put any detail you want into the motion to *Refer*. You should first check the bylaws to see if you can do what you want to do. For instance, you can't *Refer* something to a special committee if a standing committee is already authorized to take care of those kinds of issues. If you have a bylaws committee and a bylaws amendment is on the floor, it is out of order to move to *Refer* the motion to a special committee formed for this purpose. The referral must be to the bylaws committee. Here's another example: In the motion you name who should be on the committee. If the bylaws indicate that the president appoints all committees, you can't appoint the committee in the motion to *Refer* because that would be a violation of the bylaws.

Parliamentary Pearls

A special committee automatically ceases to exist when the committee gives its final report. If the group wants to have the committee cease to exist before that or to take back something it referred to a committee, it is done by a motion to *Discharge a Committee*. The committee is discharged from further consideration of the issue referred to it.

I highly recommend the inclusion of a report due date in the motion to *Refer*. In a longer project, it might even be a date for an initial report. Most of us work better when we have a deadline date, and committees are no different.

Rules for the Motion to *Commit* or *Refer*

- Needs a second
- Is debatable
- Is amendable
- Needs a majority vote

A script (cheat sheet) for a motion to *Commit* or *Refer* can be found on my website, www.nancysylvester.com.

Amend

This motion is the embodiment of the democratic process. If a motion is made and it is not acceptable as is, the amendment process gives the group the opportunity to fix it so that at least a majority can live with it. True democracy! The intent of this motion is to modify the pending motion before it is voted on. In other words, an amendment is the continuous improvement process at work.

There are many rules applicable to an amendment. I won't try to duplicate them here, so if you need the specifics go to *Robert's Rules of Order Newly Revised.*

Be Specific

An amendment to a motion can take three formats, as follows:

- **Insert or add.** This format involves inserting or adding words or paragraphs.
- **Strike out.** This format involves cutting words or paragraphs.
- **Strike and insert.** This format involves substituting a word, paragraph, or the entire text with new text.

The maker of the motion should specify in the amendment the format it should take (insert, strike out, strike and insert) and the location of the amendment, such as "I move to insert the word 'Mac' before the word 'computer.'"

Germane

We have all heard examples of bills that passed in Congress where something totally unrelated (and sometimes very stupid) was added to the bill as an amendment. When the bill passed, so did the amendment. The good news is that this cannot happen when you are following *Robert's* because *Robert's* says that an amendment must be *germane*, which means that it must relate to the subject of the motion it is amending. You cannot introduce a new, independent issue as an amendment. Makes sense to me!

def•i•ni•tion

Germane means related to the subject. An amendment must be germane to the motion it is amending. A secondary amendment must be germane to the primary amendment it is amending.

Germane, but It Doesn't Have to Agree

Although the amendment must be germane, it does not have to maintain the intent of the motion it is amending. It can even contradict the motion it is amending. The classic example used by Robert himself helps to clarify this idea:

> The motion on the floor: "I move that we censure our president."
>
> Amendment: "I move to *Amend* the motion by striking the word 'censure' and inserting the word 'thank' so that the motion will read, 'I move that we thank our president.'"

That motion to *Amend* is germane and is also allowed because it is the members who own this motion, and it is totally within their rights to change the intent of the original motion. (See Chapter 5 for more on ownership of a motion.)

Limited Number

To avoid confusion, there is a limit on the number of amendments that can be pending. There can be only one main motion, one primary amendment, and one secondary amendment pending at a time. The primary amendment amends the pending main motion. The secondary amendment can only amend the primary amendment.

Some people refer to the primary amendment as an amendment to the first degree and the secondary amendment as an amendment to the second degree.

Gavel Gaffes

Not all motions can be amended. For a list of motions that cannot be amended, refer to *Robert's Rules of Order Newly Revised*.

Remember that after a primary amendment has been voted on, if it passed, it becomes a part of the motion it was amending. At that point, a new primary amendment could be offered. The same is true for a secondary amendment.

Vote Needed

To *Amend* a motion, you must have a majority vote. This is true even if the motion it is amending takes a two-thirds vote. For example, the main motion on the floor is to *Amend* the bylaws by changing the dues from $10 to $15. If you amended the motion by striking $15 and inserting $12, the amendment to change the proposed dues increase from $15 to $12 would only take a majority vote. If your amendment passed, the bylaw amendment to raise the dues from $10 to $12 would take a two-thirds vote.

Rules for the Motion to *Amend*

- Needs a second
- Is debatable
- Is amendable
- Needs a majority vote

A script (cheat sheet) for a motion to *Amend* can be found on my website, www.nancysylvester.com.

Postpone Indefinitely

A motion is made, and you don't think it's a good idea for this particular group. If the group votes it down, however, it will make the organization look bad. You just wish you could make it go away without having to vote on it ….

Your wish is *Robert's* command! The motion you want is the motion to *Postpone Indefinitely*. As noted earlier in this chapter, this motion in effect kills the main motion for the duration of the session without having to take a vote on it. It helps you reject an ill-advised motion without risking the embarrassment of passing it or failing it. This motion gives the group the opportunity to fully discuss it before deciding whether or not to kill it.

Parliamentary Pearls

The liberal debate rules for the motion to *Postpone Indefinitely* can be used to the advantage of a member who has already spoken his or her two times on the main motion but wants to speak again. He or she can make the motion to *Postpone Indefinitely* and, while speaking on the motion to *Postpone Indefinitely*, speak on the main motion as well. Pretty clever!

Debate Rules

The rules of debate on this motion are very lenient. The rules allow you to debate the motion to *Postpone Indefinitely* as well as the main motion it applies to.

Using the Motion to *Postpone Indefinitely* as a Straw Vote

In addition to using the motion to *Postpone Indefinitely* to kill an ill-advised motion, members opposed to the main motion can use it as a straw vote to find out whether they have a majority. If the motion to *Postpone Indefinitely* passes, they have succeeded at killing the motion. If it fails, the opponents to the motion still have the vote on the main motion and can rethink their strategy.

Point of Information

The motion to *Postpone Indefinitely* is very low on the motion ladder, positioned right above main motion. It is low so that before killing the main motion, you have many other ways to fix it.

An Exception to the Ladder

In Chapter 7, we learned about the motion ladder. At that time, I mentioned that there is one exception to the motion ladder. This motion is it. If the motion to *Postpone Indefinitely* passes, you do not take the final step down the ladder. You do not vote on the main motion.

Rules for the Motion to *Postpone Indefinitely*

- Needs a second
- Is debatable
- Is not amendable
- Needs a majority vote

A script (cheat sheet) for a motion to *Postpone Indefinitely* can be found on my website, www.nancysylvester.com.

The Least You Need to Know

- Subsidiary motions are made when a main motion is already on the floor.
- The motion to *Lay on the Table* is like 911—use it only for emergencies!
- Be sure to check your bylaws before you *Refer* a motion to a committee.
- When you have a lot of motions to cover in one meeting, or should have a long discussion on one motion, the motion to *Limit* or *Extend the Limits of Debate* could be very helpful.

- The motion to *Amend* allows the group to compromise so that a majority decision can be reached.
- You can use the motion to *Postpone Indefinitely* to kill a motion without voting on it.

Chapter 13

Incidental Motions

In This Chapter

- Keeping all members in line
- Asking questions about procedure and the issues
- Appealing the chair's decisions
- Making sure the vote count is accurate

The class of motions called incidental motions usually relates to matters of the business meeting rather than directly to the main motion. They may be offered at any time when they are needed.

All incidental motions are secondary motions, meaning that they are made when a main motion is already on the floor. Some of these motions, such as *Suspend the Rules* or *Point of Order*, can be made while nothing is pending; in those situations, they are called incidental main motions.

Six Incidental Motions

The following motions are in the class called incidental motions:

- ***Point of Order.*** If a member feels the rules are not being followed, he or she can use this motion. It requires the chair to make a ruling and enforce the rules.
- ***Appeal from the Decision of the Chair (Appeal).*** This is a motion to take a decision regarding parliamentary procedure out of the hands of the presiding officer and place the final decision in the hands of the assembly.
- ***Objection to the Consideration of a Question.*** The purpose of this motion is to prevent the assembly from considering the question/motion because a member deems the motion as irrelevant, unprofitable, or contentious.
- ***Suspend the Rules.*** This motion is used when the assembly wants to do something that violates its own rules. This motion does not apply to the organization's bylaws; local, state, or national law; or fundamental principles of parliamentary law.
- ***Division of the Assembly.*** The effect of this motion is to require a standing vote (not a counted vote). A single member can demand this if he or she feels the vote is too close to declare or is unrepresentative. This motion can only be used after a voice vote or a show of hands vote.
- ***Division of the Question.*** This motion is used to separate a main motion or amendment into parts to be voted on individually. It can only be used if each part can stand as a separate question.

Parliamentary Pearls

Because leadership should be shared by all members in attendance at a meeting, it is every member's right and responsibility to call a *Point of Order* if the presiding officer fails to do so.

This is not an exhaustive list, and other incidental motions exist that relate to methods of voting and to nominations, but this chapter will only cover these more commonly used motions.

Since this is not a rulebook (that's *Robert's* job), I will not be including all of the specific rules for each of the motions discussed. For the rules, please refer to *Robert's Rules of Order Newly Revised.*

Point of Order

If something inappropriate happens in a meeting, such as a member stooping to name calling during a heated debate, it's the presiding officer's responsibility to call the member to order. If a motion is worded in a way that makes it a violation of your bylaws, the presiding officer should call the motion out of order. However, if the presiding officer fails to call the member to order or fails to call an action out of order, any other member may call a *Point of Order.* Because it might be too late if you wait until the person is finished speaking, if the point needs to be made right away, it can even interrupt the speaker.

Use *Point of Order* to Disagree with the Chair

Point of Order isn't just used when members are not following proper decorum. Members can also use it when they disagree with the presiding officer's decision. For example, let's say that the motion on the floor is to purchase a computer. A member moves to *Amend* the motion to add "and carpet the office." The chair allows the amendment, but you believe that it is out of order because the carpet for the office and the computer are really two different issues, and therefore the amendment is not germane to the computer motion. (For more on amendments and the requirement that they be germane, see Chapter 12.) You could then call a *Point of Order* and state your point. If the chair agrees with you, the amendment would be ruled out of order. If the chair does not agree with you, the amendment would be allowed.

Parliamentary Pearls

Point of Order and the next motion I'll discuss, *Appeal,* are closely related. If members do not agree with the ruling of the chair on a *Point of Order,* the members can *Appeal from the Decision of the Chair.* An *Appeal* is the democratic method of having the decision of the chair overturned.

What Does *Point of Order* Require?

So a member calls out "*Point of Order*" if he or she disagrees with something or believes that another member is acting improperly. What next? First, the presiding officer asks the person to state his or her point. Then, after the member makes the point, the presiding officer must rule on it. If the group agrees with the ruling, it is carried out and the issue is over.

Turning the Ruling Over to the Assembly

But what if the presiding officer isn't sure how to rule? Let's say that it's a tough call, and the chair isn't sure what to do. Instead of making a decision and then having it appealed, the presiding officer can turn the decision over to the members—now there's a democratic process in action!

Here's how it would work: Let's return to the motion to purchase a computer—"I move that we purchase a computer"—which now has been amended by adding "and carpet the office." A member calls "*Point of Order*." The chair asks the member to state his or her point, and the member says that "the amendment to add 'and carpet the office' is not germane to the motion 'I move that we purchase a computer.'" The chair can't decide whether it is germane or not. Instead of ruling one way or the other (and probably having an *Appeal* no matter which way the chair rules), the chair decides to put the question to the members for a decision.

Here is how it might sound. The presiding officer: "A member has raised a *Point of Order* that the amendment to add 'and a printer' is not germane to the motion. The chair is in doubt and submits the question to the assembly. The question before you is, 'Is the amendment germane?'"

This question is debatable because if an *Appeal* was filed it would be debatable. Therefore, debate occurs. At the end of the debate, the presiding officer puts the question to a vote. "Those who are of the opinion that the amendment is germane and should be allowed, say *aye*. Those who believe the amendment is not germane and should be ruled out of order, say *no*."

Parliamentary Pearls

When ruling on a *Point of Order* ...

- Use a soft voice.
- Make your concern for fairness apparent.
- Take the time to think about how to handle the issue.
- Call for a consultation with the parliamentarian, if there is one.

No matter which way the vote goes, no *Appeal* is allowed when the decision has been made by the assembly. That's because the *Appeal from the Decision of the Chair* applies only when the chair makes the decision, and in this instance, the chair turned the decision over to the membership.

Do It Now Because Later Is Too Late!

If something is so inappropriate that it is out of order, it should be clear that it is out of order when it occurs or immediately after it occurs. Therefore, you must call a *Point of Order* at the time the violation occurs, not later. In other words, you don't get a chance to mull it over.

The only exception to the rule that the *Point of Order* must be called immediately is if the breach is of an ongoing nature, such as a breach of the governing documents. In such cases, a *Point of Order* can be raised at a later time. For example, if your bylaws indicate that the finance committee will have three members, and the current finance committee has five, that is an ongoing breach and can be brought up at any time.

Rules for *Point of Order*

- Does not need a second
- May interrupt the speaker
- Is not debatable
- Is not amendable
- Is ruled on by the chair

A script (cheat sheet) for a *Point of Order* can be found on my website, www.nancysylvester.com.

Appeal from the Decision of the Chair (Appeal)

This is one of my favorite motions because it serves as a reminder to everyone that parliamentary procedure is all about a democracy. If the presiding officer ever gets bigheaded and thinks he or she decides it all, this motion quickly puts that person in his or her place.

Gavel Gaffes

When you use the motion to *Appeal*, remember that it is not the presiding officer that you are appealing, it is the *decision* of the presiding officer that you are disagreeing with. Keep the focus of parliamentary procedure on the issue, not the person.

Earlier in this chapter, I mentioned that the motion to *Appeal from the Decision of the Chair*—or *Appeal*, as it's frequently called—is closely related to *Point of Order*. That's because after the member makes a *Point of Order*, the presiding officer is required to rule on that *Point of Order*. If a member disagrees with that ruling, he or she can *Appeal from the Decision of the Chair*.

Do It Now Because Later Is Too Late!

Just as with the *Point of Order*, the *Appeal* must be made immediately. If you disagree with the decision of the chair, you must appeal it at the time of the occurrence.

Doing It

The *Appeal* can interrupt the speaker, and it can be made on any decision made by the chair. The only exception (you knew there had to be one) is when another appeal is pending. Only decisions can be appealed—if the presiding officer gives information, that is not a decision, and the information cannot be appealed.

Rules for the Motion to *Appeal from the Decision of the Chair*

- Needs a second.
- Is debatable unless it is made when the immediately pending question (motion) is undebatable. In debate, no member is allowed to speak more than one time except the presiding officer, who may speak two times and does not need to vacate the chair when speaking.
- Is not amendable.
- Needs a majority vote in the negative to reverse the decision of the chair. Therefore, a tie vote sustains the decision of the chair.

A script (cheat sheet) for a motion to *Appeal from the Decision of the Chair* can be found on my website, www.nancysylvester.com.

Objection to the Consideration of a Question

The motion to *Object to the Consideration of a Question* is rarely used. Okay, I'll confess: the only time I have ever seen it properly used was at a convention of parliamentarians! Part of the reason is that it has so many stringent requirements on it.

The purpose of this motion is to prevent the assembly from considering the question/motion because a member deems the question as irrelevant, unprofitable, or contentious. It is appropriate to use this motion if the member judges the motion to be outside of the object of the organization and the presiding officer has not ruled the motion out of order.

This is one of the few places where the distinction between original and incidental main motions (see Chapter 5) matters. An *Objection to the Consideration of the Question* can only be made on an original main motion; it cannot be made on an incidental main motion such as an amendment to the bylaws or a motion to ratify a previous action.

No Daydreaming Here

Not only do you have to be awake enough to know whether the motion is an original main motion or an incidental main motion, but you have to be quick enough to realize that you must object to it before anyone discusses it. This motion must be made before there is any debate on the motion and before any subsidiary motion on it is stated by the chair. I wasn't kidding when I said you couldn't daydream! The objection must be made right away because if the question is so objectionable, it should be obvious that it is objectionable when it is made, and the members should not need time to think it over.

Vote Needed

If at least two thirds of the group does not judge the motion to be objectionable, the assembly can consider the motion. Therefore, the chair should put the motion to *Object to Consideration of the Question* to a vote with the question, "Shall the question be considered?" It takes two thirds in the negative to have the *Objection to Consideration of a Question* pass.

Rules for *Objection to the Consideration of a Question*

- Must be made before there has been any debate on the motion and before the chair has restated any secondary motions applying to the motion
- Does not need a second
- Is not debatable
- Is not amendable
- Needs a two-thirds vote in the negative to prevent consideration

A script (cheat sheet) for an *Objection to the Consideration of the Question* can be found on my website, www.nancysylvester.com.

Suspend the Rules

The motion to *Suspend the Rules* is used when the group wishes to do something that cannot be done without violating its own rules. But even with this motion, the group cannot violate its constitution, bylaws, or fundamental principles of parliamentary law.

When you make this motion, you should include the object of the suspension. For example, some of your friends have to leave the meeting, and you want Motion Q voted on before they go. But Motion Q is not on the agenda until much later in the meeting. You might say, "I move that we *Suspend the Rules* so that we can consider Motion Q at this time." If the motion passes, the group will take up Motion Q now instead of later in the agenda.

Gavel Gaffes

When you make the motion to *Suspend the Rules,* you don't necessarily have to tell the exact rule you are suspending, but you do have to tell the object of the suspension. You can't simply say, "I move to *Suspend the Rules,*" and then ignore all of the rules and do whatever you want.

Rules That Cannot Be Suspended

Robert's has some very specific requirements regarding what can be suspended and what can't. Remember that the constitution and bylaws of the organization are meant to be the rules that cannot be changed at the whim of the group attending one meeting. As a result, the constitution and bylaws cannot be suspended. The only exception to that rule is if the constitution or bylaws include a rule allowing for their own suspension.

Other rules that cannot be suspended are the fundamental principles of parliamentary law—in other words, rules that protect the basic rights of individual members, deal with voting rights, and so on. For example, rules that protect absentee members are not suspendable. If a rule requires previous notice, the members in attendance at the meeting cannot suspend that rule and consider the motion without previous notice.

Rules That Can Be Suspended

Rules that relate to business procedures and to priority of business can be suspended. In addition, rules that are in your standing rules or policies and procedures can be suspended.

Vote Needed

Here is where this motion gets a little confusing. I would like to tell you the vote is always a majority or always two thirds, but I can't. The kind of vote you need depends on the kind of rule you're suspending.

If the rule is in the nature of a parliamentary rule of order, a two-thirds vote is required. So a motion to *Suspend the Rules* and not allow debate on the motion would require a two-thirds vote.

If the rule is in the nature of guidelines relating to the way your organization carries out its business, a majority vote is all that is required. These include things like the hour the meeting begins, the order of business, and so on. Most of the rules that are contained in the organization's standing rules (see Chapter 4) need a majority vote to suspend.

Parliamentary Pearls

Instead of treating the *Suspend the Rules* motion as a formal motion that needs to be voted on, consider handling it by general consent. In most cases, there is no objection to *Suspend the Rules*. When that is the case, instead of processing it, the presiding officer should say, "Is there any objection to *Suspending the Rules* and taking up Motion Q at this time?" [Pause] "Hearing no objection, we will now proceed to Motion Q."

Rules for the Motion to *Suspend the Rules*

- Needs a second.
- Is not debatable.
- Is not amendable.
- May be made while another motion is pending as long as it applies to that motion.

- A vote is needed: If the rule is in the nature of a parliamentary rule of order, a two-thirds vote is required. If the rule is in the nature of guidelines relating to the way the organization carries out its business, a majority vote is required.

A script (cheat sheet) for a motion to *Suspend the Rules* can be found on my website, www.nancysylvester.com.

Division Motions

There are two division motions: *Division of the Assembly* and *Division of the Question*. Just as the two names indicate, *Division of the Assembly* "divides" the members who are voting (by having members voting one way stand and members voting the other way remain seated) and *Division of the Question* divides the motion. We will examine them separately.

Division of the Assembly

Imagine that you are sitting in a meeting and a vote is conducted. The presiding officer says, "All those in favor, say *aye*. All those opposed, say *no*. The *ayes* have it and the motion passes." You are sitting there thinking, "No way do the *ayes* have it. They just have bigger mouths and louder voices!" In that situation, this is the motion for you. All you have to do is call out "*Division*" and your problem is solved.

This motion requires the presiding officer to conduct the vote again, this time by a standing vote. It does not have to be a counted standing vote because in large conventions/meetings, a vote can take hours to count, and that would possibly be only a delay tactic.

This motion has a lot of unusual rules: It can only be called on a voice vote or a show of hands and no other kind of vote. It only takes one person to call it out, it does not require a second, it cannot be debated, it is not amendable, and it can have no other subsidiary motions applied to it. It does not require a vote because one person calling out "*Division*" is enough to require a standing vote. It's based on the idea that if one person is unclear on the outcome of the vote, that is enough. It is part of the concept of protecting the rights of the minority.

Like most of the other motions in this chapter, the window of opportunity for using this motion is very small. It can only be called after the vote is taken and before another motion has been stated. Also, it is applicable only to a voice vote or a show of hands vote. It is not applicable to any other kind of vote, even though people try to use it that way.

Division of the Question

Sometimes, for the sake of speed, one motion includes multiple ideas. For example, a committee recommends that "we buy the outgoing president a gavel and the outgoing treasurer a calculator." If you agree with both, it works beautifully to offer them both in one motion. However, if you only like the idea of a gavel for the president and think it is a stupid idea to buy a calculator for the treasurer, you can use the *Division of the Question* motion to split them up.

The question under consideration must be dividable, so be sure to give it some thought before moving to have it divided. For example, if the motion under consideration is that "we purchase a computer and a printer" and you currently own neither, the motion is not dividable. Even though a computer without a printer is useful, a printer without a computer would be of absolutely no use. If you want the computer without the printer, then you should use the motion to *Amend* and move to strike "and a printer."

To divide the motion a member should say, "I move to *Divide the Question*," and then state exactly how he or she wants it divided. This motion takes a majority vote but is usually handled by general consent. Once the question is divided, each part is treated as a separate motion, with discussion on each followed by the vote on each.

Rules for the *Division of the Assembly*

- Does not need a second
- Is not debatable
- Is not amendable
- Is required on the demand of one member

A script (cheat sheet) for a *Division of the Assembly* can be found on my website, www.nancysylvester.com.

Rules for the *Division of the Question*

- If there is an objection, it must be processed as a motion.
- Needs a second.
- Is not debatable.
- Is only amendable as to how the motion is divided.
- Needs a majority vote.
- If the question is divided, each section is treated as a separate motion that has already been made. So you discuss one, vote on it, and then go to the next one, discuss it, and vote on it.

A script (cheat sheet) for a *Division of the Question* can be found on my website, www.nancysylvester.com.

Requests and Inquiries

Many motions fit into the category of "requests and inquiries." However, you are likely to come across only three of them, so I will only cover those three:

- ***Parliamentary Inquiry.*** A question directed to the presiding officer concerning parliamentary law or the organization's rules as they apply to the business at hand.
- ***Point of Information.*** A nonparliamentary question about the business at hand.
- ***Withdrawal of a Motion.*** A request by the maker of a motion to remove the motion from consideration. After the motion has been stated by the presiding officer, it belongs to the assembly, and the assembly's permission (majority vote) is needed to withdraw the motion.

For details on other requests and inquires, please refer to *Robert's Rules of Order Newly Revised.*

Parliamentary Inquiry

You're in a meeting. You want to do something, but you don't know how to do it. This is the motion for you. All you have to do is rise and say, "Mr. Chairman, I rise to a *Parliamentary Inquiry.*" The presiding officer should then say, "Please state your inquiry." You state your inquiry, and the presiding officer answers the inquiry. It is at that exact moment that the presiding officer is glad he or she got this book, which will help in answering the inquiry.

> **Point of Information**
>
> When making a *Parliamentary Inquiry* or *Point of Information,* you can interrupt the speaker, but only if doing so is absolutely necessary. Neither motion requires a second, and they are not debatable or amendable. There is no vote taken since the inquiries are responded to by the chair or by someone the chair appoints.

Point of Information

You are in a meeting. This time you are listening to the debate and believe that it would be helpful to have additional information on the motion that surely someone knows but you don't. To find out if anyone else has this information, you simply rise and say, "Mr. Chairman, I rise to a *Point of Information.*" The presiding officer should then say, "Please state your point." You state your question, and the presiding officer answers the question or calls upon someone else to answer it.

Withdrawal of a Motion

You made a motion. Now that you have heard the debate, you think that making that motion wasn't the wisest move you've ever made. You're in luck—all you have to do is request permission to withdraw your motion.

Does this motion need a vote? That depends! I'm not trying to be a smart aleck. It really depends on when you want to withdraw it. Let's briefly review the six steps of a motion:

1. A member makes a motion.
2. Another member seconds the motion.
3. The chair states the motion, formally placing it before the assembly.
4. The members debate the motion.
5. The chair puts the question to a vote.
6. The chair announces the results of the vote.

If you remember that at the completion of Step 3 the ownership of the motion is turned over from the individual who made the motion to the assembly, you probably already know when the motion needs a vote and when it doesn't. If the member wants to withdraw the motion during Steps 1, 2, or 3, the member can withdraw the motion without anyone else agreeing. Of course, someone else could turn around and make the same motion.

Parliamentary Pearls

If a member were to request to withdraw his motion during Step 4, the presiding officer would say, "Is there any objection to allowing the maker of the motion to withdraw his motion?" [Pause] "Hearing no objection, the motion is withdrawn. The next business in order is …"

If the member wants to withdraw the motion during Step 4, it now belongs to the assembly, and the mover must get permission from the assembly. This is usually handled by general consent, but if anyone objects, the member then makes the motion to *Withdraw the Motion*, and it takes a majority vote for it to pass.

The Least You Need to Know

- It's up to the chair to call a member to order, but if he or she fails to do so, any member can make a *Point of Order.*
- The motion to *Appeal from the Decision of the Chair* ensures that the chair doesn't abuse his or her power.

- Even parliamentarians find the *Objection to the Consideration of a Question* motion confusing.
- Use *Parliamentary Inquiry* when you just don't know the best way to do something using parliamentary procedure.
- Withdrawing a motion is allowed, but you may have to vote on it.

Chapter 14

The "Bring Back" Motions

In This Chapter

- How to take back a motion
- How to clear off the table
- Ways to update motions
- What to do if you change your mind

The "bring back" motions are a group of motions used to bring back a motion that has already been before the assembly for reconsideration, just in case once wasn't enough.

These motions are methods of properly getting around two of the basic principles of parliamentary procedure. The first principle is that an assembly cannot be asked to decide the same (or substantially the same) question twice during one session unless a special motion is made to allow that. The second principle is that a motion that conflicts with a motion adopted at the same session or one previously adopted that is still in effect is not in order.

Four "Bring Back" Motions

The following motions are classified as "bring back" motions:

- *Rescind*
- *Amend Something Previously Adopted*
- *Take from the Table*
- *Reconsider*

Since this is not a rulebook (that's *Robert's* job), I will not be including all of the specific rules for each of the motions in this chapter. For the rules, please refer to *Robert's Rules of Order Newly Revised.*

Rescind

This motion is used to cancel something that the voting body did at a previous meeting. Life changes, we change our minds, circumstances change, and this is the motion that allows you to respond to that change.

Vote Needed

A member should not be able to wait until just the right number of people who voted in favor of the motion is absent and then move to *Rescind* that motion. That would be a violation of the rights of the absent members. To protect those rights, a higher than normal vote is needed.

For the motion to *Rescind*, any of the following votes are needed:

- A two-thirds vote
- A majority vote if previous notice is given
- A majority of the entire membership

If any of these three votes is reached, the motion passes.

Point of Information

Here is an example of the vote needed for *Rescind:*

> An organization has 45 members. At the April meeting, the members in attendance approved the motion to hold a road race in August as a fundraiser for the organization. At the May meeting, members realize that absolutely nothing has been done to start the fundraiser, and besides that, another local organization is also having a road race fundraiser the same weekend in August. A member moves to *Rescind* the motion adopted at the April meeting to have an August fundraiser. At that May meeting, 30 members are present and all 30 vote either *aye* or *no*. What is the vote needed at the May meeting to pass the motion to *Rescind?*
>
> - A two-thirds vote: 20 in favor, 10 against.
> - A majority vote if previous notice was given. Previous notice was not given, but if it had been given, only 16 votes would be needed.
> - A majority of the entire membership: 23 votes.

Therefore, in this situation, if there are 20 votes in the affirmative, the motion to *Rescind* passes.

What Can't Be *Rescinded?*

Here are some of the things that you cannot *Rescind:*

- A vote after something has been done as a result of that vote and it is too late to undo it. If, for example, the motion was made at the March meeting to buy ice cream treats for the next three monthly meetings, and you are at the April meeting and the ice cream treats have been served and eaten, it is not possible to undo the buying and serving of ice cream treats for the April meeting.
- An action in the nature of a contract, once the other party in the contract has been informed (if, for example, a contract is signed or verbally committed to).
- A resignation that has been acted upon. For example, if the treasurer submits his resignation and that resignation is formally accepted by the assembly.

- An election to or expulsion from membership if the person was present or has already been notified.
- A motion that could still be *Reconsidered.* (See *Robert's Rules of Order Newly Revised* for a list of these motions.)

Rules for the Motion to *Rescind*

- Needs a second
- Is debatable
- Is amendable
- A vote is needed: a two-thirds vote, a majority vote if previous notice is given, or a majority of the entire membership

A script (cheat sheet) for a motion to *Rescind* can be found on my website, www.nancysylvester.com.

Amend Something Previously Adopted

"Ditto" is the word here. Everything that applied to the motion to *Rescind* applies to the motion to *Amend Something Previously Adopted.* If you understand one, you understand the other.

Two Differences

There are only two differences. First, instead of canceling a previously adopted motion, this motion changes it. Second, you must include how you propose to change the previously adopted motion in the motion to *Amend Something Previously Adopted*, just as you would in any other motion to *Amend.*

Rules for the Motion to *Amend Something Previously Adopted*

- Needs a second
- Is debatable

- Is amendable
- A vote is needed: a two-thirds vote, a majority vote if previous notice is given, or a majority of the entire membership

A script (cheat sheet) for a *Motion to Amend Something Previously Adopted* can be found on my website, www.nancysylvester.com.

Gavel Gaffes

It is very easy to get the motion to *Amend Something Previously Adopted* mixed up with the motion to *Amend*. The main difference is that the motion to *Amend* is a secondary motion and the motion to *Amend Something Previously Adopted* is a main motion. Because the motion to *Amend* is a secondary motion, it can only be applied to a main motion. So if the motion on the floor is to purchase a computer, a secondary motion to *Amend* might be to insert the word "Mac" before the word "computer." No other motions can be pending when the main motion to *Amend Something Previously Adopted* is made.

Take from the Table

You'll recall from Chapter 12 that the motion to *Lay on the Table* allows a group to set aside a pending motion in order to attend to more urgent business. To bring the tabled motion back before the group, a member must make the motion to *Take from the Table* before the end of the next regularly scheduled meeting.

Time Restrictions

A motion that was *Laid on the Table* can only be *Taken from the Table* during the remainder of the meeting at which it was *Laid on the Table* or before the conclusion of the next regularly scheduled meeting. For example, let's say your group meets on the first Thursday of each month. In February, a motion was *Laid on the Table* early in the meeting. That motion can be *Taken from the Table* during the remainder of the February meeting or up until the end of the meeting held on the first Thursday in March. The "next regular meeting" must be within a quarterly time interval. Therefore, if you have an annual convention,

Point of Information

Have you ever wondered what table you're laying a motion on or taking it from? The table is the secretary's table. In essence, the motion is placed in the care of the secretary (symbolically on his or her table) until it is needed again.

you can't *Lay on the Table* at one convention and *Take from the Table* at the next.

What happens to it after the March regular meeting? It falls off the table. If you want to bring it up again at the April or May meeting, it is as though it was never moved in the first place and must come up as new business.

Other Restrictions

The motion to *Take from the Table* can be made by any member, and it requires a majority vote to pass.

If the motion is *Taken from the Table* at the same meeting, individual debate restrictions apply. So if you already spoke on it two times before it was *Laid on the Table*, you cannot debate it again after it is brought from the table. But if it is brought from the table on a later day, the restrictions do not carry over. So even if you spoke on it two times on the first day, at a later day you can debate it two more times.

As noted in Chapter 12, when you *Lay a Motion on the Table*, all pending motions go with it. Take the motion to purchase a computer as an example. Let's say that a motion is made to *Amend* by inserting "Mac" before the word "computer." It is then moved to *Refer* the motion to a committee. Then it is moved to *Lay on the Table*, and that motion passes. When the motion is *Taken from the Table*, all those subsidiary motions still apply to it, and you must first deal with the motion to *Refer*, then the amendment, and finally the main motion to purchase a computer (as amended, if the motion to *Amend* passed).

Rules for the Motion to *Take from the Table*

- Needs a second
- Is not debatable
- Is not amendable

- Needs a majority vote
- May be made during the unfinished business or new business portion of the agenda

A script (cheat sheet) for a motion to *Take from the Table* can be found on my website, www.nancysylvester.com.

Reconsider

This motion clearly wins the award for the most complicated of all of the motions. If you want to understand all of the intricacies of this motion (and there are plenty of them), you need to check out *Robert's*. With that disclaimer, let's proceed.

Parliamentary Pearls

The motion to *Reconsider* is recognized as a uniquely American motion. Actually, it is the only motion of American origin. It is universally accepted by all of the major American parliamentary authorities. But when you realize how complicated it is, it may be something we don't want to put the "Made in USA" brand on!

Effect

The effect of the adoption of this motion is to erase the original vote on the motion and put the assembly in exactly the same place it was in right before that vote occurred. If the motion to *Reconsider* passes, the motion is put back on the floor, as if the original vote had not occurred, and discussion continues.

Who and When

The motion to *Reconsider* can be made only by a member who voted on the prevailing side. So if the motion passed, you had to have voted aye on it to move to *Reconsider* it; if the motion failed, you had to have voted no to move to *Reconsider* it. The whole idea is that at least one person in the group has to have changed his or her mind before the entire group should have to go back and consider this motion again.

The motion to *Reconsider* can be made only on the day that the original motion was made. There is one exception: during a convention or when you are meeting for multiple days in a row, it can be made on the next day as well.

Two Parts: Make It, Call It Up

Here's the part that's really unusual. This motion can be made at one time and processed (or called up) at another time. So even if you can't process the motion for whatever reason, such as time constraints, you can still make the motion and then call it up to discuss it at a later time. This is covered in detail in *Robert's Rules of Order Newly Revised.*

What Can't Be Reconsidered

The motion to *Reconsider* is not a free-for-all, and a lot of motions can't be reconsidered. You will find them listed in *Robert's Rules of Order Newly Revised.*

Rules for the Motion to *Reconsider*

- Is debatable only if the motion being reconsidered was debatable
- Is not amendable
- Needs a majority vote
- Can only be made by a person who voted on the prevailing side
- Can be moved only on the same or next succeeding day after the original vote was taken

A script (cheat sheet) for a motion to *Reconsider* can be found on my website, www.nancysylvester.com.

Reconsider, Rescind—I Get Those "R" Words Mixed Up!

It's easy to get these two motions confused, yet the rules that apply to them are very different. The following snapshot of both motions might help clear up some of the confusion.

Clarification of *Reconsider* and *Rescind*

Motion	Timing	Maker of Motion	Outcome of Original Motion	Timing of Consideration of Motion	Second Needed	Debatable	Amendable	Vote Needed
Reconsider	Same session	Must have voted on the prevailing side	Passed or failed	If made at one time, can be called up later	Yes	Yes, only if motion being reconsidered is debatable	No	Majority
Rescind	Later session	No restrictions of vote on original motion	Passed	At time the motion is made	Yes	Yes	Yes	Two-thirds, majority with notice, majority of members

For specific information on rules, see *Robert's Rules of Order Newly Revised*, Chapter IX.

The Least You Need to Know

- You cannot *Rescind* a motion that the group has taken action on that can't be undone.
- If you don't move to *Take a Motion from the Table* by the end of the next regularly scheduled meeting after it was *Laid on the Table*, the motion falls from the table. If you then want to consider the motion, it must be brought up as a new item of business.
- The rules for the motion to *Rescind* are almost identical to the rules to *Amend Something Previously Adopted.*
- To move to *Reconsider* a motion that has already been voted upon, you must have voted in favor of it if it passed or against it if it failed.

Part 4

Let's Get to Order

There's more to displaying leadership in a meeting than knowing the motions. Leadership is about preparing for the meeting, conducting it in an orderly fashion, and handling any difficult situations in a manner that's perceived to be fair.

This part covers some of the fine details of a meeting. If you are already a leader or if you would like to be one, this part is crucial for you. It will give you the guidance you need to prepare for and run your meeting, no matter what kind of meeting you are leading.

Chapter 15

On the Agenda

In This Chapter

- The correct order for agenda items
- Moving right along on the minutes
- Receiving reports
- Where special orders come from
- Distinguishing between new and unfinished business

The agenda is a predetermined sequence of items of business to be covered at a specific meeting. An agenda, which is sometimes referred to as an order of business, can be a huge timesaving tool—but only if it is prepared and used correctly. All too often, the chair creates an agenda but fails to stick to it. It takes discipline to follow an agenda, but that discipline will pay off in time saved.

The idea behind the agenda is to look at all the elements of business that need to come before a group and then put them in order of importance. Items should be ordered from most to least important so that, if a meeting is cut short, the most important things will have (hopefully) already been resolved. Let's take a closer look at that order.

The Order of Business

If your group meets at least quarterly (four times a year), has *Robert's* as its parliamentary authority, and has not adopted a special order of business, the following is your order of business for your meetings:

1. Reading and Approval of Minutes
2. Reports of Officers, Boards, and Standing Committees
3. Reports of Special (Select or Ad Hoc) Committees
4. Special Orders
5. Unfinished Business and General Orders
6. New Business

Let's look at each of these business items in turn.

Approval of Minutes

If this agenda item is done correctly, it can and should take only a minute or two.

Ideally, the secretary prepared the minutes from the previous meeting immediately after that meeting and sent them out to the members—either by e-mail or regular mail—before this meeting. When the minutes are printed and distributed in advance of the meeting, there is no need to have the minutes read during the meeting, and the members can quickly move to approve them.

Approval Verbiage

Approval of the minutes could be this simple: the presiding officer says, "You have received the minutes of the last meeting. Are there any corrections to the minutes? [Pause] Hearing none, if there is no objection, the minutes are approved as printed and distributed to the members." (By the way, this is an example of voting by general consent, which you learned about in Chapter 9.)

Changes to the Minutes

Notice that the verbiage suggested is, "Are there any corrections to the minutes as printed?"

If a member suggests a correction to the minutes, it is usually best to handle it by general consent. After a member offers a change, the presiding officer would say, "Is there any objection to making that change? [Pause] Hearing no objection, the change will be made."

If there is an objection, the change is handled by following the amendment process: The motion to approve the minutes is on the floor, and a member states exactly how the minutes should be amended. The amendment is seconded, restated by the presiding officer, discussed, voted on, and announced. The approval of the minutes, as amended, requires a majority vote. It is unusual to have to vote on a change in the minutes. If your group's minutes are changed on a regular basis, you're probably including too much information in the minutes. See Chapter 18 for help.

Gavel Gaffes

You might have heard presiding officers ask, "Are there any additions or corrections to the minutes as printed?" It is not necessary to ask for additions as well as corrections because an addition *is* a correction.

Reports

Not every officer and committee will have a report at each meeting unless it is an annual meeting, at which all officers and committees might be required by the bylaws to present a report.

Reports are divided into four different groups and are given in the following order:

1. Officers
2. Boards
3. Standing committees
4. Special committees

The reports within the four groups should be given in the order in which they are listed in the bylaws or, in the case of special committees, in the order they were created.

Printed Reports

If everyone gets in the habit of putting all of the reports in writing and distributing them before the meeting, this part of the agenda could move along very quickly. As with the minutes, if all members have received printed reports in advance of the meeting, all the presiding officer has to do when he or she gets to a specific officer is to ask, "Do you have any additions to the report as printed and distributed to the members?" Most of the time the answer is no, and then the meeting can move right along.

Point of Information

A motion arising from an officer, board, or committee report must be taken up immediately.

Motions to adopt or implement any recommendations made by an officer should be made from the floor by a member other than the reporting officer.

Motions to implement any recommendations made by a committee should be made by the committee chairman or other reporting member.

Saying "Thank You" Is Enough

After a member gives a report, the presiding officer should simply acknowledge receipt of the report by thanking the member who presented the report and moving on to the next agenda item.

With regard to reports, the three "a" words—accept, adopt, and approve—all mean the same thing. When you adopt, accept, or approve a report, you are making it a permanent official document of the organization. Very seldom should a report become an official document of the organization. Therefore, very seldom should there be a motion to adopt, approve, or accept a report.

When a report is said to be received, it simply means that it was heard. So if, after a report has been given, a member makes the motion, "I move to receive the report of the finance committee," that member is a day late and a dollar short. The report has already been heard and therefore received. Again, it is usually best simply to thank the person giving the report and announce the next item of business.

Gavel Gaffes

You should never approve the treasurer's report because it should always be audited after the treasurer presents it. If you feel the need to approve, accept, or adopt a financial report, it should be the auditor's report that is approved. After the treasurer's report is given, the chair can say, "Thank you, the report will be filed for audit."

For complete information on the content of the officers' reports and guidance on what to include in committee reports, see Chapter 20.

Special Orders

The special orders category of the agenda allows a group to specify a certain time for considering a specific subject and gives it an absolute priority for that time.

A two-thirds vote is required to make something a special order. Such a high vote is necessary because the special order takes away from members the right to follow the typical agenda, and when the time of the special order arrives, it forces them to stop what they are doing and take up the special order. When the time for the special order arrives, it has the effect of suspending the current business so that the members can take up the special order.

Bylaws Give Special Orders

In most organizations, the only time you will see special orders on the agenda is when the bylaws require that a particular item be handled at a specific meeting. A good example is the election of officers—it's common for the bylaws to indicate at which meeting the election of officers is to be conducted. When that is the case, the election of officers comes on the agenda under special orders.

Convention Special Orders

You might also see the special orders item of business used at a convention or a meeting that will take place over several days. People frequently travel to conventions and might need to know which day and time a specific issue will be brought up so they can be in attendance at that time.

Order of the Special Orders

When there are multiple special orders for the same time, the special order that was made first is considered first. For specific information on how to handle multiple special orders, refer to *Robert's Rules of Order Newly Revised.*

That Business Is Unfinished, Not Old

The most misunderstood and abused section on the agenda is unfinished business. Not familiar with that term? Probably because you have heard it referred to as old business, which is incorrect. There is no category called "Old Business." The category is actually called "Unfinished Business and General Orders." Let's look at each of these subsections separately.

Unfinished Business

Unfinished business is just that—business that was previously started but hasn't been finished.

Gavel Gaffes

The term "old business" gives no indication of whether that business was finished or not. Referring to it as "unfinished business" makes it clear that the business was started but not yet finished. "So what?" you ask. Remember that the agenda is in order of priority. If a group started business at the previous meeting and didn't finish it, that business should have a higher priority than something completely new or a new spin on an old subject.

In order for something to be included in the unfinished business section of the agenda, it must be something that the group started at a previous meeting but didn't complete. For example, in a group that meets monthly, if an item was on the agenda at the March meeting and the group did not get to it before time to adjourn, it would come up automatically at the April meeting under unfinished business.

Point of Information

The only business that comes up under unfinished business and general orders is …

- A motion that was pending when the previous meeting was adjourned.
- Items that were on the agenda at the previous meeting but didn't get taken up before that meeting was adjourned.
- Items that, at the previous meeting, were postponed to this meeting.
- Any item that was *Laid on the Table* at the current or previous meeting. When a motion is taken from the table, it does not automatically come up under unfinished business, but the motion to *Take from the Table* could be made during the unfinished business portion of the meeting.

However, just because a group discussed a topic at last month's meeting doesn't give it higher priority at this month's meeting. For example, let's say that at the March meeting a motion was made and passed to have a fundraiser in August. After the March meeting, you got the idea to have a raffle and have the drawing at the August fundraiser. At the April meeting, you move that the group have a raffle and have the drawing at the August fundraiser. That motion would come up under new business. The decision at the March meeting was to have an August fundraiser, and that decision was voted on and passed at the March meeting. The motion at the April meeting was a subject the group had discussed before (the August fundraiser), but the raffle had not been discussed before, so in April it is new business.

General Orders

If, at the March meeting, a motion was postponed to the next meeting, it would be included in the general orders section of the agenda at the

April meeting. The general orders section includes any motion that, usually by postponement, has been made an order of the day (item of business) without being made a special order. Translated, this means that if an item is postponed until a certain day or after a certain event, it fits in this category. Unlike special orders, general orders do not suspend any rules and therefore cannot interrupt business. To make an item a general order requires a majority vote.

When it gets to the point in the agenda for unfinished business and general orders, the presiding officer should not announce this category unless there is business in the category. Unlike the next category, new business, there is no possibility for surprise here. If nothing was postponed or not completed at the last meeting and nothing was laid on the table at the last meeting or the current meeting, there is no possibility for unfinished business.

If there is no unfinished business or general orders, when that time comes on the agenda, the presiding officer should say, "Since there is no unfinished business or general orders for this meeting, we will now proceed to new business." If there is unfinished business or general orders, then when it comes to that time in the agenda, the presiding officer should simply announce the first item of unfinished business. Business in this category is taken up in the order of the time to which it was postponed, regardless of when the general order was made.

> **Point of Information**
>
> During a convention, the agenda is approved early in the first meeting of the convention. During regular meetings of a group that meets weekly or monthly, the agenda does not have to be approved unless it has specific times for specific items.

New Business

It's easy to determine what fits in this category. Basically, anything that the group can properly take up and that doesn't fit anywhere else fits in new business. This is where you present to the members for their consideration any new items of business.

If a motion was laid on the table at this meeting or the previous meeting, it can be taken from the table under new business. It does not automatically come up under new business, but the motion to *Take from the Table* can be made during new business.

The presiding officer cannot refuse to allow business to come up under new business as long as the business is within the purpose of the group.

Taking Business Out of Order

There are four ways that business can be considered out of the order given in the printed agenda:

- **General consent.** Sometimes it is clear that it is the will of the group to change the order of business. It might be because of the arrival of a special guest or the lateness of the hour. The presiding officer might simply say, "If there is no objection, we will change the agenda and have our guest speak now. Immediately after his or her presentation, we will continue with this item of business and the remainder of the agenda. Is there any objection to changing the order of business? [Pause] Hearing none, the order will be changed."
- ***Suspend the Rules.*** When some members want to change the order and it is obvious that others do not, it will take a motion to change the order. That motion would be to *Suspend the Rules* (see Chapter 13). It should state exactly how the order should change. This motion takes a two-thirds vote.
- ***Lay on the Table.*** When a motion is pending and an urgent matter comes up, a member may move to *Lay on the Table* the pending motion (see Chapter 12). This motion is undebatable and takes a majority to pass. If there are many items on the agenda between where you are and where you want to be, you can repeat this motion for each item.

  Once a motion is laid on the table and you have finished the next item of business, if someone wants to discuss the tabled item, it requires a motion to *Take from the Table* (see Chapter 14).
- ***Reconsider* the making of an item a general or special order.** If an item has been made a general or special order and you want to bring it up before the time specified, you can either *Suspend*

the Rules, which takes a two-thirds vote, or you can reconsider the motion that made it a special or general order. All the rules of the motion to *Reconsider* must be followed (see Chapter 14).

Consent Agenda

Some organizations that have routine business find that an efficient way of handling that business is to include it on a *consent agenda*, which is also called a consent calendar. This is an agenda category that includes a list of routine, uncontroversial items that can be approved with a single motion, no discussion, and one vote.

The consent agenda is most frequently used by governmental bodies that have routine business that must be approved. If you are going to follow this process, you may want to have a section in your rules explaining the procedure.

When you get to this part of the agenda, the presiding officer first asks whether any member wants to remove any item from the consent agenda. The items are usually numbered or lettered, and the member simply states which number he or she would like removed. No explanation is necessary. A member can ask to remove an item if that member wants to discuss it, ask questions on it, or have a separate vote on it.

After members have had plenty of opportunity to remove any item from the consent agenda, either a member moves to approve all of the remaining items on the consent agenda or the chair assumes this motion. There can be no discussion or amendment of this motion. The vote is taken, and all items that were on the consent agenda are approved by the one vote.

Tips on Agenda Preparation

Presiding officers over the years have developed many ways to make preparing the agenda easier. Some of these tips are based on electronic tools, others on good old common sense. Let's take a look at a few of them.

Use Past Minutes

Agenda preparation can be made easier by referring to two sets of past minutes: the minutes of the previous meeting and the minutes of the meeting held one year ago.

The minutes of the previous meeting are very helpful in reminding you of any business that was begun at the last meeting but not yet concluded and that should be included on the agenda for the next meeting.

The minutes of the meeting one year ago will shed light on what annual items should be put on the agenda for this meeting, such as the annual audit.

Create a Template

Many people who use a computer to prepare the agenda open the file of the agenda from the previous meeting and then make changes in that file. The problem is that sometimes you miss the obvious (like changing the date of the meeting). Instead, create a template. All major word processing programs allow users to create templates, which can then be stored and pulled up each time you are ready to create a new version of that document. Simply go to the "Help" section of your word processing program and put in "Create a Template." It will instruct you how to create the template, and you'll find that you not only save a lot of time, but produce more accurate agendas!

Warning Flags

Members can prepare more easily for a meeting if they can determine with a quick glance at the agenda which items will require action and which items have material included in the agenda packet. If members know that they are going to have to vote on an issue, they will probably give it more attention before the meeting, particularly if they only have limited time to prepare.

You can simply place a designated symbol in front of each item that requires a specific action (in this case I'm using an asterisk) and another symbol in front of each item that has material included in the premeeting packet (in this case I'm using the pound sign). The following is an example of the first three items on an agenda using these symbols (note there is no symbol for the vice president):

1. (*#) Approval of minutes
2. (*) President's report
3. Vice president's report

The Least You Need to Know

- *Robert's* specifies the order in which items of business should be taken up.
- Only business that the group has previously discussed should be included as unfinished business.
- Your group can change the order of the agenda, but it requires a vote to do so.
- Create and use a computer template to prepare the agenda for every meeting.

Chapter 16

Presiding Secrets

In This Chapter

- How to facilitate instead of dictate
- Observing nonverbal cues
- How 10 minutes of prep can save hours of meeting time
- Preparing and using scripts

Unfortunately, all too many presiding officers take what I like to call the "dictator approach" to presiding. In other words, they like to be in complete control of the meeting, to the point that it inhibits the parliamentary process. Let me qualify that. When a person has the dictator approach and you ask him or her about it, the person will quickly deny it. But if you pursue the topic further, you will hear him or her say things like, "The chair can close debate," or "The chair doesn't have to call on someone if he or she doesn't want to." These are examples of the dictator philosophy.

However, as I noted in Chapter 3, the role of the presiding officer is to facilitate the meeting, not to dictate what happens in the meeting. To facilitate means to "make easier," and that is clearly the role of the presiding officer. In this chapter, we'll consider the skills that a presiding officer needs to be an effective but fair leader.

Presiding Qualities

Every effective presiding officer should have the following qualities: credibility, neutrality, judgment, and fairness.

Credibility

Members won't give someone a fair hearing if they don't judge that person as knowledgeable, honest, and fair. Presiding officers must establish their credibility early and reinforce that credibility often by taking actions that are perceived as fair and honest.

Neutrality

Members will put up with a lot of faults in a presiding officer, but one thing they won't forgive is showing obvious partiality in a controversial issue. Presiding officers must stay neutral and should go out of their way to demonstrate neutrality to the members.

One way of displaying neutrality is never to enter into the debate. If presiding officers can't stay neutral, they are obligated to have someone who can stay neutral preside.

Gavel Gaffes

Don't hesitate to admit when you have made a mistake, but then make sure you take steps to correct it. People don't expect perfection from their presiding officer—honesty, yes; perfection, no.

While presiding officers can't make motions, they can suggest motions. For example, if an issue is being discussed, someone suggests a possible solution, and the nonverbal reaction is very positive, the presiding officer might at that time ask, "Would you like to put that in the form of a motion?"

Judgment

Being an effective presiding officer is all about making the correct judgment calls, particularly during a vote. For instance, presiding officers shouldn't indicate whether the vote passed or failed unless they are absolutely positive of the outcome. If there is any doubt, the vote should be retaken.

Presiding officers should also recognize when it is time to let group members have a moment to clear their heads. In the latest edition of *Robert's*, this is referred to as a "stand at ease." If things are very sensitive or difficult, a presiding officer shouldn't hesitate to give the members time to take a deep breath by asking them to stay in their place and "stand at ease."

Parliamentary Pearls

The words "If there is no objection ..." are very helpful. If as the presiding officer you do something that isn't exactly according to parliamentary procedure, and you preface it with these five words and no one objects, then you have gotten general consent to proceed. Of course, if there is one objection, you have to proceed to process it as a motion.

Fairness

Fairness is a lot like beauty—it's in the eye of the beholder. Therefore, presiding officers should do all that they can to make sure their actions are perceived as fair by others.

Consistency in how presiding officers address the members can dramatically impact the appearance of fairness. Presiding officers should pay attention to their tone of voice and facial expressions when they recognize a member to speak. Even if that person is very irritating, it's important to not display that irritation. In addition, presiding officers should avoid calling on some people by first name and not others.

Presiding Skills

In addition to personal characteristics, presiding officers must have certain skills to be effective at their job. The good news is that skills can be developed. If you want to be a good presiding officer, following are the skills you should develop.

Communication

Presiding is one of those times when it is good to remember that we were given two ears and one mouth for a reason. The verbal part of communication is helpful to the presiding officer, but the part that is most crucial is listening, observing, and sensing the mood of the group. If you can do this, you can overcome almost any other fault you might have as a presiding officer. When a member is speaking, give that member your full attention. Make sure you are not distracted by all the other things happening around you.

Parliamentary Pearls

Make sure the members know that they are being listened to! One of the most interesting things I have learned about communication is that people who are upset usually calm down when they feel that they are being heard. Notice that I did not say "when they feel they are being agreed with." Most people only ask that they receive a fair hearing, not agreement. Once the member feels heard, he or she is more likely to calm down and listen to others.

If you are listening to what the members are saying and how they are saying it, you will be able to summarize their ideas and help them focus on what they want to do. They are usually very impressed when they observe you display this skill.

More than half of what we communicate is communicated nonverbally. Therefore, when presiding you must be tuned in to the nonverbal communication that is occurring throughout the meeting. To do that, you must listen not only with your ears but also with your eyes. Look at the participants. Emotions are communicated but only if you are watching for them.

When you have seen, heard, or sensed something, check it out by asking, "I'm sensing that you feel uncomfortable with moving ahead with the vote. Is that correct?"

Facilitation

Facilitating is a difficult but important skill. It entails figuring out what group members want to do and then assisting them in doing what they (not you) want to do. The skill of facilitating a meeting includes focusing on procedure and keeping the meeting moving. Good facilitation means that you put aside your personal agenda and realize that this meeting is not all about you.

Organization

Remaining organized during the meeting will make your meetings more efficient. One of the greatest organizational tools for the presiding officer is to follow the six steps of processing a motion (refer to Chapters 5 and 6). Steps 3, 5, and 6 (discussed again later in this chapter), when done well by the presiding officer, can help the presiding officer be perceived as well organized. Another organizational tool that should not be underestimated is the agenda. When everyone in the meeting knows the agenda and the presiding officer is assisting the group to stay faithful to the agenda, the presiding officer is perceived as organized.

Presiding Techniques

The techniques in this section can help you improve your presiding skills.

Parliamentary Pearls

Confidence is the name of the game. Even though you may not always feel confident when you are presiding at a meeting, you should always display confidence. However, remember that there is a fine line between confidence and arrogance, and few things are more annoying than an arrogant chair.

Share the Ownership

The presiding officer who approaches the meeting with the mindset that it is his or her meeting is approaching it very differently from the presiding officer who approaches the meeting with the mindset that it is the members' meeting.

If you and the members see the meeting as belonging to the members and not to the presiding officer, the members are much more likely to own the meeting. When they feel ownership in the meeting, they share the responsibility with the presiding officer for running it. For instance, if the members feel as if the meeting belongs to them, they will be more likely to use peer pressure to help maintain decorum in the meeting. But if the members feel the meeting belongs to the presiding officer, they will wait for the presiding officer to call the members to order.

Set the Tone

When the presiding officer sets a tone of fairness and respect for the members, the members usually follow suit. If the minority point of view is treated with the same level of decency as the majority point of view, the atmosphere of the meeting will remain very positive. Toleration by the presiding officer of even the least bit of disrespect will change the tone of the meeting. As presiding officer, do not tolerate any disrespect! Put a stop to it immediately.

Reduce Confusion

One way to keep the meeting moving is to keep confusion out of the meeting. In Chapters 5 and 6, we discussed the six steps of a motion. Three of those steps, if done correctly, will help keep the meeting moving and keep the confusion out:

- **Step 3: The presiding officer states the motion.** You will be amazed at how much confusion restating the motion will eliminate. When members know exactly what the motion is before the discussion begins on that motion, they will be much more likely to stay focused.
- **Step 5: The presiding officer restates the motion and puts it to a vote.** Being reminded of exactly what the group is voting on right before the vote makes the whole voting process less confusing, especially for the members who were daydreaming. (And believe me, some members *will* be daydreaming.)

- **Step 6: The presiding officer announces the result of the vote.** When the members know which side prevailed, the implication of the vote, and what the next item of business is, there will be far less confusion. For the content of a complete announcement of the results of a vote, refer to Chapter 6.

Reduce Extraneous Debate

When the debate is dragging on and on and on, it's up to the presiding officer to help move it along. Let's say that the motion on the floor is to purchase a computer, and the issue has been debated for 45 minutes. In addition, members are beginning to stray off topic just a bit. The presiding officer can move things along by making any of the following statements:

- "Is there any further discussion on the motion to purchase a computer?"
- "Please limit your discussion to the specific motion, which is to purchase a computer."
- "We've heard many good points of view but are beginning to repeat some of the same ideas. Are there any new opinions on the motion to purchase a computer?" or "Please limit your comments to new opinions."

Another way of reducing extraneous debate is to recognize alternate sides when speaking. After someone has spoken in favor of the motion, before calling on the next person, simply ask, "Is there anyone who would like to speak against the motion?" Alternating between an affirmative speaker and a negative speaker sometimes helps reduce the debate, especially when the debate has been rather one-sided.

Call Members Out of Order as Politely as Possible

There's an old saying that goes something like this: "It isn't what you say, but how you say it." That has never been truer than in ruling comments of a member out of order. Calling a member to order is one of those times when your communication skills will be tested. Don't just rule the comments of the member out of order; instead, explain why the comments are out of order and how the member can do what he or she wants to do and still be in order.

> **Gavel Gaffes**
>
> Humor is a wonderful quality for a presiding officer to possess. It can be used positively to release tension during a difficult meeting. But use humor wisely! Never use humor at the expense of any member, even the member who has been a thorn in your side throughout the meeting.

Focus on Procedure

Knowing and displaying knowledge of parliamentary procedure can go a long way in helping the members see you as a skillful presiding officer. They will have more confidence in your presiding skills when they see you smoothly handle the processing of a motion. When they watch you help the group through a difficult procedural issue, they will trust you to appropriately handle any situation.

Expediting the Meeting

People don't want to be in a meeting any longer than is judged absolutely necessary. So if you can be seen as expediting the meeting, that is a good thing.

> **Parliamentary Pearls**
>
> E-mail can be a very effective tool in agenda preparation. For example, if you are going to prepare the agenda next weekend, e-mail the members during the early part of the week and ask them to e-mail agenda items to you by Friday.

But here's a word of caution. Remember that it is important to establish credibility early in the meeting. One of the best ways to do that is to start the meeting slowly. You don't want to look like you are trampling on the members' rights to get the group out on time.

Early on in the meeting, go slowly, be deliberate, and do things that help members see that you are fair. Make sure everyone has had a chance to speak before going to the vote. Take the first few votes slowly and deliberately. Once you have established credibility, you can pick up the pace. How do you know when that time has come? The members will tell you, if only through nonverbal cues.

Share the Agenda Preparation

If you get other members involved in agenda preparation, you will soon find that the members are taking ownership of the agenda and the meeting. Have in place and known to all members a system for them to contact you with an agenda item. If the members know the day on which they must have items to you in order to get them placed on the agenda, they are more likely to participate in the agenda preparation.

Prepare in Advance

I know this is going to sound like typical parliamentarian advice, but it is a good idea to review the bylaws and rules of the organization before the meeting. I can't tell you how many times I have seen a presiding officer become embarrassed when a member called to the attention of the chair a rule that the chair was obviously not aware of.

Advance preparation by the presiding officer should also include going through the agenda and trying to second-guess what might come up during the meeting. Then, if you think that a motion might come up that you are not comfortable with, you could take with you a copy of the script on how to handle that motion. My website, www.nancysylvester.com, contains numerous scripts to aid you in preparing for the meeting.

Follow the Rules

My favorite *Robert's* quote is, "Where there is no law, but every man does what is right in his own eyes, there is the least of real liberty." I like that quote because it reminds us why rules are so necessary and why relying on everyone's good judgment just doesn't work. Therefore, it is important to follow the established rules of the group (probably *Robert's*) instead of following "rules according to the current chair."

Parliamentary Pearls

You should always have an agenda for the meeting. The agenda should be shared with all of the members, ideally before the meeting. Follow the agenda religiously. If you don't follow it, you can't expect the members to follow it. If the group decides not to follow the agenda, do it in an orderly fashion—*Suspend the Rules* (see Chapter 15).

Starting the meeting on time is an excellent way to display your respect for the rules. When you wait to begin the meeting because certain people are running late, you have rewarded those who did not follow the rules and have punished those who did.

If you are presiding over the meeting of a group that has never followed any rules, be careful not to shock them by a sudden, strict application of the rules. Be proactive by first explaining that you are going to apply the rules. Determine in advance the most important rules to have the group follow and explain them and how you intend to follow them. Then begin with those. For example, you might state, "The chair wants to be sure that all members who wish to speak are heard. Therefore, before a member will be recognized to speak a second time on a motion, the chair will recognize other members who have not yet spoken on that motion."

Preparing and Using Scripts

I've already told you that successfully presiding at a meeting of any size requires preparation and practice. Like many sports and professional activities, those who do it well make it look much easier than it really is. Because presiding officers are the focus of attention, sometimes even a simple question can throw them off—it's as if you can't remember your own mother's name, much less what you are supposed to say next.

There is a solution to this problem. No, not the one about your mother's name but what to say next. Use a script. A script is a document that states what is to be said, when it is to be said, and by whom it is to be said. The amount of detail in the script varies with the person writing the script and the person using it.

Types of Scripts

Scripts vary from parliamentarian to parliamentarian and organization to organization, but here are the three most common kinds:

- **Gavel to gavel.** The gavel-to-gavel script includes words that will be said from the beginning of the meeting to the end. This kind is most frequently used in conventions but is also used in meetings where controversy is expected. This script includes all that will be said, not only by the presiding officer but by reporting officers and presenters as well. Obviously it does not include the discussion of the motions, but other than that, much of what will happen can be prepared for and included in the script.
- **Difficult situation scripts.** Sometimes a presiding officer will only want a script to cover parts of the meeting where difficulty is anticipated. Sometimes those problems are parliamentary in nature, such as how to handle the opening of the convention and the necessary parliamentary business needed for that opening. (You can find a sample script for the opening of a convention at my website, www.nancysylvester.com.) Other times the script is nonparliamentary in nature, such as the list of dignitaries, along with their titles, that will be used for introducing those people.
- **Motion scripts.** These provide the presiding officer with the words to say when handling a specific motion. (Go to my website, www.nancysylvester.com, for numerous motion scripts.)

Why Script?

Even if you don't usually need a script, it might be reassuring just to know you have it in case a difficult situation comes up. In addition, relying on scripts can save an organization a lot of time by helping the presiding officer avoid mistakes that could take time to fix. You may also find that scripts serve as much-needed confidence builders while you are presiding.

An added benefit of having a script for a meeting is that you can write the script in the peace and quiet of your office while your head is clear and you are thinking logically. That is very much unlike trying to think of what to say during a meeting when others, with their personal agendas, are suggesting solutions.

Point of Information

Imagine you are facing a difficult election in your organization. There are many people running for office, and getting a majority vote on the first ballot for some of the positions is unlikely. The election is for president, vice president, secretary, treasurer, and two directors-at-large. You are concerned about getting confused, so you want to prepare a script for any possible situation. You might prepare scripts for the following potential scenarios:

- If there is a tie for any officer position
- If more than two candidates are running and no one candidate receives a majority vote
- If only one candidate for the position of director-at-large receives a majority vote
- If no candidate for the position of director-at-large receives a majority vote
- If no candidate for the position of director-at-large receives a majority vote on the second (or any other number) ballot

How to Script

You will find many examples of scripts in Appendix C and on my website (www.nancysylvester.com). They are designed for you to copy and use. Although they cover many scenarios and motions, you might decide you want to create scripts for other situations.

When you are building that first script for your organization, consider using the following documents for guidance:

- The minutes of previous meetings.
- The agenda of the current meeting.

- The court reporter's document from last year's convention. (Some conventions hire a court reporter to record every word said at the convention.)
- Scripts used by other organizations.
- The organization's governing documents. Many times the rules that apply to a specific situation are included in the governing documents. Quoting them in the script helps make the members secure that you are following the rules of the organization. It also helps the members understand why you are doing something a particular way.

One of the most beneficial parts of the script is in the preparation for its use. For conventions or important meetings, I encourage the president, vice president, president-elect, executive director, secretary, parliamentarian, AV technicians, and any committee chairmen who will be reporting to get together and read through the script and make any changes that are needed.

Parliamentary Pearls

Your script should be adapted to the situation and the group. When writing a script, keep the following in mind:

- The size of the group
- The level of formality you wish to use
- The personality of the presiding officer
- The typical language of the presiding officer

When they get to any part of the script that might be controversial, they can stop and discuss all that might happen during that part and how to handle any of the issues that might surface. You can assign someone to think and act like a difficult or challenging member and have that person bring up issues or questions during the preparation. That is a great way to get the presiding officer ready for a contentious meeting.

The script review meeting not only helps the presiding officer determine what to expect, but it usually also increases his or her confidence.

The Least You Need to Know

- Presiding officers should be facilitators, not dictators.
- As a presiding officer, don't be afraid to make mistakes—members will respect you more for admitting you're not perfect.
- A good presiding officer listens to what a member is saying while also observing the member's nonverbal communication for clues.
- While it may seem simple, starting the meeting on time sets the tone for the meeting—you show that you follow the rules and expect others to as well.
- Don't be afraid to use scripts to keep the meeting running smoothly.

Chapter 17

Cast Your Ballot! Nominations and Elections

In This Chapter

- Documents governing nominations and elections
- Common nominating methods
- The nominating committee in action
- Who counts the ballots?

In parliamentary procedure, selecting leaders of an organization is a two-step process: Members first nominate candidates for positions, and then members hold an election for the offices. Since the choice of leaders frequently determines the future direction of the organization, these two steps are of utmost importance.

Don't Jump in Without Reading Your Organization's Rules!

Before you begin the nomination and election processes, you should first check your organization's bylaws, as they usually contain important information about these activities. If rules regulating your elections and nominations are in the bylaws, you *must* follow them.

In addition to the bylaws, you should review the following information:

- **Other printed rules.** These include standing or special rules of the organization. If it is in the other rules and those rules don't conflict with the bylaws, you must follow those rules.
- **Organizational customs.** If your organization has handled the nomination and election process a certain way for a while and that process doesn't conflict with the bylaws or other rules, then that is the way you should do it unless directed otherwise by the members.

If a way of proceeding isn't in the bylaws or other rules and you don't have a custom established, or if you don't like the custom and want to change it, a member must make a motion to establish how the nomination or election process will work.

Parliamentary Pearls

The timing of the nomination and election process is frequently indicated in the bylaws. For example, if the bylaws provide that the election shall occur at the November meeting or at the annual meeting, at that meeting the election comes up under the agenda heading of "Special Orders." It comes after the reports and before unfinished business. Think of it as a special order from the bylaws.

Who Nominates and How Do You Do It?

Nominating candidates for office is the process of narrowing down the field and focusing the election on those members who were nominated. However, it's important to note that a person who was not nominated for a position can be elected.

There are many different methods of nominating candidates for office. They include …

- Nominations by a committee
- Nominations from the floor
- Nominations by the chair
- Nominations by ballot
- Nominations by mail or e-mail
- Nominations by petition

Nominations by committee and from the floor are by far the most frequently used methods. They are usually done in connection with each other. The nominating committee first gives its report, and then the presiding officer asks for nominations from the floor.

Since the first two are most frequently used, I will cover them here. To get additional information on the other methods of nomination, I refer you to *Robert's Rules of Order Newly Revised.*

Nominating Committee

The nominating committee is the most important committee in an organization because it is responsible for helping choose the future leaders of the organization. What an awe-inspiring job!

Gavel Gaffes

If you can't keep your mouth shut, don't become a member of a nominating committee. Confidentiality is a necessary part of the nominating committee process. The process works best when members come together, openly discuss the strengths and weaknesses of each candidate for each of the offices, and then determine which candidate to slate for each office. If committee members cannot talk freely in the candidate discussion, the whole purpose of the nominating committee has been defeated.

I strongly recommend that your organization prepare a procedures manual for the nominating committee. It should include all the rules applicable to the nominating committee, the roles of each member of the nominating committee, and what forms the committee should use. I guarantee that members of the nominating committee will find such a manual to be invaluable.

In addition, many nominating committees are given a candidate qualities checklist, in which they can rate each candidate for particular qualities that an organization seeks for each office. Here's a sample checklist—if you want to create one of your own, simply use this format but include only the qualities that you are seeking:

Candidate Qualities Form

Instructions: Rate each candidate from 1 through 5 on each quality (5 is the highest score possible).

Candidates for (office name) ____________:

Rating of Qualities of Candidates for Office

Candidate Qualities	Candidate's Name and Rating			
	Name A	Name B	Name C	Name D
Meets all of the requirements of the bylaws and standing rules				
Demonstrates commitment to the organization				
Demonstrates leadership skills				
Commitment to the leadership team				
Ability to professionally represent the organization				
Ability to distinguish between major and minor issues and focus on the major issues				

Candidate Qualities	**Candidate's Name and Rating**			
	Name A	**Name B**	**Name C**	**Name D**
Ability to serve as a role model within and outside of the organization				
Ability to work with staff				
Compatibility with officers' team				
Past history of work for this organization				
Timeliness of output of expected work				
Ability and willingness to work as a team player				
Interpersonal communication skills				
Public communication skills				

Who Can Be Nominated?

To be properly nominated for an office, a member must meet the qualifications for office as they are described in the bylaws. For instance, the bylaws might require that someone be a member for a minimum length of time before he or she can hold office or that a candidate must have been on the board of directors for a specified amount of time before holding the office of president or vice president. If the qualifications are stated in the bylaws, they cannot be suspended.

Parliamentary Pearls

The bylaws are meant to ensure members' rights. If a member is given a right in the bylaws, it cannot be taken away without changing the bylaws. Running for an office is a membership right. If there are no qualifications for a specific office stated in the bylaws, an organization can't require that a candidate have any particular qualifications to hold an office. Otherwise, you would be adding a qualification to the membership right that is not stated in the bylaws. The only exception is if the laws of the state include qualifications, which is highly unlikely.

Can Nominating Committee Members Be Nominated?

If your organization uses a nominating committee, the members of that committee are not barred from being nominated for an office. Being a member of the committee should not prevent someone from being nominated for a position.

Nominations from the Floor

Unless the rules of the organization say otherwise, the presiding officer must call for nominations from the floor. If there is a nominating committee, this part of the process would come after the committee report. Organizations usually allow for nominations from the floor to give each member a chance to exercise his or her right to fully participate in the selection of the nominees.

After the presiding officer calls for nominations from the floor, any member may make a nomination. The nomination does not require a second, although in some organizations there is a tradition of allowing for one or two seconding speeches.

It's Election Time!

When the nomination process is completed, it is time for the election—which means that it's time to check the bylaws again to see whether there are any rules applicable to the election. There usually are. The following are some election rules frequently found in bylaws:

- **Requirement for ballot election.** If the rules indicate that the election must be by ballot, it must be by ballot. You cannot waive having a ballot vote—even if there is only one candidate for an office—unless the bylaws allow you to do so.
- **Requirement for a majority vote.** Unless the bylaws indicate otherwise, it takes a majority vote (more than half of the votes cast) to elect a person to office. Sometimes the bylaws specify a plurality vote. In that case, the candidate who receives the highest number of votes is said to have a plurality. The advantage of a plurality vote is that you usually can complete an election on the first ballot. The disadvantage is that it means a person might be elected to office without the vote of a majority of the members.
- **You can't drop the lowest vote-getter.** Sometimes the election doesn't happen on the first ballot—for example, if there are a lot of candidates running for one office and no one candidate gets a majority vote on the first ballot. Another example is if there are three board positions open and only two candidates get a majority vote on the first ballot. Then a second ballot is needed. The second ballot must have the same names (minus those elected) on the ballot unless someone withdraws. You can't drop the name of the person(s) who received the fewest votes unless the rules authorize doing so.

  The reason for this rule? Since elections are so important, we need to preserve all options. One option is that the person farthest behind could be elected as a compromise candidate.
- **No mail ballot without a rule.** You can conduct an election by mail ballot only if the bylaws authorize it.
- **One ballot or multiple ballots.** There are two ways to conduct a ballot vote when multiple offices are up for election. The first involves a single ballot with all the offices to be elected appearing on that ballot. The second is to conduct a ballot vote for each office, one at

> **Parliamentary Pearls**
>
> There are many different methods of conducting an election. In this chapter, we have focused on the most common method, the ballot election. Other methods are listed and explained in *Robert's Rules of Order Newly Revised.*

a time. The bylaws may specify which system to use. To illustrate the difference between these two processes, consider an election in which the offices for president, vice president, secretary, and treasurer are to be filled. The first method would have a single ballot with each office and the candidates for each office listed. The members would vote on all four offices on a single piece of paper.

The second system would first call for the election of the president and issue ballots for that office. When that election was completed, ballots would be issued for the office of vice president, and so on. These elections should occur in the order that they are listed in the bylaws.

The advantage of the one-ballot system is efficiency—you can usually have the election of all four officers done on one ballot, all at one time. However, the multiple-ballots method allows a person to run for more than one position if he or she isn't elected for one office. For instance, someone who was not elected president may choose to run for vice president, secretary, or treasurer.

1-2-3—Count Those Ballots!

The group of people responsible for counting ballots is usually referred to as the tellers. They are usually appointed to the committee before or at the beginning of the election meeting. Only members whom the membership considers to be honest, accurate, and dependable should be appointed. In addition, ballot counters should not be personally involved in the election. Tellers should be familiar with the bylaws, standing and special rules, and the parliamentary rules regarding election process.

During an election, tellers distribute, collect, and count the ballots and then report that count. (In Appendix D, you will find procedures for tellers and a sample tellers' report.) The committee also frequently assists in counting a standing vote as well.

When counting ballots, follow these rules:

- Blank ballots don't count; they can be thrown away.
- Illegal ballots cast by legal voters are listed as illegal votes. They count in determining the number of votes cast. An example of an illegal vote is a vote for someone who is ineligible.
- In determining whether or not a ballot should be counted, use common sense. If it is clear for whom the person intended to vote but, for example, the voter misspelled the candidate's name, the ballot counts.
- When the ballot has places for elections for multiple offices or multiple votes allowed for a particular position, blank spaces do not affect the rest of the ballot. In other words, your vote will count if you vote for too few candidates, but it will not count if you vote for too many.
- It is okay to have fewer ballots than the number of eligible voters; it is not okay to have more ballots than the number of eligible voters.

The tellers make sure that only members eligible to vote receive ballots and that no extra ballots are floating around. After the ballots are marked, at the instruction of the chair, tellers collect the ballots, go to a secluded place, and count them. *Robert's* includes specific instructions on the process of counting ballots; see *Robert's Rules of Order Newly Revised* and Appendix D.

Tellers' Report

The tellers prepare and sign a report that is read to the assembly and is used by the presiding officer to declare who is elected. That report is entered in full in the minutes. In Appendix D, you will find a tellers' tally form and a tellers' report form. The tellers' report should include the following information:

- The number of votes cast
- The number of votes needed for election or for the proposal to pass

- The number of votes each candidate or side received, each listed separately
- Any illegal votes cast, including the reason they were illegal and the number of illegal votes

Chair Declares

The chairman of the tellers reads the tellers' report, but the presiding officer declares who is elected for each office. Here's how the process works: after the tellers' chairman reads the tellers' report, he or she hands it to the presiding officer, who reads it again and then declares who was elected to each position.

Chair Presides

We learned in Chapter 8 that if the presiding officer is going to debate a motion, he or she should relinquish the chair to the vice president, who presides in his or her absence. But if the presiding officer is a candidate for an office, he or she stays in the chair for the election. No need to relinquish the chair.

When the Election Is Final

The election for each office is considered final when the candidate who won the election is notified and accepts the position. The only exception to this rule is if the candidate is not present but has, in advance, consented to the candidacy, in which case the election is final at the completion of the election. If the candidate is not present, has not consented in advance, and declines the election, an election to fill the vacancy can take place immediately unless the bylaws give other instructions.

What happens if a person is elected to two offices but can only hold one? If the member is present, the member can decide which office he or she wants, and then another election should be held to fill the other office. If the member is not present, the members who are present will select, by majority vote, which office the person will take. Makes you want to be in attendance if you are up for a couple of offices!

The bylaws should specify when newly elected members take office. In organizations that meet monthly, it's not unusual for a member to be elected at one meeting but not take office until the next.

The Least You Need to Know

- If you can't keep a secret, don't be on the nominating committee—it requires strict confidences.
- Check your bylaws for your organization's voting processes.
- Although there are several acceptable methods for nominating members to office, the two most common are nominations by committee and nominations from the floor.
- The chairman of the tellers reads the results of the vote, but the chair declares who is elected.

Part 5

Officers, Committees, and Meetings

This part covers a lot of material that will be helpful to you as you prepare for meetings. If you are an officer or a committee chairman, you'll find help in preparing your reports or the meeting minutes. If you serve on a committee, you'll find a chapter that will help you understand the committee process and how to make the most of it.

Maybe you picked up this book because you have a responsibility in an upcoming convention. If so, you're in luck because I've included a chapter on conventions and their unique demands. If your group is thinking about holding electronic meetings, the final chapter is for you.

Chapter 18

Just a Minutes

In This Chapter

- What the minutes should and shouldn't include
- Making minutes easier to prepare
- Reviewing and approving the minutes
- Dealing with executive session minutes

People make preparing minutes out to be a lot worse than it really is. They often think of the minutes as a daunting document to create because they believe that they must note everything everyone said at the meeting. Since it's hard to keep track of everything, they frequently don't keep track of *anything*. But the minutes aren't that bad. They are simply the written record of the proceedings of a deliberative assembly. They serve to record the actions taken at a meeting, not what was *said* at that meeting.

Minutes serve as the institutional memory for the organization. Because you have them to refer back to, they prevent a group from doing the same thing over and over.

In addition, minutes serve as a record of what was decided at the meeting. If the organization gets involved in a lawsuit, the minutes are one of the first documents that all parties will request. When ruling, a judge or jury will give much more weight to the official minutes of the meeting than to what any particular individual recalls happening.

What to Put in the Minutes (and What to Leave Out)

Robert's recommends that minutes contain the following items:

- The kind of meeting (regular, special, and so on).
- The name of the organization.
- The date, time, and place of the meeting.
- The names of the presiding officer and secretary or, in their absence, the names of their substitutes.
- The approximate number of members present (optional).
- The establishment of a quorum (optional).
- Record of the action taken on the minutes of the previous meeting.
- The exact wording of each main motion as it was voted on and whether it passed or failed, along with the name of the maker. In addition, if the vote was counted, the count should be included, as well as the tellers' reports, if any. In roll call votes, the record of each person's vote is included.
- Any notice given at the meeting. Previous notice is sometimes required, such as with amendments to the bylaws. If any such notice was given at the meeting, it should be included in the minutes.
- Points of order and appeals, including the reason given by the presiding officer for the ruling.

Parliamentary Pearls

Although it's not necessary to include the full report of the treasurer in the text of the minutes, many groups find it helpful to include the previous balance, income totals, disbursement totals, and current balance.

- For committee reports, the name of the committee and the reporting member. If the committee provides a printed report, attach it to the minutes and note that it is attached.
- The name and subject of any guest speakers.
- The hour of adjournment.

Robert's is equally clear about what should *not* be included in the minutes:

- The opinion or interpretation of the secretary.
- Judgmental phrases such as "heated debate" or "valuable comment."
- Discussion. Minutes are a record of what was *done* at the meeting, not what was *said* at the meeting.
- Motions that were withdrawn.
- The name of the person who seconded a motion.
- Flowery language.
- Reports in detail.
- Transcripts of the meeting. While some groups choose to have a transcript of the meeting, it should never substitute as the minutes of the meeting.

Getting the Minutes Approved

The minutes are made official only after they are approved, which usually takes place at the next meeting.

If your organization frequently makes changes to the minutes, you might want to send out the initial, unapproved set with the word "draft" clearly printed on it. Then, when the minutes have been changed and approved, the official minutes can be sent out.

If your organization seldom has changes to the minutes, two sets, one draft and one approved, will probably be unnecessary.

Sign 'em

After the minutes have been corrected and approved by the membership, they should be signed by the secretary. (The president's signature isn't required.) The word "approved" and the date of the approval should also be included.

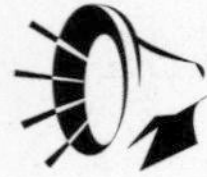

Gavel Gaffes

Although including the words "respectfully submitted" right before the secretary's signature used to be common practice, it is considered outdated to do so today. Instead, simply sign your name.

Book 'em

The official copy of the minutes is the property of the organization. They should be entered in the *minutes book* and kept by the secretary if the organization doesn't have a headquarters office. If there is an office, the official copy of the minutes should be kept there.

def•i•ni•tion

The **minutes book** is usually a three-ring binder that contains a complete copy of all of the minutes.

The official copy of the minutes should have attached to it the original signed copies of each of the following:

- Committee reports
- Officers' reports
- Written motions
- Tellers' reports
- Correspondence

If the secretary distributes copies of the minutes to the members, it isn't necessary to include all of the attachments with them. Instead, you can include a brief summary of the attachments or at least a reference to them. Members can get a copy of them from the secretary if they wish to review them.

Parliamentary Pearls

Just because the minutes are an official document doesn't mean that they have to be hard to read. Some simple formatting can make the minutes easier to read. Here are a few suggestions:

- Set off each section with a boldfaced heading, ideally the same heading used in the agenda.
- After each motion, bold the words that indicate if it passed or failed.
- Turn on the line-numbering feature so that each line of the minutes is numbered.

Make a Minutes Template

In Chapter 15, I suggested creating a template for the agenda. Creating and using a template for the minutes also saves a tremendous amount of time. The following document is a sample of a minutes template. You can find a similar template in electronic form on my website: www.nancysylvester.com. You will also find sample minutes in Appendix D.

Sample Minutes Template

MINUTES of [Organization name]

Meeting date: _____

Call to order: A ____________ [kind of meeting] meeting of the ______________ [organization name] was held in __________ [place, city, state] on _________ [date], 20__. The meeting convened at _____ [time] with President ________________ [name] presiding and ____________________ [name] as secretary.

[Some small organizations choose to list attendees. This works well for boards of directors.]

Members in attendance: [optional item]

Members not in attendance: [optional item]

continues

continued

Approval of minutes: Motion was made by ________________ [name] and seconded to approve the minutes of the ____________ [date] meeting. **MOTION CARRIED.**

Officers' reports:

President

Vice president

Secretary

Treasurer

Board and committee reports:

Unfinished business:

[Subject title]

Motion: Moved by ________________ [name] that ___________ [state motion].

MOTION CARRIED. MOTION FAILED. [leave only one of these]

New business:

[Subject title]

Motion: Moved by ________________ [name] that _____________ [state motion].

MOTION CARRIED. MOTION FAILED. [leave only one of these]

Announcements:

Adjournment: The meeting was adjourned at __________ [time].

________________________ ________________________

Secretary Date of approval

[Organization Name]

Skeletal Minutes

Skeletal minutes are minutes prepared in advance of a meeting or convention. They include everything that will occur, in the order it will occur, based on the agenda and the script for the meeting. The person in charge of the minutes can fill in the details during the meeting. Skeletal minutes can be used at any type of meeting, but they are probably of greatest assistance at conventions, when a lot of issues will be covered.

Since skeletal minutes may be a whole new concept to you, I thought some samples might be helpful. You will find them in Appendix D. The first sample is the first few paragraphs of skeletal minutes of the third meeting of a convention. The second example is the first few paragraphs of the minutes for that meeting. You will also find other examples of minutes in Appendix D.

Minutes Approval Committee

When you don't meet very often, it might be difficult to recall what happened at the previous meeting, much less what order it was done in. Some of us have trouble remembering what we had for lunch yesterday, much less how the wording ended up on that controversial motion at the annual meeting last year. Worse yet, people sometimes remember very clearly, but different people have a very different memory of what occurred.

When there is going to be at least a few months between meetings, it's probably best for the organization to have a minutes approval committee. Essentially, this is a small group of members who work with the secretary to create an acceptable set of minutes immediately after the meeting. If office equipment is available, they can enter the minutes into a computer, print them out, and make

Gavel Gaffes

When there is a minutes approval committee, the minutes don't need to be approved by the membership at the next meeting because they have already been approved by the minutes approval committee. The minutes approved by the committee are the official minutes of the meeting.

photocopies so that the final copy can be proofed, agreed upon, and signed before the minutes approval committee members go home.

Shhh! Minutes of Executive Session

As explained in Chapter 2, a meeting (or a portion of a meeting) in which the proceedings are secret and the only attendees are members and invited guests is considered to be executive session. Since all that was said or done in executive session is confidential, the minutes of executive session meetings, or portions of meetings, should be handled differently than the minutes of other meetings.

Executive session minutes should be treated with extreme confidentiality. The good news is that, as I have repeated in this chapter, minutes are a record of what was done, not what was said. Therefore, anything said in confidence at a meeting held in executive session is not going to get out via the minutes.

The meeting or the portion of the meeting held in executive session should have its own set of minutes. The uniqueness of these minutes is not in their content, but in how they are handled and distributed. Those minutes should be prepared exactly like other minutes but should be clearly marked "executive session" and also marked "confidential." These minutes are only for the eyes of members of the body that met in executive session and any persons the body chooses to share them with. Notice the operative words in the last sentence: the body. No individual member or group of members who are a part of the body can independently determine to share these minutes with other people. The only way these minutes can be shared with other people is if, in a meeting, the body votes to share them with particular other people.

There is an exception—you know there has to be one! If the group is governed by the state open meetings act, as discussed in Chapter 2, it is the rules contained in the act that determine when and if these minutes can be shared with someone outside of the membership of the body that met.

How to Approve Them

Since the minutes are confidential, they must be approved in executive session. The good news is that, when you go into executive session for the sole purpose of approving the minutes of the previous executive session, you do not have to then go into executive session at the next meeting to approve those minutes and so on. *Robert's* indicates that the brief minutes of the meeting to approve the executive session minutes are assumed to be approved as part of the minutes of the current executive session meeting. Thank goodness! Or, once started, executive sessions would have a life of their own just approving minutes.

How to Distribute Them

Distribution of executive session minutes may vary based on the level of confidential material included within them. As a general rule, they are distributed in the same manner as other minutes.

When the information contained in the executive session minutes is extremely confidential, special distribution methods might be needed. For example, when they include the review of the executive director and specific steps decided on by the board that will be followed if the executive director is to remain employed, extreme confidential handling of them is warranted. Under those and like circumstances, only one set of the minutes should be made, and the electronic file of them should either be deleted or password protected. Then at the meeting, instead of passing out the minutes, they should be read and then approved. After approval and signature, they should be kept under lock and key. This method prevents copies of extremely confidential minutes from lying on someone's desk for wandering eyes to view or being left on the copy machine.

Oops! Someone Shared the Minutes

As explained in Chapter 2, deliberations of an executive session are secret, and all attendees are honor bound to maintain confidentiality. That also applies to the minutes. A member who violates that secrecy can be punished following the disciplinary procedures outlined in *Robert's*. If a nonmember, such as a staff member, violates that secrecy, he or she should be seriously reprimanded.

The Least You Need to Know

- The minutes should be a record of the actions taken by the group, not a record of what was said at the meeting.
- If your organization makes frequent changes to the minutes, create an unofficial version marked "draft" to send out to members for review.
- Once minutes are accepted by the membership, they become the official record of the meeting.
- Organizations that meet infrequently should consider using a minutes approval committee, which prepares and approves the minutes immediately after the meeting.
- The portion of the meeting that is held in executive session should have its own set of minutes and those minutes must be treated with utmost confidentially.

Chapter 19

Committees in Action

In This Chapter

- What committees are really all about
- Standing committees versus special committees
- Keeping a procedures manual
- Common committee pitfalls

Ever hear the joke about committees? They're the only human organisms that have multiple stomachs and no brain.

Unfortunately, this punch line describes many committees that I have worked with. My challenge for you after you have read this chapter is to prove this joke wrong!

What a Committee Is *Supposed* to Be

A committee is a group of one or more persons who are appointed or elected to carry out an assignment. The responsibility that goes with the assignment is sometimes referred to as its charge. The charge can be to investigate, to recommend, or to take action. There are two important components in that definition, so let's break it down.

- To say that committee members are appointed or elected indicates that the committee is usually not an autonomous group—in other words, they are responsible for and must answer to someone or some body.
- The committee's charge is what it was told to do. A committee can only do what it is charged to do—it should do no more and no less than its charge. A committee is charged with a task through the motion to *Commit* or *Refer* (see Chapter 12).

Committees are used when the membership feels it would be more appropriate to have a smaller group of people research, study, and discuss an issue and report their findings to the parent body rather than leave it up to the entire membership to do this. In some cases, the membership might also ask the committee to recommend an action.

Kinds of Committees

Although committees can have countless names, they all fall into one of two categories: standing or special.

Standing Committees

A standing committee exists from one year to the next and is typically charged with a continuing function. A typical standing committee is the finance committee. As long as you have money coming in and going out, you will always need a finance committee.

Standing committees are usually established by the bylaws, and the committees' functions are usually laid out there as well.

Parliamentary Pearls

An executive committee is a form of standing committee. It is usually made up of the officers of the organization. An executive committee exists only if it is authorized in the bylaws. Go to the bylaws to determine if there is an executive committee for your organization, who is on it, and exactly what power it has. The executive committee is usually a subsection of the board of directors, and when it is, it is frequently allowed to act on behalf of the board between meetings of the board.

Special Committees

A special committee is formed to perform a specific task. It comes together, completes the task, gives its final report, and then ceases to exist. It cannot be appointed to perform a task that falls within the assigned function of a standing committee.

A special committee is sometimes referred to as a select committee, an ad hoc committee, a task force, or a work group. No matter what name it goes by, it is still a special committee.

Special committees are formed when a task comes up that doesn't fit the job description of any of the standing committees. Special committees are, or should be, short lived and specific in focus. For example, if your group decides to have a fundraiser, you might appoint a special committee to take charge of the fundraiser.

Gavel Gaffes

Before you form a special committee, check out the bylaws and make sure there isn't a standing committee that is assigned that task or a similar task. If there is, the task should be handled by the standing committee.

Committee of the Whole Is Special

A version of a special committee is a committee of the whole and its variations. This is a parliamentary tool that is not used very much in deliberative assemblies. You will find it used more frequently in legislative bodies and governmental bodies. It allows the entire group to discuss an issue with the freedom of a committee.

The committee of the whole comes in the following three versions:

- Committee of the whole
- Quasi committee of the whole
- Informal consideration

Parliamentary Pearls

The committee chairman is usually named by the same body that named the committee. The chairman of a committee is the leader of the committee, is responsible for calling and conducting the meetings, and should make sure that people follow up on tasks they volunteered for or were assigned to.

How a Committee Works

Unless a committee is so large that it needs to function as a full assembly, a committee can follow the more relaxed rules described in Chapter 2. However, a committee cannot adopt its own rules unless authorized to do so in the instructions the committee was given or in the bylaws. In addition, committees don't have the power to punish a member. If a member is doing something that he or she shouldn't do, the committee should report that fact to the assembly.

The Committee's Charge

Since a committee is not an autonomous group, it should get its charge from the parent body, whether that's the board or the membership. The charge might entail investigating an issue with no power to act, or it might give the committee full power to act. The exact nature of the charge can be spelled out in the motion that creates the committee in the first place, or for standing committees, it can be spelled out in the bylaws.

Whoever has the power to appoint a committee has the power to fill vacancies on the committee and to remove members from the committee. So if a committee member was appointed by the president and that member isn't doing his or her job, the president can remove that person from the committee and appoint someone else to serve on the committee.

Keep Your Mouth Shut

Committee meetings are open only to members of the committee and anyone else the committee invites to attend. Just because you are a member of the organization does not give you the right to attend a committee meeting. The whole idea is to give the assignment to a small, focused group. Allowing everyone to come and go as they wish would defeat the purpose.

In addition, whatever is discussed within the committee is confidential. If a member can't speak up in a committee meeting without fear of everyone in the organization knowing what was said, the freedom of discussion is lost.

Subcommittees: Committees Within Committees

A committee can appoint a subcommittee made up of members of the committee to undertake particular tasks. This is a useful technique for dividing the labor.

Point of Information

Frequently you will find in the bylaws a statement that the president is ex officio a member of all committees (hopefully it adds, "except the nominating committee"). That is, the president is a member of that committee by nature of the office he or she holds. When the president is ex officio a member of all committees, he or she has the right to attend committee meetings, discuss issues, and vote, but isn't required to do an equal share of the work and is not counted in determining a quorum. Note that the rules for a president as ex officio are different from a nonmember being ex officio.

Committee Procedure Manual

It is tough to hit a target if you don't know where the target is located. Similarly, it is difficult for a committee to be successful if it isn't really clear on what its responsibilities are and what is expected of it. That is why I am a firm believer that every committee should have an updated procedure manual.

The committee's procedure manual should be created by the committee, approved by it, and then approved by whomever that committee reports to, usually the board of directors. In Chapter 17, I discussed the nominating committee procedure manual and how helpful it can be. Each committee should have a manual, and every member of the committee should have a copy of the manual.

There is no universally accepted manual format for committee procedure manuals. Each committee and each organization has its own needs. The following subjects should be covered in any procedure manual:

- Background information
- Governing document requirements for the committee
- Responsibilities of the committee chairman
- Responsibilities of the committee
- Forms used by the committee
- Information on meetings of the committee

Other optional items include the following:

- Past reports
- Past committee minutes

Committee Pitfalls

All those jokes about committees exist for a reason. Unfortunately, a lot of committees are ineffective, and many organizations use committees inappropriately. Being aware of the following committee pitfalls can help you avoid them:

- **The committee does the work, and then the body does the work again.** This is a terrible waste of time and energy, but it happens all too frequently. A group gives an assignment to a committee. The committee does the work and reports back to the group. Then, because the larger group didn't do the work, it isn't comfortable authorizing the committee to proceed, and the entire body does again all of the work done by the committee.

- **The committee does its work but doesn't prepare an adequate, succinct report to the body.** The report is the only evidence the body will have of the committee's work, so if the committee doesn't prepare a complete report, the body won't know what the committee did. All that work will have been wasted effort.

- **Work but no recommendation.** The committee prepares a report but fails to include specific recommendations. The main body needs to know what action the committee recommends in order for the committee to have been effective.

- **No work.** The group assigns a committee to undertake a particular task, but the committee doesn't do the work it was charged with.

Parliamentary Pearls

A committee should keep notes of what was decided, but it may not need to keep formal minutes. Usually the committee chairman keeps notes, but it would be appropriate for the committee chairman to request that a member be responsible for the notes.

Discharging a Committee

Think of a committee's assignment as an object—for our purposes, we will think of it as a ball. Only one group of people can be in possession of the ball at a time. If one group doesn't like the way the other group is handling the ball and thinks it can do a better job, then in order to do something with it, it must first gain possession of the ball.

Similarly, if an assembly assigns a task to a committee and the assembly doesn't like the way the committee is handling it, or if the assembly decides that it wants to do the task, then the only way the assembly can get the task back is to take possession of it. This is done through a motion to *Discharge the Committee*. By using this motion, the assembly can end the existence of a special committee or take back the task from a special or standing committee.

The motion to *Discharge the Committee* is not necessary in the case of a special committee that has completed its task and has given its final report because that committee ceases to exist. But if the committee hasn't completed its work and the assembly wants the task back, then the assembly must use the motion to *Discharge the Committee.*

def•i•ni•tion

Discharge the Committee is a motion that relieves a committee from further consideration of the task that has been assigned to it.

Since the motion to *Discharge the Committee* is the parliamentary equivalent of getting mad, taking your ball, and going home, this motion should be reserved for special situations.

The Least You Need to Know

- A committee is a group of one or more persons who are appointed or elected to carry out a charge.
- Standing committees' charges are determined by the bylaws; special committees' charges are determined by the membership or board through the motion to *Commit* or *Refer.*
- Committees are required to report on their work. If charged to make a recommendation, that recommendation should be included in the report.
- Every committee should have an updated procedure manual.

Chapter 20

Officers' and Committee Reports

In This Chapter

- When officers need to prepare a report
- The special nature of the treasurer's report
- What to do when an officer or a committee makes a recommendation
- How committees prepare and present their reports

Officers and committees must have a system to keep the appointing/electing body informed of their activities. That information should take the form of a report, which can be given orally or in writing and might or might not include specific recommendations.

Officers' Reports

The bylaws usually require the officers to give an annual report. If so, that report should be done in writing. At all other meetings, officers only report if they have specific information or recommendations to share with the group. It is not unusual for an officer to prepare only the one formal report—the annual report—each year.

Gavel Gaffes

Frequently officers of the organization are also assigned as chairman of a particular committee. In that situation, the officers' report must be separate from the committee report. Sorry, you can't get away with preparing only one report!

Parliamentary Pearls

Even though the secretary is responsible for the minutes, the minutes are not referred to as the secretary's report. They are an agenda item all by themselves and are not considered a part of the secretary's report.

Most of the time, the officers' reports are informative in nature. If officers wish to include recommendations in their reports, they may do so. However, an officer should not make the motion to adopt that recommendation during his or her report. After an officer finishes his or her report, another member may put the recommendation in the form of a motion.

Although *Robert's* doesn't specify a format for the officers' reports, it is standard to include the following information in them:

- A heading that includes the name of the office, the name of the officer, the date of the report, and the time period the report is covering.
- A description of what the officer has done since the last report that fulfills the responsibilities of the office.
- Actions that the officer plans to take in the future.
- Any recommendations that the officer wants to make to the membership. If there is more than one recommendation, they should be numbered for ease of reference.

Treasurer's Report

The treasurer's report is so specialized that it warrants a discussion separate from the other officers' reports.

The treasurer usually reports at each meeting. The level of detail to include in the report depends on the kind and size of the organization. Usually the information included in a treasurer's report is very similar to the information you receive from the bank in your monthly account statement. No matter what the format, whether it's done by hand or on a fancy spreadsheet, it should include the following items:

- Balance on hand at the beginning of the reporting period
- Receipts (money that came in)
- Disbursements (money that went out)
- Balance on hand at the end of the reporting period

The monthly treasurer's reports on the organization's finances are for informational purposes only and should not be approved, adopted, or accepted by the organization.

At some point after the report has been received, the organization should arrange to have it reviewed by an auditor or the organization's own audit committee. The purpose of the audit is to certify the accuracy of the report.

The treasurer also must give an annual report. It should include the balance at the beginning of the reporting year, all receipts, all disbursements, and the balance at the end of the reporting year.

Gavel Gaffes

If you are the presiding officer, be sure to use the right words at the end of the report of the treasurer.

Wrong words: "Is there a motion to approve the report of the treasurer?"

Right words: "Thank you. The report will be filed for audit."

Audit

The purpose of the audit is to certify the correctness of the financial reports. It does not indicate the financial situation of the organization. It makes sure that the proper accounting principles and practices are being used.

Who does the audit is determined by the size of the organization and any state or federal regulations that apply to the organization. If the organization is too small to have a formal audit done by an independent accounting firm, then there should at least be an audit committee whose job it is to review the financial records and certify their correctness.

Whether the audit is done by a committee or an independent audit firm, it should include two parts:

- One part is the certification of the accuracy of the financial records.
- The second part is more subjective. It is an examination of the current accounting procedures of the organization and recommendations for improvement. If, for example, the current reimbursement form does not have all of the information that is needed to practice proper accounting procedures, this part of the audit would recommend a change to the current reimbursement form.

Parliamentary Pearls

Have available for the auditors:

- Bank statements
- Checkbook registers and bank books
- The treasurer's books
- Minutes of meetings
- The adopted budget
- The report of the audit committee or auditor from the previous year
- Periodic and annual financial reports
- Bylaws and other rules
- *The Finance Committee Procedure Manual*

Budget

The treasurer usually works with the finance committee and/or the staff to create and maintain the budget. As with the preparation of any other budget, the budget of the organization should look first at what amount is reasonable to expect as an income and then at how the members want to spend that income.

The budget is usually approved by the board of directors and sometimes by the membership. Once a budget has been approved, expenditures of specific amounts that are within the budgeted amount do not have to be approved.

Gavel Gaffes

For a report to bear the stamp of a committee, the committee members must have met and agreed upon the report (by general consent or formal majority vote). In other words, the committee chairman can't just decide something on behalf of the committee and report it as the committee's report.

Committee Reports

A committee report is an official statement that is formally adopted by a majority vote of the committee and that is presented to the parent body (either the entire membership or the board of directors) in the name of the committee. It contains information obtained, information regarding actions taken, or recommendations on behalf of the committee. Don't worry: It's not as complicated as the definition makes it sound. Let's break it down a bit.

If the committee was charged with obtaining information on an issue, it should report that information to the group that gave it the charge. The report should also include a description of how the committee went about carrying out its assigned task. In addition, sometimes committees are charged with making a recommendation based on their research. If so, the committee's recommendation should be part of the report.

Point of Information

A detailed committee report should include the following elements:

- A description of the way the committee performed the task
- Any information and facts obtained
- Conclusions drawn from the obtained information
- Recommendations of the committee (if there are any)

The Format of the Report

Committee reports are most effective when they are put in writing, although many groups accept oral reports. If the committee submits a written report, the chairman of the committee should sign it and add the word "chairman" after his or her name. The chair's signature indicates that the committee has approved the report and directed the chairman to sign the report on its behalf.

Presenting the Report

The chairman of the committee presents the report to the parent body on behalf of the committee. If the chairman is unable to give the report, another member may present the information.

At the conclusion of the report, the reporting member makes a motion to implement the recommendation of the committee. The suggested wording is, "On behalf of the committee, I move that …." Because the recommendation comes from a committee, no second is needed.

The following is a sample committee report. You will find a committee report format in Appendix D.

Report of the American Association of Fun-Loving People

National Nominating Committee

February 14, 20XX

During the months of November and December, the AAFLP nominating committee sought nominations from the membership through the AAFLP Newsletter, *Fun Fun Fun.*

The nominating committee met January 11 and 12, 20XX in Ain't-It-Fun, North Dakota. After deliberation and ballot votes, the committee selected its slate of candidates for office for AAFLP for the upcoming year. The nominating committee's slate of candidates is as follows:

President	Charlie Cheery
Vice President	Joan Jovial
Secretary	Ellen Ecstatic
Treasurer	Einer Elated

The nominating committee will include the slate in the March newsletter, as specified in the AAFLP Bylaws.

The nominating committee also agreed upon the following recommendations:

1. To *Amend* the standing rules by inserting a new 11.03 and renumbering the succeeding subsections:

    11.03 Within six months after its election, the committee shall meet, either in person or by telephone conference call, to develop criteria for offices and a program to encourage candidates to seek office.

2. That the convention standing rules provide that immediately after nominations are completed, each candidate for each office will be given three minutes to address the convention.

Polly Positive, Chairman

AAFLP Nominating Committee

The Least You Need to Know

- Officers' reports are usually informative in nature, although they can also include recommendations.
- An officer should not make a motion to adopt one of his or her own recommendations; that should be up to another member after the officer has finished presenting the report.
- The treasurer's report should not be approved—it is presented and filed for audit.
- The committee chair presents the committee report to the parent body on behalf of the entire committee.

Chapter 21

Making the Most of Conventions

In This Chapter

- What makes conventions special
- Delegates' roles and responsibilities
- Convention committees in action
- Tips for keeping the convention running smoothly

Every convention is unique. Conventions vary in length, formality, number of attendees, and even the kinds of committees they have. In this chapter, I'm going to explain some of these unique aspects of conventions.

It's Convention Time!

Most conventions are attended by a voting body made up of delegates who are chosen by a subordinate group to represent them. Democratic and Republic national conventions, for instance, fall into this category. Smaller organizations often open their conventions up to all members and give them all the right to vote.

Point of Information

A convention by any other name is still a convention. What I'm referring to as a convention might also be called a conference, congress, house of delegates, delegate assembly, general assembly, house of representatives, or annual meeting. Each group puts its particular spin on the gathering and gives it a name.

Convention FAQs

Members frequently have questions about the convention process. I will try to address those frequently asked questions in the following sections.

What's the Convention Session, and When Is It a Meeting?

In Chapter 2, we discussed the difference between a meeting and a session. A meeting is an assembly of members gathered to conduct business during which there is no separation of the members except for a short recess. A session is a meeting or a series of connected meetings.

A convention is one session but usually many meetings. Let's use an example of a convention that runs from Sunday through Thursday. On each of those five days, there are two business meetings. That convention has 10 meetings but only one session. Each business meeting is its own meeting, but all the meetings combined make up one session.

What Must Be Done to Officially Open a Convention?

Since each convention is truly a separate entity, each convention must officially form itself as a single voting body. This official formation is necessary before any business can be transacted. The official organization of a convention consists of the adoption of three reports: the credentials report, the rules committee report, and the program committee report (sometimes referred to as the agenda). In other words, before a convention can conduct business, it must first decide who has the right to be in attendance and to vote (credentials report), what rules will be followed (rules committee report), and what order business will be conducted in (program committee report or agenda).

Conventions frequently open with ceremonies of an inspirational nature, including an inspiration and the pledge of allegiance to the flag. These preliminary ceremonies are not considered business, so they can be included before the official organization of the convention.

Should Delegates Come to a Convention with Their Decisions Already Made?

A delegate is a member who is chosen to represent a particular group of people at a convention. The delegate is a voting member of the convention. Delegates should be sent to the convention informed as to how the group they represent feels on issues that are to come up during the convention.

Unfortunately, delegates are often sent to a convention instructed on how to vote on a particular controversial issue. However, doing so is contrary to the basic concept of parliamentary law. Conventions are held to bring everyone together so that everyone can hear the same information, discuss the issue together, and then make a group decision. When a delegate is instructed on how to vote ahead of time, all the discussion is wasted. A delegate is a human being with a brain, and that person should be allowed to use his or her brain.

Gavel Gaffes

Frequently groups send alternate delegates to conventions. They are sent to take the place of delegates in case those delegates are sick or unable to attend. Unless the rules state otherwise, when an alternate replaces a delegate, the replacement is permanent. The former delegate cannot come back as a delegate.

Some groups abuse the alternate concept by having the alternate sit in the place of the delegate for short periods of time. This happens multiple times during the convention, and it's almost like watching the delegation play musical chairs. Unless the rules indicate otherwise, *Robert's* requires that once an alternate replaces a delegate, there is no coming back.

What Are the Delegates' Responsibilities?

Unfortunately, some delegates treat attendance at a convention as a paid vacation. Being selected as a delegate entails many responsibilities that need to be taken care of before, during, and after the convention.

Before the convention, the delegate should fill out and send in all credential and registration forms. Material regarding the business to come before the convention is usually sent out in advance of the convention. The delegate should read all that information in preparation for the convention. The delegate should discuss all controversial issues with the members he or she represents and find out their points of view on the issues.

During the convention, the delegate should attend all the business meetings as well as any informative sessions designed to educate delegates on issues to come before the convention. At the business meetings, the delegate should take an active role in the deliberations of the convention body. When it is time to vote, the delegate should vote, although the delegate cannot be forced to vote.

After the convention, the delegate should report back to the group he or she represented. That report may be oral, written, or both. It should be an informative report of key business that transpired at the convention.

Convention Committees

The following five committees are somewhat convention specific and worth separating out:

- **Credentials.** Establishes who can vote during the meeting.
- **Rules.** Establishes the rules that the group will follow during the meeting.
- **Program.** Determines the order of business for the meeting.
- **Resolutions.** Screens, consolidates, and edits resolutions that are to come before the convention body.
- **Minutes Approval.** Approves the minutes of the convention on behalf of the convention body.

Let's look at each in turn.

Point of Information

In Chapter 17, we discussed the role of the tellers' committee in counting the ballots and reporting the count to the members. The tellers' committee, along with the presiding officer and parliamentarian, should determine in advance the best way to conduct a vote count if one is needed. Then, during the convention, the committee should be ready to assist with that count.

Credentials Committee

The function of the credentials committee is to receive members' credential forms, certify delegates and alternates, and register delegates and alternates at the convention.

In advance of the convention, this committee or the headquarters' staff sends out credential forms that include the information the committee needs in order to determine whether members are qualified to vote. Then, when members arrive at the convention, they go to the credentials desk to receive their badges, voting cards, or ribbons for the badges that prove they are voting members.

Point of Information

At the end of the credentials committee report, the chairman moves the adoption of the report. The report may sound something like this:

"Madam President, attached is the list of the names of the voting delegates who have registered up to this time." [Specific statistics would be given here such as the number of delegates, alternates, etc.] "On behalf of the committee, I move that the roll of delegates hereby submitted be the official roll of the voting delegates at this time."

After the motion is adopted to approve the credentials report, it is a good idea to remind the body of the number of voting delegates or members.

At the beginning of the convention, the credentials committee reports the list of voting members who have registered and the number of voting members. That number is used to determine the total possible number of votes that could be cast on any one motion. This report must be approved by the membership; once it is, the list of voting members becomes the official list for the remainder of the convention. Conventions that last more than one day should begin each day with an updated report of the credentials committee. If the number of voting members has increased from the day before, a motion should be made to approve the updated report. Since members who leave the convention or simply do not show up for a meeting do not have to report that to the credentials committee, the number of voting members does not decrease.

Rules Committee

Once the credentials committee establishes who can vote, it's time for the rules committee to establish what are called the convention standing rules. These are parliamentary rules as well as other rules that relate to the administration of the convention. Some of the possible subjects covered in the convention standing rules include …

- Credentials committee report information.
- Any requirements for admission into the convention room, such as badges.
- Seating requirements, such as a designated delegates area.
- Procedures for an alternate to replace a delegate.
- Information on badges and voting cards.
- Processes and requirements for presenting motions or resolutions, such as that they must be in writing.

Parliamentary Pearls

At the end of the report, the rules committee chairman moves the adoption of the convention standing rules. It might sound something like this: "Mr. President, on behalf of the rules committee, I move the adoption of the convention standing rules as just read and as printed on page 12 of the convention program."

- Time limits on individuals speaking in debate.
- Debate rules.
- Nomination and election rules.
- Establishment of a minutes approval committee.
- Cell phone and pager regulations.
- The parliamentary authority (*Robert's*, I hope!).

The rules are usually printed in the convention information and read by the rules committee chairman at the beginning of the meeting.

Program Committee

Once the rules committee completes its report and recommends the adoption of the convention standing rules, the program committee makes its report. The program committee report should include the order of business, the meeting schedule, and any special events. At the end of its presentation the committee chairman, on behalf of the committee, moves its approval.

Resolutions Committee

Every convention handles the resolutions committee and its responsibilities differently. The purpose of the convention resolutions committee is to screen, consolidate, and edit resolutions that are to come before the convention body. Proper use of this committee can significantly reduce the time spent in business meetings because the committee reviews and discusses each resolution and makes its recommendation regarding each resolution to the convention body. Then, at the time of its report, it presents each resolution to the convention body along with its recommendation.

Some resolution committees can originate motions or resolutions, others can choose to not present a resolution to the convention body, and still others can't change even a small word without the agreement of the maker of the resolution.

Point of Information

The chairman of the resolutions committee moves the adoption of each resolution and gives the committee's recommendation as to how the convention body should vote on the motion. It may make any of the following recommendations:

- Vote yes, in favor of the resolution.
- *Amend* the resolution and then vote yes after the convention body amends it.
- Vote no, in opposition of the resolution.
- No recommendation (which means the committee is choosing to avoid giving the convention body a recommendation on how to vote).
- Referral to a committee. (This should be used sparingly.)

Minutes Approval Committee

This committee is described in detail in Chapter 18. Please refer to that description, which includes a method to help make convention minute-taking easier, the skeletal minutes. A sample of skeletal minutes in action can be found in Appendix D.

Little Things That Make a Big Difference at a Convention

There are many little touches at a convention that can ensure that it's run smoothly. The larger the convention, the more important these things become:

- **Pages.** In a convention, pages are people, not pieces of paper. Pages are assigned in advance of the meeting and usually wear something to distinguish themselves during the meeting. Before the meeting, pages are responsible for seating delegates in their designated area and other members in their assigned area. During the meeting, pages are responsible for passing notes and messages in the meeting room (all that practice in grade school finally pays off), making sure members who wish to speak can reach a microphone, assisting in the maintenance of order, and being sensitive to and helping fill the needs of the members.

- **Timekeepers.** If the convention rules include time limits on the speeches, timekeepers are a must. It is their job to keep time during the business meetings, so they must be familiar with the speaking and debate rules of the convention. Timekeepers should sit so that the presiding officer and the member speaking can both see them.

Parliamentary Pearls

If speakers get three minutes per speech, at the end of two and a half minutes, the timekeeper should hold up a yellow flag. At three minutes, the timekeeper should hold up a red flag. When the red flag goes up, the presiding officer should allow the speaker to finish his or her sentence and then interrupt the speaker and indicate that time is up.

- **Briefings, forums, informational sessions.** There are many different names for these optional, informal meetings, and they can make a huge difference in the success of the convention. When controversial issues come before the convention body, sessions should be held to give the group the opportunity to discuss the issue for a day or two before they have to vote on it. Giving the group that time to process the different sides of the issues not only makes them more informed voters, but usually adds to the quality of their decisions.

The Least You Need to Know

- Each group may call its convention something different, but they are all conventions by nature.
- A convention is one session but usually many meetings.
- Delegates should be sent to the convention informed as to how the group they represent feels on issues that are to come up during the convention. They should not, however, be instructed how to vote on particular issues.
- Because of the unique nature of conventions, they often have their own committees and rules of debate.

Chapter 22

Electronic Meetings

In This Chapter

- Why e-meetings can come in handy
- Synchronous versus asynchronous meetings
- E-meeting venues
- Rules for running an e-meeting

The negative people of the world frequently say that the time will come when electronic meetings (e-meetings) will totally replace in-person meetings. I don't agree with such predictions. I believe that the more we are surrounded by technology, the more we will need and want the personal contact of in-person meetings.

I do believe, though, that we will see a significant increase in the use of electronic meetings, as they have their time and place. As a consequence, it's worth taking a look at this new breed of meetings.

Why E-Meetings?

Why do people use electronic meetings? Here are some of the reasons that e-meetings are becoming more popular:

- **Time-sensitive issues.** Some issues need to be addressed before the group can come together for an in-person meeting. Sometimes, if an issue isn't dealt with immediately, it becomes a moot point. For example, say your group wants to take a stand against a bill that is scheduled to be voted on by your state legislators in two weeks. Your next in-person meeting is three weeks away. If you take a stand on the issue at your next in-person meeting, it will be after the bill has been voted on and therefore a moot point.
- **Cost.** If all of the people in your group live in the same area, the cost of conducting a meeting is minimal. But when the attendees are from all over the country or even the world, you can save everyone money by conducting an e-meeting.
- **Comfort.** There is a whole generation or two who have become so comfortable with electronic communication that they are at least as comfortable, if not more so, with electronic meetings as they are with in-person meetings.

Same Time, Different Place vs. Different Time, Different Place

E-meetings can take place during a set time, just like regular meetings, or they can take place at different times. Meetings that take place at the same time are called *synchronous meetings*. So if you are on a conference call with members from New York, California, Alabama, and Illinois, you are in a synchronous meeting. You are interacting in real time. *Asynchronous meetings* are meetings that occur with the participants in different places at different times.

def•i•ni•tion

Synchronous meetings occur when participants are in different places at the same time. **Asynchronous meetings** occur with the participants in different places at different times. These are also referred to as nonsynchronistic meetings.

So if your bylaws allow you to debate and take a vote by e-mail, you are participating in an asynchronous meeting.

If you understand these two concepts, you will understand the basis of the rules for your electronic meetings. When you attend a synchronous meeting, you can, for the most part, follow the rules established in *Robert's* with only a few variations. But that is not true of asynchronous meetings. Because of the nature of asynchronous meetings, the basic rules of *Robert's* will work, but they must be adapted, sometimes significantly.

You Need an Okay from the Bylaws

Any kind of meeting that is not an in-person meeting must be authorized in the bylaws or higher-level governing documents.

If, in an extreme emergency, you conduct a meeting electronically that is not authorized in the bylaws, the best thing to do is to ratify those actions at the next legal meeting. Be sure to specifically list each action in the minutes of the meeting in which you ratify those actions.

Gavel Gaffes

If your bylaws don't authorize an electronic meeting, any action you take during an electronic meeting is not a legal action taken by the group.

If your bylaws don't authorize e-meetings and your organization wants to add a clause addressing them, here is some wording that might work for you. These are actual examples from existing bylaws. Notice that each example authorizes particular groups to have specific kinds of electronic meetings.

- "The Board of Directors, Executive Committee, standing committees, and special committees are authorized to meet by telephone conference or through other electronic communications media so long as all the members may simultaneously hear each other and participate during the meeting."
- "The Legislative Council, including its Assemblies or committees, may conduct its business by electronic or conventional means, including mail, telephone, fax, computer, or other appropriate

means, provided that all members have access to the information and/or debate through one or more of the means listed."

- "The Board of Directors, Executive Committee, standing committees, special committees, and subcommittees of the Board of Directors are authorized to meet by electronic communication media so long as all members may participate."

E-Meeting Venues

There are many different formats for electronic meetings. I will list a few here, but by the time you read this chapter, someone will have created at least one new way to meet electronically. The developments in technology are so rapid that it is very difficult to keep up.

Synchronous meetings include …

- **Telephone conferencing.** This is probably the most frequently used e-meeting venue. Each participant in the phone conference is on a telephone at his or her own location. The advantage of this format is that all members can hear each other; the disadvantage is that they can't see each other. That doesn't seem like much of a disadvantage until you realize that nonverbal communication constitutes more than half of what we communicate.
- **Videoconferencing.** This format gives the participants the advantage of being able to hear and see the other meeting participants. It is wonderful technology, but don't let it fool you. It is not the same as being in the same room. It can also be very expensive.
- **Web conferencing.** This format works similar to videoconferencing except it harnesses the power of the Internet as a platform to conduct the meeting. It, too, is a wonderful technology, but since it depends on the Internet—an unstable technology—it can have technical issues that can get in the way of the e-meeting. It can also be cost prohibitive.
- **Chat rooms.** Some groups use chat rooms and/or instant messaging (IM) to conduct meetings. In order for it to be a synchronous meeting, all attendees must be in the chat room or instant messaging at the same time. The group must have rules for how members

are recognized. For instance, it might require members to type in "hand" when they want to speak, and the chair might recognize a member by typing the word "go" with that individual's name next to it. This method is a much more cost-effective way, but similar to telephone conferencing, it has no visual communication. It also has no vocal communication and can be problematic for those members who are not fast typists.

Asynchronous meetings include …

- **E-mail.** All members of the meeting are listed in the "to" part of the e-mail. When you reply to a message in the e-mail, you should reply to all so that all of the participants receive the same information.
- **E-mail lists.** These are sometimes referred to as e-mail groups or Listservs. All of the participants in the meeting are on the electronic list and therefore get all of the e-mails. You send an e-mail to the e-mail list, and it is automatically sent out to all of the participants in your group.
- **Facsimile/fax.** Although the fax machine is used most frequently as a way of voting electronically, it is sometimes also used as a method of having a "discussion" within a group.

E-Meeting Techniques

In a regular meeting, if you get confused about which document the person speaking is referring to, you simply look at which document the person next to you is looking at. But when you're in an e-meeting, it's not so easy!

There are some techniques that can help everyone involved in the e-meeting spend less time looking for the document in question or locating the sentence that was just read. Spending time trying to find your place during a meeting is not only time consuming but also frustrating for meeting attendees.

Every document that members will be referring to during the e-meeting should be easily distinguishable using only a couple of words. Let's say you have four documents that are going to be used during the e-meeting. If you were to send out the documents to each of the participants via postal mail, you could put each on different-colored paper. This way, the second document is easily referred to as the yellow document. If you're going to send the documents out electronically, use the header or footer and the title page to title the document in a shortened way, such as Document B. This way, the second document can be referred to as Document B, and it's easy to find the correct one.

Another problem occurs when a meeting participant refers to a long document and people get lost in all the pages—another meeting time waster. There's an easy solution: number each line on each page. So referring to something in the middle of the document might sound like this: "I have a comment about the paragraph that begins on page 4, line 22." Then pause while everyone quickly finds his or her place and make your comment. People are now able to listen to your comment instead of spending your talking time looking for the paragraph you're referring to.

E-Meeting Rules

Synchronous meetings can rely on the rules already in *Robert's* and need only a few additional rules to account for the unique situation. Asynchronous meetings require detailed new rules because *Robert's* doesn't cover them.

The one principle that should be adhered to in the writing of any e-meeting rules is that the proposed procedures should replicate, as much as possible, the way business is conducted in in-person meetings. For example, a rule for an e-mail list for a board of directors might be that "Each message posted by a director shall be a message written by the director. Forwarding a message from a member is prohibited." The issue is whether to allow forwarded messages. To determine the rule, compare this rule to what happens when a member wants to debate a motion on the floor. In an in-person meeting, the member who is not a director cannot just go to the meeting and speak in debate. Therefore, in an electronic meeting, a member who is not a director should not be able to send a message directly to each and every director. In an electronic meeting and an in-person meeting, if a member wants to share a message, it must first be shared with the director, who then puts the message in his or her own words and includes it in the debate.

Rules to Consider for Synchronous Meetings

Some of the rules that you might consider incorporating into a set of rules written for synchronous meetings include …

- Members shall state their name upon joining the meeting. Upon establishing a quorum, the chair will announce the names of all of the members in attendance.
- The meeting must be arranged at least 48 hours in advance.
- Each member should seek recognition from the chair before beginning to speak. (Here identify the method in which it is acceptable to seek recognition. This will vary according to the technology used. If an acceptable method is difficult to determine, simply going through the list of attendees in alphabetical order works well for a small group.)
- Before recognizing a member to speak a second time on a motion, the chair shall ask if all who wish to speak a first time have spoken.
- Before processing a *Previous Question* motion, the chair shall first determine if all who wish to speak a first time have had the opportunity to do so.
- Each member should identify himself or herself prior to speaking.
- Motions will be voted on by voice vote. If the chair has a problem determining the vote, he or she may call for a roll call vote. The roll call vote is for determination of the outcome of the vote and shall not be recorded in the minutes.
- The minutes of the meeting shall be approved at the next in-person meeting.

> **Point of Information**
>
> Because it might be very difficult to determine a majority or two-thirds vote by voice during a conference call, groups might need to rely on the roll call vote more frequently in those situations. However, it is only appropriate to record each member's vote in the minutes when each member represents a constituency, and even then it's not always appropriate.

Rules to Consider for Asynchronous Meetings

Because *Robert's* was created for synchronous meetings, much of what is contained in *Robert's* must be adapted to asynchronous meetings. Therefore, there are questions that need to be answered before writing the rules for an asynchronous meeting. Some of those questions include …

- **Does the meeting have a start and end time, or is it an ongoing meeting?**

  There appear to be at least two different approaches to e-mail list meetings. The first approach is to have a start and stop time/date for the meeting. This start and stop time is similar to the start and stop time of an in-person meeting, but it is much longer because there's no guarantee that people will check their e-mail at the same time.

  The second approach is to have the meeting be an ongoing process. In that case, the group establishes a time period for processing each motion. With this approach, it would be possible to have more than one motion being processed at a time. While that is not desirable, it may be the only practical way to be able to deal with multiple motions in a timely manner.

- **Is only one main motion allowed to be processed at a time?**

  Because it could easily take weeks to process a motion, some groups allow for more than one main motion to be processed simultaneously. If that is the case, some rules need to be in place to keep track of which motion the individual is commenting on. A simple rule requiring the name of the motion in the subject line can make a huge difference.

- **Who is going to serve as chair of the meeting, and who is going to take care of the administrative tasks for the meeting?**

  Someone needs to serve as the presiding officer for the meeting, as with in-person meetings. Is that same person going to take care of the administrative tasks for the meeting, or are they assigned to someone else? Some of those tasks include timelines for each motion, order of the presentation of motions, voting procedures, removal of inappropriate comments, etc.

- **Is someone or a committee authorized to receive all motions and consolidate multiple motions on the same subject?**

  Many organizations have such committees, sometimes referred to as the resolutions committee or the reference committee. These committees significantly improve the flow of the meeting.

Parliamentary Pearls

Be sure to give some thought as to how the voting occurs in your e-mail group meetings. If the members have to send their vote to the entire group, will that affect how they vote? It might be best to have them send their votes to an independent third party who tallies the votes and reports the results to the chair.

The following are some of the rules you might consider incorporating into a set of rules written for asynchronous meetings:

- **Rules regarding the administration of the meeting, such as …**

  The meetings shall be held in executive session.

  ________________ shall serve as the presiding officer of electronic meetings.

  ________________ shall have the authority to rule that a message is out of order and notify the members of the ruling.

  The ______________ shall have the authority to postpone a motion to the next face-to-face meeting of the membership based on the following criteria:

  a. the complexity and number of secondary motions applied to the main motion;

  b. determination by ________________ that it is in the best interest of the organization to postpone taking action on the motion.

  The secretary shall securely maintain the thread for each main motion, including secondary motions, until the minutes including that motion have been approved.

- **Rules regarding the timeline of both the meeting and the processing of motions, such as ...**

  A proposed timeline for discussing and acting on a motion shall be established by ____________________ and communicated to the members at the beginning of the processing of any motion based on the following considerations (these should be adapted to your organization):

  a. The content, urgency for acting on the motion, and internal and external timing demands;

  b. If there is time and/or need for a draft of the motion to be made available so that members can suggest changes to or request clarification from ____________________. When time does not permit posting of a draft motion, ____________________ shall forward an explanation to the members; and

  c. The time when the membership shall be notified of the motion using a communication vehicle available to all members.

  NOTE: The proposed timeline can be modified by ________________________ based on the complexity and number of secondary motions that need to be discussed and voted upon.

- **Rules regarding process, such as ...**

  The process for discussing and acting on motions shall include the following:

  a. Main motions shall be submitted to the chair, posted, and discussion shall begin. The posting shall include the motion name, number, who submitted the motion, the rationale included with the motion submission, and the timeline for processing the motion.

  b. At a designated time, discussion on the main motion shall stop, and secondary motions shall be presented and acted upon.

  c. After the period for secondary motions has been completed, the motion in its final form shall be posted for discussion and voting, and no additional secondary motions shall be allowed.

Proposed secondary motions must be submitted to the chair within the required time limits. ______________________ is authorized to consolidate, reword, prioritize, and not present to the members the secondary motions that are submitted. The ____________ may decide to prioritize and present to the members more than one secondary motion at a time. Prioritization shall be based on parliamentary principles and efficient and effective conduct of business. The decision to not present a secondary motion to the membership can only be made after notification to the membership with opportunity for members to object. If __________ [number] members object, the secondary motion shall be presented to the membership.

Posting of secondary motions shall include the motion letter, main motion number that it applies to, submitter's name, and timeline for processing the secondary motion.

When posting an electronic message related to a motion, members shall use a format that includes:

a. a heading indicating the motion name, number, whether the member is speaking for the motion (pro), in opposition to the motion (con), or asking for information (*Point of Information*);

b. a closing for each message that includes the member's name.

Each message posted by a member shall be a message written by the member. Forwarding a message from a nonmember is prohibited.

- **Rules regarding voting, such as …**

Voting shall be conducted only during the voting period, which shall be a minimum of one week for main motions and three business days for secondary motions.

Point of Information

It is very unusual to count the abstentions when counting votes. But they are counted in some electronic meeting rules to determine whether enough members were involved in the decision to make it a binding decision. *Robert's* allows a member to abstain from voting, and this rule does, too.

Any *Appeal from the Decision of the Chair* must be submitted to the chair, who shall forward it to the ________________ [committee name]. The ______________________ [committee name] shall make the decision on the *Appeal* within three business days and report its decision to the members through the e-mail list.

- **Rules regarding determination of a quorum, such as …**

  A quorum shall be a majority of the members. The number of votes cast, including abstentions, determines verification of a quorum.

Rules That Adjust *Robert's* to E-Meetings

The sample rule regarding an *Appeal from the Decision of the Chair* was included because, if it were not there, two members could defeat a motion that was time sensitive without that motion coming to a vote. Here is how that would work: Let's say that a motion is pending, and voting on it is scheduled to begin in three days. The motion is that the group supports an activity that begins in 10 days. A member makes a *Point of Order*, saying that he or she feels that the group should not consider the resolution. The chair rules that the point is not well taken and that the group will proceed to process the resolution.

The same member who made the *Point of Order* then moves to *Appeal from the Decision of the Chair*, and that motion is seconded. There are now only 10 days left until the proposed activity, and the group must now discuss and vote on the *Appeal* and then, if the *Appeal* fails, still discuss and vote on the main motion. There simply isn't enough time to do all of these things. If the group can't quickly resolve the *Appeal*, the motion will not get voted on in time to support the activity, thereby rendering the motion moot. Two people who are against a motion could prevent the majority from voting on it simply by using the motion *Appeal from the Decision of the Chair* as a delay tactic.

To prevent this sort of situation, the *Appeal from the Decision of the Chair* can be resolved by the specified committee. That way, it can be resolved in a timely manner, and the vote on the main motion can proceed.

Let's Ease Into This E-Mail Group Meeting Thing!

Before your group amends its bylaws to authorize electronic meetings, I strongly encourage you to create an e-mail list and use it for discussion purposes only. Then, after you have had a chance to see how well it works for you, you can write the rules so that you can make your e-meetings decision-making meetings instead of discussion-only meetings.

An organization needs no special rules to discuss issues on an e-mail list—it's similar to discussing issues casually before or after the meeting. However, until you have rules in place, you cannot make decisions on the list. Since the rules for asynchronous meetings are not covered in *Robert's*, you will need to write rules that are specific to your organization. Use the suggestions included here as a starting point for your rules.

Even if you never use the electronic meetings venue to make decisions, it can still be an effective venue for your group. Think about the time you could cut out of in-person meetings if everyone had a chance to "discuss" the issues electronically before the meeting. If you meet by a synchronous method, such as telephone conference call, think of the time you could save on the call if the discussion occurred over a period of days before the call.

The Least You Need to Know

- Meetings that are not held in person must be authorized in the bylaws.
- Synchronous meetings occur when participants are in different places at the same time. Asynchronous meetings occur with the participants in different places at different times.
- Put serious thought into how voting will work in your e-meetings.
- Have a trial run for your e-meetings before changing your bylaws.

Appendix A

Glossary

absentee voting Voting by mail or by proxy by a person who is not in attendance at the meeting. The bylaws must expressly authorize it before it is allowed.

abstain To refrain from voting, thus giving consent to the decision made by the group. Frequently the reason for abstaining is a conflict of interest.

abstention The result of abstaining from voting. Because the abstention is not voting, it does not count as a vote cast.

accept To adopt or approve a motion or report. The effect of accepting, adopting, or approving a report is that the assembly endorses the report in its entirety, every word of it.

acclamation An election by unanimous consent.

ad hoc A special committee. The term comes from a Latin term meaning "to this" and refers to a committee formed for a particular purpose.

adhering to the motion A motion is considered adhering to the motion or question if it is made while the motion it is adhering to is pending. For example, a main motion is made. While it is being discussed, an *Amendment* is made to that main motion.

The *Amendment* is adhering to the main motion. Adhering motions remain connected to the main motion even if the motion is interrupted, *Referred*, *Postponed*, or temporarily disposed of.

Adjourn A motion to close the meeting.

adjourned meeting A meeting that is a continuation of a previous meeting. It occurs when the work was not completed at a regular or special meeting, and there was a motion to continue the meeting at a different time. The original meeting and the adjourned meeting make up a single session. Because it is a continuation of a previous meeting, special notice of the meeting doesn't need to be sent to the membership. The adjourned meeting begins on the agenda where the meeting it is continuing left off.

adjournment sine die It is the final adjournment of an assembly. The last meeting of the convention is said to adjourn sine die.

administrative year While not a parliamentary term, this term refers to the time period in which the officer remains in office without need for re-election.

adopt To accept or approve a motion or report. The effect of accepting, adopting, or approving a report is that the assembly endorses the report in its entirety, every word of it.

affirmative vote A vote in favor of the adoption of the motion.

agenda A predetermined sequence of items of business to be covered at a specific meeting; an order of business. The prescribed agenda for organizations that have regular meetings at least quarterly and have *Robert's Rules* as their parliamentary authority is as follows: approval of minutes; reports of officers, boards, and standing committees; reports of special committees; special orders; unfinished business and general orders; and new business.

alternate A member authorized to substitute for another member.

Amend A motion to modify the pending motion before it is voted on.

***Amend* by adding** One of the forms of a motion to *Amend.* This form places a word or consecutive words or a paragraph at the end of a motion.

***Amend* by inserting** One of the forms of a motion to *Amend.* This form places a word or consecutive words or a paragraph in the beginning or the middle of a motion.

***Amend* by striking out** One of the forms of a motion to *Amend.* This form takes out a word or consecutive words or a paragraph in a motion.

***Amend* by striking out and inserting** One of the forms of a motion to *Amend.* This form strikes out a word or consecutive words and inserts a word or consecutive words in its place.

***Amend* by substituting** One of the forms of a motion to *Amend.* This form strikes out a paragraph or more and inserts another paragraph or more.

Amend Something Previously Adopted A motion that allows the assembly to change an action previously taken. This motion can be applied to a motion adopted at a previous meeting provided that none of the action involved has been carried out such that it is too late to undo.

amendable When a motion is amendable, it can be modified during the time it is pending (the fourth step in the processing of a motion).

amendment A motion that proposes a change to the wording of a pending motion.

American Institute of Parliamentarians (AIP) A professional organization of parliamentarians that emphasizes knowledge of *Robert's*, *Sturgis*, and other parliamentary authorities.

announcement of the vote The sixth step in the processing of a motion. In a complete announcement, the chair states the following: the results of the vote, a declaration of whether the motion passed or failed, the effect of the vote, and the next item of business.

annual meeting A meeting held yearly, usually for the purpose of electing officers and receiving the annual reports of current officers and committees. The annual meeting is usually specified in the bylaws. You may also find in the bylaws what business can be brought up at the annual meeting as well as whether the annual meeting is considered a regular meeting, thus having the flexibility of a regular meeting. Sometimes certain subjects—for example—bylaw amendments, can only be acted on at the annual meeting.

annual meeting rules Rules that are adopted for a single meeting and which may include parliamentary rules.

Appeal from the Decision of the Chair (Appeal) A motion to take a decision regarding parliamentary procedure out of the hands of the presiding officer and place the final decision in the hands of the assembly.

appoint To name or assign a person to an office, a position, or a committee.

approve A term synonymous with ratify, confirm, adopt, or accept. The effect of accepting, adopting, or approving a report is that the assembly endorses the report in its entirety, every word of it. The text becomes an act or statement of the assembly.

articles of incorporation Also referred to as the corporate charter, it's the legal instrument required by the state to incorporate an organization.

assembly A group of people meeting together to openly discuss issues and make decisions that then become the decision of the group. Also referred to as a deliberative assembly.

assessment A fee that is imposed on the members. It must be specifically authorized in the bylaws.

asynchronous meetings Electronic meetings that occur with the participants in different places at different times. Venues include but are not limited to e-mail, e-mail list groups, and facsimile/fax. Also referred to as nonsynchronistic meetings.

attendance via a communication method There are various methods by which a person can attend a meeting electronically, but only as specifically authorized in the bylaws. For example, if a member must miss a meeting because they physically cannot be in the meeting room, then some bylaws authorize that person to attend by video or audio conferencing methods. Unless the bylaws indicate otherwise, that person is considered in attendance at that meeting.

audit An examination and verification of the financial records of the association. Depending upon the size of the organization, an audit may be required by federal or state law. The size of the organization also determines whether the audit can be done by an internal group, usually referred to as the audit committee, or an external, independent auditor.

aye A word frequently used in a voice vote to vote in the affirmative. For example, "All those in favor of the motion, say 'aye' …."

ballot vote A method of voting in which ballots—usually pieces of paper—are passed out to each voting member, the member fills in the ballot, and the ballot is collected. Instructions from the chair might be: "Please mark your ballots clearly, fold them one time, and hand them directly to a teller."

board of directors A specified group of members who make decisions on behalf of the organization. The membership, authority, and limitations of this group are specified in the bylaws. Meetings of the board are usually only open to members of the board and their invitees.

board of directors meeting Because it takes a lot to run an organization, and all the members do not have a tremendous amount of time to devote to the organization, the members give some of the responsibilities of running the organization to a group of people frequently referred to as the board of directors. Thus, the board meeting is a meeting of a specified group of members who make decisions on behalf of the organization. The membership, authority, and limitations of this group are specified in the bylaws. Because this group has been given total authority over specific aspects of the organization, meetings of the board are usually only open to members of the board and their invitees and the meetings are usually held in executive session.

budget The itemized estimate of income and disbursements.

business An item or matter brought up at a meeting in the form of a motion, for action by the assembly.

bylaws A governing document that, when used without a constitution, comprises the highest body of rules of the organization, except for rules from a higher governing authority such as a parent body or laws. In the bylaws, an organization is free to adopt any rules it may wish, subject to a higher governing authority such as a parent body or laws, even rules deviating from the organization's established parliamentary authority.

Call for the Orders of the Day By the use of this motion, a single member can require the assembly to follow the order of business or agenda or to take up a special order that is scheduled to come up, unless two thirds of the assembly wish to do otherwise.

call of the house A motion used only in bodies that have the legal power to compel the attendance of their members, such as legislative bodies. This motion requires the unexcused absent members to be brought to the meeting, following the established procedures.

call of the meeting The official notice of a meeting given to all members of the organization.

call the roll A method of taking a vote or of determining attendance of members in which each member's name is called out and members publicly announce their vote or their presence.

call up the motion to *Reconsider* The motion to *Reconsider* can be divided into the making of the motion and the actual consideration of the motion, referred to as calling up. Words used: "Madame President, I call up the motion to *Reconsider* the vote on the motion …" *See also* making the motion to *Reconsider*.

called meeting Another term for a special meeting.

calling a member to order An order from the presiding officer to a member to stop an inappropriate action and be seated. If the presiding officer does not call to order a member behaving inappropriately, another member may call that member to order.

caucus A meeting to plan strategy toward a particular issue or motion.

censure A motion to reprimand or admonish a member. The only consequence of this motion is the admonishment or reprimand.

chair The person who is in charge of the meeting. Presiding officer and chair are interchangeable terms. They both are sometimes used to refer to the president of the organization when the president is conducting the meeting.

charter A document issued by a parent organization authorizing the establishment of a subordinate unit.

close debate Termination of Step 4 in the processing of the motion. It occurs when the chair ends debate because no one else wants to speak or with the adoption of the *Previous Question* motion.

close nominations A motion that puts an end to nominations. The motion is out of order if any member is seeking the floor to nominate a candidate. This motion should not be used. Instead, when there is no one seeking the floor to nominate a candidate, the chair should close nominations, without a motion.

Commit or ***Refer to a Committee*** This motion sends the main motion to a smaller group (a committee) for further examination and refinement before the body votes on it.

committee A group of one or more persons who are appointed or elected to carry out a charge. The charge can be to investigate, to recommend, or to take action.

committee meeting The larger group frequently assigns specific tasks to a committee. When they assign the task, they usually give the committee a specified level of authority to carry out the task. That authority may be to research the subject and make a recommendation to the larger group or it may be to make a decision for the larger group and carry out that decision. That group comes together to meet and, based on the authority given them, takes the action directed by the larger group.

committee of the whole The entire assembly acts as a committee to discuss a motion or issue more informally. The presiding officer vacates the chair and another member is appointed to serve as chairman. This motion is usually reserved for large assemblies, particularly legislative bodies.

committee report An official statement that is formally adopted by a majority vote of the committee and that is presented to the parent body (either the entire membership or the board of directors) in the name of the committee. It contains information obtained, information regarding any action taken, or recommendations on behalf of the committee.

conflict of interest A situation in which a member has a direct personal interest not common to the other members.

consent agenda or **consent calendar** An agenda category that includes a list of routine, uncontroversial items that are approved with one motion, no discussion, and one vote.

Consideration by Paragraph or Seriatim The effect of this motion is to debate and *Amend* a long motion paragraph by paragraph.

consideration of a question The discussion that occurs during Step 4 of the processing of a motion while the motion is pending.

constituent unit Organizations, particularly national organizations, are frequently made up of units at regional, state, or local levels that are referred to as constituent units. The bylaws should establish their relationship within the organization's structure.

constitution A governing document that contains the highest body of rules of the organization, except for rules from a higher governing authority such as a parent body, or laws. Some organizations have both a constitution and bylaws, but the single bylaws document is recommended.

continued meeting A term interchangeable with adjourned meeting.

convene To initiate a meeting by calling the meeting to order.

convention An assembly of delegates usually chosen for one session. The participants frequently attend as representatives of a local, state, or regional association. The convention participants come together to make decisions on behalf of the entire organization. Some smaller organizations give all members the right to attend the convention as voting members. Thus, the voting members of the convention are the individual members of the organization who are registered and attend the convention.

convention standing rules Rules that are adopted for a single meeting or series of meetings and that may include parliamentary rules.

corporate charter A legal document that includes the name and object of the organization in compliance with state statutes for the state in which the organization is incorporated. It may also be referred to as the articles of incorporation.

corresponding secretary An officer who is responsible for the general correspondence of the organization.

counted vote A method of voting in which the members express their vote by standing or raising their hand, and then those standing or with their hands raised are counted and the number is reported to the presiding officer. "Those in favor of the motion, please stand and remain standing until counted. [pause] You may be seated. Those opposed to the motion, please stand and remain standing until counted. [pause] You may be seated."

CP Certified Parliamentarian through the American Institute of Parliamentarians (AIP). To become a CP, a person must pass a written examination that covers the rules in various parliamentary authorities and must earn service points.

CP-T Certified Teacher of Parliamentary Procedure through the American Institute of Parliamentarians (AIP). In addition to being a CP, the person must complete a teacher education course and must show evidence of successful teaching experience.

CPP Certified Professional Parliamentarian through the American Institute of Parliamentarians (AIP). To become a CPP, a person must pass a rigorous oral examination and demonstrate expertise in presiding.

CPP-T Certified Professional Teacher of Parliamentary Procedure through the American Institute of Parliamentarians (AIP). In addition to being a CPP, the person must complete a teacher education course and must show evidence of successful teaching experience.

Create a Blank A method used to change a motion that allows an unlimited number of choices for a specific portion of a motion to be considered at the same time. For example, if the motion is to purchase an item for $50 and there are several choices for the amount of money to spend, a member could first move to strike $50 and *Create a Blank*. *See also* fill a blank.

credential A certificate that shows a person is authorized to serve as a delegate or alternate delegate or a representative of a specific body.

credentials committee The committee that has the duty to certify the credentialed delegates or members and report that number to the membership. That number then becomes the highest number of votes that can be cast at the meeting.

cumulative voting A voting method used when there are multiple positions or propositions and each member may cast a vote multiplied by that number of positions or propositions. The member may assign those votes however he or she chooses among the various positions or propositions, including multiple votes to one position or proposition. To be used, this method of voting must be specifically authorized in the bylaws or the state statutes.

custom A long-established practice of an organization. If a custom is found to be in violation of the organization's bylaws, rules, or parliamentary authority, and a member challenges that, the custom must cease.

dark horse A nominee who may not be the first choice of most, but on whom most may prefer to agree.

debatable When a motion is debatable, the members may discuss it during Step 4 of the processing of the motion. Undebatable motions must skip Step 4 and go immediately to the vote on the motion.

debate The discussion of a motion that occurs after the presiding officer has restated the motion and before putting it to a vote.

decorum To conduct oneself in a proper manner. Usually refers to debate, as in decorum in debate.

decorum in debate Appropriate behavior during debate. *Robert's Rules* lists nine such debate rules, including not attacking another member's motives, addressing comments through the chair, and so on.

defer action Using specific motions to delay action on a motion.

delegate body In organizations that are large and/or spread throughout the country or the world, it's not practical for all the members to come together for a meeting. To still maintain decision-making that represents the membership, this type of organization may have delegates who come together and meet on behalf of the entire organization. The participants frequently attend as representatives of a local, state, or regional association. The convention participants come together to make decisions on behalf of the entire organization.

deliberative assembly A group of people meeting together to openly discuss issues and make decisions that then become the decision of the group.

dilatory A motion, action, or statement the purpose of which is to delay action. It is an attempt to obstruct the will of the assembly.

Discharge a Committee A motion that relieves a committee from further consideration of the task that has been assigned to it.

disciplinary procedures An organization has a right to make and enforce rules, and to require members to refrain from conduct that hurts the organization. Therefore, a society has the right to discipline its members, following very specific procedures that are outlined in *Robert's Rules.*

discussion Debate that occurs after the presiding officer restates the motion and before the vote is taken on the motion.

Dispense with the Reading of the Minutes This motion, if adopted, delays the reading of the minutes to a later time in the meeting. In most contemporary organizations, the minutes are distributed in advance of the meeting and, therefore, there is no need to read them at the meeting.

dispose of Action on a motion that removes it from consideration by the assembly. A motion is considered permanently disposed of when it has been approved or defeated by vote of the assembly.

Division of the Assembly The effect of this motion is to require a standing vote (not a counted vote). A single member can demand this if he or she feels the vote is too close to declare or is unrepresentative. This motion can only be used after the voice vote or show of hands vote where there is a reasonable doubt of the results.

Division of the Question This motion is used to separate a motion into parts to be voted on individually. It can only be used if each part can stand as a separate question.

entertain a motion A request, usually from the presiding officer, for a formal motion on the subject under discussion.

ex-officio A person is a member by virtue of an office held. An ex-officio member has full voting and speaking rights, unless otherwise indicated in the bylaws.

executive board A term usually synonymous with board of directors or board of trustees.

executive committee An executive committee is to the board of directors what the board of directors is to the membership. It is a smaller group, usually the officers, who are given specific authority in the bylaws. They have only the specific authority that is given to them in the bylaws, even though some executive committees assume a lot of authority. Like the board, their meetings are open only to members of the executive committee and their invitees and are held in executive session.

executive session A meeting or a portion of a meeting in which the proceedings are secret and the only attendees are members and invited guests. Deliberations of an executive session are secret and all attendees are honor-bound to maintain confidentiality. You may have already figured out that this may be an incredibly useful tool in a controversial issue and/or when you want the members to feel free to say things without worry of what they have said being repeated outside of the meeting.

expunge from the minutes Upon the adoption of the motion to *Rescind and Expunge from the Minutes*, the secretary draws a line through the portion of the minutes covered in the motion and writes the words "*Rescinded and Ordered Expunged*" with the date and his or her signature. This should be used rarely as a method of expressing strong disapproval of the action taken.

federal laws Most organizations are governed by federal laws, such as the federal Internal Revenue Code.

fill a blank A method used to change a motion that allows an unlimited number of choices for a specific portion of a motion to be considered at the same time. For example, if the motion is to purchase an item for $50 and there are several choices for the amount of money to spend, a member could first move to strike $50 and *Create a Blank*. If that motion is adopted, then members could list any number of recommendations for the amount of money. The body votes on those recommendations one at a time, in a specified order, until one receives a majority vote and thus fills the blank. Then the main motion of the purchase is voted on.

fiscal year The financial year of the organization. It's the period of time between the opening of the treasurer's books for the year and the closing of them for the year.

Fix the Time to Which to Adjourn This motion sets the time for another meeting to continue business of the session. Adoption of this motion does not adjourn the present meeting or set the time for its adjournment.

fixed membership Refers to the number of memberships established in the bylaws. If the bylaws established a board of nine and there are currently two vacancies, a majority of the fixed membership would be five. A majority of the entire membership would be four.

floor A member has the floor when he has been recognized by the chair to speak. A member is "assigned the floor" by the presiding officer. During that time no one else is to speak until the floor is assigned to another. A motion is considered on the floor when it is in Step 4 of the processing of a motion; when it is pending.

forum An informal meeting or portion of a meeting that allows the members to openly discuss issues.

friendly amendment A proposed amendment that is perceived to be acceptable to the entire assembly. This amendment should be processed just like any other amendment, following the steps of any other motion, even if the maker of the motion "accepts" the amendment. If it is obvious all members are in agreement with the minor change, it can be adopted by unanimous consent.

frivolous motion A motion proposed that is not significant or is dilatory (intended to delay or obstruct business).

fundamental principle of parliamentary law Rules in parliamentary procedure that protect the basic rights of the individual member. These rules cannot be suspended. An example is that the right to vote is limited to the members as defined in the bylaws. Therefore, the rules cannot be suspended to allow nonmembers to vote.

gavel A mallet used by the presiding officer to bring order to the meeting and keep order throughout the meeting. A gavel is a symbol of parliamentary procedure and of the presiding officer.

general consent or **unanimous consent** A method of voting without taking a formal vote. The presiding officer asks if there are any objections, and if none are expressed, the motion is considered passed. If any objection is expressed, the motion must be processed using the six steps.

general orders A category of the agenda that includes any motion that, usually by postponement, has been made an order of the day without being made a special order. Translated, that means that if an item is *Postponed* until a certain day or after a certain event, it fits into this category.

germane Related to the subject. An amendment must be germane to the motion it is amending. A secondary amendment must be germane to the primary amendment it is amending.

good of the order Business that refers to the general welfare of the organization. It frequently includes announcements and other informal information. Some organizations have this category as part of their agenda.

governing documents The rules of the organization. They include federal law, state law, corporate charter, articles of incorporation, constitution, bylaws, rules of order, standing rules, and policies and procedures.

governing documents of parent organization If the organization is a local or state branch of an organization (referred to as the parent organization) and they are authorized to exist in the governing documents of the parent organization, then the rules contained in the governing documents of the parent organization that apply to the local are higher in authority than the rules of that state or local organization.

hand-counted vote A method of voting in which the votes of the members are actually calculated instead of estimated. The members raise their hands, and someone counts the hands raised.

hearing An informal meeting of a group that allows members to express their views and listen to the views of others on a particular subject.

honorary Applied to a membership or an officer. This form only exists if so authorized in the bylaws. The rights that come with this form of membership or officer must also be authorized in the bylaws.

house An assembly. Most frequently used with legislative bodies or delegate bodies.

illegal vote A vote that is not credited to any candidate or choice but is counted as a vote cast. An example is a ballot cast for a fictional character, such as Sylvester the Cat.

immediately pending A motion is considered immediately pending when several motions are pending and it is the motion that was most recently stated by the chair and that will be first disposed of.

in order An action following correct parliamentary procedures.

incidental main motion A main motion that is incidental to, or related to, the business of the assembly or its past or future action.

incidental motions Motions that relate to matters that are supplementary to the conduct of the meeting rather than directly to the main motion. They may be offered at any time when they are needed. Motions in this classification include: *Point of Order*, *Appeal from the Decision of the Chair*, *Objection to Consideration of a Question*, *Suspend the Rules*, *Division of the Assembly*, *Division of the Question*, *Consideration by Paragraph or Seriatim*, *Parliamentary Inquiry*, *Point of Information*, *Motions Relating to Methods of Voting and the Polls*, *Motions Relating to Nominations*, *Request to Be Excused from a Duty*, *Request for Permission to Withdraw a Motion*, *Request to Read Papers*, and *Request for Any Other Privilege*.

incoming president A person who has been elected president but has not yet taken the office of president. This is different than president-elect, because president-elect is an official title for a particular office.

indecorum Improper or disorderly behavior.

informal consideration A form of *Committee of the Whole*. This motion allows the assembly to exchange ideas on an informal basis with more freedom of debate than in a formal assembly.

item of business An agenda item, including a report or a motion. The chair usually announces it by stating "the next item of business …."

Lay on the Table This motion in essence puts aside a main motion until a later, unspecified time. It places in the care of the secretary the pending question and everything adhering to it. If a group meets quarterly or more frequently, the question *Laid on the Table* remains there until taken off or until the end of the next regular session. This motion should not be used to kill a motion without debating it. The motion to *Take from the Table* is used when the assembly wants to continue considering the motion.

legal vote A vote cast by a member entitled to vote.

Limit* or *Extend Limits of Debate This motion can reduce or increase the number and length of speeches permitted or limit the length of debate on a specific question.

lost motion A motion rejected by a vote of the assembly.

main motion A motion that brings before the assembly any particular subject and is made when no other business is pending. If passed, it commits the assembly to do or say something. Motions in this classification include original main motion and incidental main motion.

majority More than half of the votes cast.

majority of the entire membership More than half of all the members of the entity that is meeting. For example, in a meeting of a convention, a majority of the entire membership refers to a majority of all the registered convention attendees entitled to vote.

majority report An incorrectly used term for the report of the majority of the members of a committee. Instead, it should simply be referred to as the committee report.

majority vote More than half of the votes cast.

making the motion to *Reconsider* The motion to *Reconsider* can be divided into the making of the motion and the actual consideration of the motion, referred to as calling up. The making of the motion to *Reconsider* has higher ranking than the consideration of the motion. Therefore, there are times that the motion can be made but not yet considered. Just the making and seconding of the motion to *Reconsider* temporarily suspends actions stemming from the vote it is proposed to *Reconsider.* That suspension lasts until the vote on *Reconsider* is taken. *See also* call up the motion to *Reconsider.*

mass meeting An open and informal meeting of a group of people with a common interest but no formal organization. These meetings happen for many different reasons, one of which is that it's the very first step in the beginning of an organization. Because a mass meeting is not a meeting of an organized group, the rules applicable to a mass meeting are very different from those of other meetings. If you are going to attend a mass meeting or you are the person calling the mass meeting, you should review the section in *Robert's* regarding mass meetings. If the purpose of the mass meeting is to form a new organization, there is another section in *Robert's* that you will also want to review that walks you through the process of organizing a permanent society.

meeting An assembly of members gathered to conduct business during which there is no separation of the members except for a short recess.

member A person who belongs to an organization.

membership Members of an organization who get together to meet and make decisions on behalf of the organization. As a general principle, usually the members of the organization have the rights to control the organization, unless they choose to assign those rights and responsibilities to another group. The place they assign those rights and responsibilities is in the bylaws. The entities that they assign those rights and responsibilities to varies, but most frequently include staff, the board of directors, the executive committee, or other committees.

minority report A formal expression of the views of a portion of a committee or group that are not in agreement with the majority stand on an issue.

minutes The written record of the proceedings of a deliberative assembly. They are a record of what was done at the meeting, not what was said at the meeting.

mock minutes A tool to assist in the minutes-writing process. They are minutes prepared in advance of a meeting or convention that include all that will be occurring and the order in which it will occur. They contain many blank spaces that are filled in during the meeting by the person(s) in charge of the minutes. They are prepared using the agenda and/or the script for the meeting.

motion A proposal that the group take a specific action or stand. Motion and question are interchangeable terms.

motions relating to methods of voting and the polls These motions are used to demand a ballot vote, count a vote, or close or reopen polls.

motions relating to nominations These motions are used in relation to nominations of candidates for office. They include motions relating to the method of nomination, closing nominations, and reopening nominations.

motions that bring the question again before the assembly Motions that are used to bring back a motion that has already been considered by the assembly. Motions in this classification include *Rescind*, *Amend Something Previously Adopted*, *Take from the Table*, and *Reconsider*.

move The word used to make a motion: "I move that …."

mover The person who makes the motion.

National Association of Parliamentarians (NAP) A professional organization of parliamentarians that emphasizes *Robert's* as the parliamentary authority.

nay A word frequently used in a voice vote to vote in the negative—"All those opposed to the motion, say 'nay' …." *Robert's Rules* recommends simply using the word "no."

negative vote A vote against the adoption of the motion.

new business A heading on the agenda for items that are new items of business.

nominate To propose an individual for an office or position.

nomination Naming a person as a candidate for an office or position.

nominee A person who has been nominated.

notice An official announcement, given verbally or in writing, of an item of business that will be introduced at the meeting. Certain motions require previous notice.

null and void Without legal force or effect.

objection A formal expression of opposition to a matter or procedure.

Objection to Consideration of a Question The purpose of this motion is to prevent the assembly from considering the question/motion because a member deems the question as irrelevant, unprofitable, contentious, or simply objectionable. The member believes it is undesirable for this motion to come before the assembly. This motion is only applicable to an original main motion, not an incidental main motion.

obtain the floor To secure recognition from the presiding officer to either speak or make a motion.

officer A person who has been appointed or elected to an official position in the organization.

old business An incorrect and misleading term for the part of the agenda properly called unfinished business. Old business is misleading because it indicates that anything that the group once talked about fits here. The only business that fits in unfinished business is business that was started but not yet finished.

on the floor A motion is considered on the floor when it has been stated by the presiding officer and has not yet been disposed of either permanently or temporarily. Pending and on the floor are interchangeable terms.

order of business The schedule of business for the meeting; the agenda.

order of the day A business item that is scheduled to be taken up during a particular meeting.

original main motions Motions that bring before the assembly a new subject, sometimes in the form of a resolution, upon which action by the assembly is desired.

out of order A motion, action, request, or procedure that is in violation of the rules of the organization.

ownership of a motion A concept that refers to whose property the motion is at a given time and, therefore, who has a right to make any changes to it. In the six steps of the motion process, the maker of the motion owns the motion up until the completion of Step 3. After Step 3, the ownership of the motion is transferred to the assembly.

parliamentarian A person who is an expert in parliamentary procedure and is hired by a person or an organization to give advice on matters of parliamentary law and procedure. Sometimes a parliamentarian is a member of the organization who has some knowledge of parliamentary procedure and is used as a parliamentary resource during the meeting.

parliamentary authority The set of rules a group adopts as the rules that will govern them. The parliamentary manual adopted by the organization, usually in its bylaws, to serve as the governing authority. *Robert's Rules* is the parliamentary authority for the vast majority of the organizations in the United States and for many organizations in other countries.

Parliamentary Inquiry A question directed to the presiding officer concerning parliamentary law or the organization's rules as they apply to the business at hand.

parliamentary law The established rules for the conduct of business in deliberative assemblies. The terms parliamentary law and parliamentary procedure are frequently used interchangeably.

parliamentary procedure A system of rules for the orderly conduct of business. The terms parliamentary law and parliamentary procedure are frequently used interchangeably.

pending A motion is considered on the floor when it has been stated by the presiding officer and has not yet been disposed of either permanently or temporarily. Pending and on the floor are interchangeable terms and refer to Step 4 in the processing of a motion.

plurality vote A method of voting in which the candidate or proposition receiving the largest number of votes is elected or selected. Use of decision by plurality vote in an election must be authorized in the bylaws.

Point of Information A nonparliamentary question about the business at hand.

Point of Order If a member feels the rules are not being followed, he or she can use this motion. It requires the chair to make a ruling and enforce the rules. Avoid overuse; save it for when someone's rights are being violated.

Point of Personal Privilege Another phrase used for a *Question of Privilege*. An urgent request or motion relating to the privileges of a member of the assembly.

policies and procedures Some organizations have additional detailed rules and guidelines regarding the administration of the organization.

poll A place where voting is conducted.

Postpone Definitely *See Postpone to a Certain Time.*

Postpone Indefinitely This motion, in effect, kills the main motion for the duration of the session without the group having to take a vote on the motion. If the motion passes, there is no vote on the main motion, which means there is no stand taken for or against the motion.

Postpone to a Certain Time or ***Postpone Definitely*** If the body needs more time to make a decision or if there is a time for consideration of this question that would be more convenient, this motion may be the answer. If a group meets quarterly or more frequently, the postponement cannot be beyond the next session.

preamble The first part of a resolution that contains the "whereas" clauses. It's the portion of the resolution that explains the reasons for the motion.

precedence of motions Pronounced *pre-SEED-ens*, it is a rank of motions indicating the order in which specific motions should be processed. When a motion is immediately pending, any motion above it on the Precedence of Motions is in order and any motion below it is out of order. In this book, the terms ladder of motions and precedence of motions are used interchangeably. Precedence of motions applies only to the following motion, in the following order: 1. *Fix the Time to Which to Adjourn.* 2. *Adjourn.* 3. *Recess.* 4. *Raise a Question of Privilege.* 5. *Call for the Orders of the Day.* 6. *Lay on the Table.* 7. *Previous Question.* 8. *Limit or Extend Limits of Debate.* 9. *Postpone Definitely.* 10. *Commit* or *Refer to a Committee.* 11. *Secondary Amendment—Amend* an amendment. 12. *Primary Amendment—Amend* a motion. 13. *Postpone Indefinitely.* 14. *MAIN MOTION.*

precedent A decision or course of action that serves as a rule for future determinations in similar cases.

preferential voting A method of voting in which members may express more than one preference on a single ballot. It's useful in ballot voting when it's impractical to reballot if no candidate was elected on the first ballot. This method of voting can only be used if authorized in the bylaws.

present A member who is physically in attendance in the meeting.

present and voting A member who is physically present at the meeting and who casts a vote on a motion. A member who abstains is not considered present and voting.

preside The chairing of a meeting.

president The chief officer of an organization. One of the duties of the president is usually to serve as presiding officer at the meetings of the organization.

president-elect A person elected to the office of president one full term before serving as president. By being elected to the office of president-elect, the person is elected to serve a term as president-elect and then a term as president.

presiding officer The person in charge of the meeting. Presiding officer and chair are interchangeable terms. They both are sometimes used to refer to the president of the organization when the president is conducting the meeting.

prevailing side The affirmative if the motion passed and the negative if the motion failed. A person is said to have voted on the prevailing side if that member voted yes on a motion that passed or no on a motion that failed.

previous notice An official announcement, given verbally or in writing, of an item of business that will be introduced at the meeting. Certain motions require previous notice.

Previous Question The effect of this motion is to immediately stop debate on the primary motion and any amendments and to move immediately to a vote on the motion. It must be seconded, no debate is allowed, and a two-thirds vote is needed to close debate.

primary amendment A proposed change to the main motion.

privileged motions Motions that don't relate to the main motion or pending business but relate directly to the members and the organization. They are matters of such urgency that, without debate, they can interrupt the consideration of anything else. Motions in this classification include *Fix the Time to Which to Adjourn*, *Adjourn*, *Recess*, *Question of Privilege*, and *Call for the Orders of the Day*.

pro tem Temporary or for the time being, as in secretary pro tem.

professional parliamentarian An expert in parliamentary procedure who has earned one or both of the following designations: Professional Registered Parliamentarian (PRP) through the National Association of Parliamentarians; Certified Professional Parliamentarian (CPP) through the American Institute of Parliamentarians.

program A schedule of the business to be considered at a meeting or convention. Program can also refer to a nonbusiness portion of the agenda in which a guest speaker gives a presentation.

proviso A condition that is applied to a change in the bylaws. It usually delays the effective date of the change made in the bylaws. It's not a part of the bylaws. All provisos should be put on a separate sheet of paper at the end of the document and removed after they are no longer in effect.

proxy voting A proxy vote can be cast when one member has given written authorization for another member (or nonmember) to vote on his or her behalf. The format of the written authorization for a proxy vote may be given in the bylaws. When the bylaws include a provision for proxy voting, they frequently limit the number of proxy votes one person may carry, as well as whether the person carrying the proxy must be a member, so be sure to check that in advance of the meeting. The proxy vote is only counted in determining a quorum for the meeting if so stated in the bylaws. Proxy voting is not allowed unless expressly authorized in the bylaws. Many state statutes have rules regarding proxy voting.

PRP A Professional Registered Parliamentarian; an individual who has been registered by the National Association of Parliamentarians on the basis of passing a course covering advanced knowledge of parliamentary law and procedure according to *Robert's Rules of Order Newly Revised.* During the examination the person must demonstrate abilities in presiding, serving as parliamentarian, and teaching parliamentary procedure.

putting the question Step 5 in the processing of the motion. It involves the presiding officer placing the motion before the members for a vote.

qualified The limiting of a motion or a vote in a specific manner. For example, if a main motion, a primary amendment, a secondary amendment, and a motion to *Postpone Definitely* are all pending and a member moves the *Previous Question* on the motion to *Postpone Definitely*, the secondary amendment and the primary amendment. In this example the *Previous Question* motion is qualified because it does not apply to all four pending motions, only three of them. It does not apply to the main motion.

quarterly time interval Two meetings are considered to be held within a quarterly time interval if the second meeting is held any time during the calendar month three months later than the calendar month in which the first meeting was held.

quasi committee of the whole "As if in" committee of the whole. The entire assembly acts as a committee to discuss a motion or issue more informally. Unlike the committee of the whole, the presiding officer remains in the chair.

question A proposal that the group take a specific action or stand. Motion and question are interchangeable terms.

Question of Privilege An urgent request or motion relating to the privileges of the assembly or a member.

quorum The number of voting members who must be present in order that business can be legally transacted.

Raise a Question of Privilege To bring an urgent request or a main motion relating to the rights of either the assembly or an individual up for immediate consideration. It may interrupt business.

ratify A motion that confirms or validates a previously taken action that needs assembly approval to become legal.

receive a report To permit or cause a report to be presented; to hear a report.

recess A short interruption that does not close the meeting. After the recess, business resumes at exactly the point where it was interrupted.

recognize a member The acknowledgement by the presiding officer that a member has the right to address the assembly.

recommendation A proposal that the body take a specific action. It's usually made by a committee, a board, or an officer.

recommit A motion to *Refer* an issue or a motion back to a committee.

Reconsider This motion enables the majority of the assembly to bring back for further consideration a motion that has been voted on. Limitations: only a member who voted on the prevailing side can make this motion, and in an ordinary meeting of an organization this motion can be made only on the same day the vote to be *Reconsidered* was taken.

Reconsider and Enter in the Minutes An incredibly unusual form of the motion to *Reconsider.* The effect of this motion is that action on the motion to be *Reconsidered* stops and the original motion cannot be *Reconsidered* until a later day. Thus, it prevents an unrepresentative group from making a decision on an issue.

recount To count the vote again.

Refer to a Committee or ***Commit*** This motion sends the main motion to a smaller group (a committee) for further examination and refinement before the body votes on it. Be sure to be specific—which committee, size of committee, the report-back date, and so on.

regular meeting A business meeting of a permanent group that is held at regular intervals (weekly, monthly, quarterly, and so on). The meetings are held when prescribed in the bylaws, the standing rules, or through a motion of the group, usually adopted at the beginning of the administrative year. Each meeting is a separate session. Any business that falls within the organization's objects can be conducted at a regular meeting.

renewal of a motion A motion is considered renewed if it was made and disposed of without being adopted and then made again. The rules concerning renewal of a motion are extensive and are based upon the principle that an assembly should not have to deal with the same motion or substantially the same motion more than one time in a single session.

Repeal Another word for the motion to *Rescind.*

report A formal communication from a committee, board, or officer to the assembly. The report can be written or oral.

reporting member The member of the committee or board that is presenting the committee or board report to the members. The chairman of a committee is usually the reporting member.

Request Any petition by a member—through the presiding officer—to the assembly that is growing out of the business of the assembly.

Request to Be Excused from a Duty If a member believes he or she cannot fulfill a required duty, either as a member or as an officer, he or she can move to *Request to Be Excused from a Duty.* If the motion passes, he is excused from the duty.

Request to Read Papers A call from a member to the assembly for permission to read from any paper or book. Reading from a paper or book is not allowed without permission from the assembly.

Rescind This motion allows the assembly to *Repeal* an action previously taken. This motion can be applied to any previously adopted motion, provided that none of the actions involved have been carried out such that it is too late to undo.

resignation A request, usually written, to relinquish an office, position, appointment, or membership.

resolution A formal form of a motion that usually includes reasons as "whereas" clauses and the action as a "resolved" clause(s).

resolved clause The last part of a formal resolution. This part is the portion that specifies the action or position to be taken.

revision of the bylaws A complete rewrite of the bylaws that is presented as a new document. When presented, the proposed revision can be amended without limitation. There is a single vote taken at the end to determine if the proposed revision, as amended, will replace the current bylaws.

rising counted vote A method of voting in which the members express their vote by standing, and then those standing are counted and the number is reported to the presiding officer. "Those in favor of the motion, please stand and remain standing until counted. [pause] Please be seated. Those opposed to the motion, please stand and remain standing until counted. [pause] Please be seated."

rising vote A method of voting in which the members express their vote by standing. "Those in favor of the motion, please stand. [pause] Please be seated. Those opposed to the motion, please stand. [pause] Please be seated."

Robert's Rules A term used to refer to any of the manuals on parliamentary procedure written by Henry M. Robert or based on the manuals he wrote.

roll call vote A method of voting in which the voting members' names are called and each member states his or her vote: "The secretary will now call the roll." This method of voting has the exact opposite effect of a ballot vote in that it places in the record how each member voted. It should only be used when the members are responsible to a particular constituency who has a right to know how they voted. It is frequently required of public bodies, such as city councils or school boards.

RP A Registered Parliamentarian through the National Association of Parliamentarians (NAP). To become an RP, a person must pass a written examination covering *Robert's Rules of Order Newly Revised.*

rules of order Written sets of laws of parliamentary procedure by which an organization conducts its business.

ruling A decision made by the presiding officer. If members of the assembly disagree with the decision, they can *Appeal* the decision.

scope of notice A concept that applies to motions that require previous notice. It requires that the amendment fall within the range that is created by what currently exists and by what is proposed in the advance notice of the amendment.

script Written directions of what is to be said, by whom, and when during the meeting. A script serves as a cheat sheet for the presiding officer or the member as he or she tries to conduct or participate in a meeting. The amount of detail in the script varies with the person writing the script and the person using the script.

second An indication by a voting member, other than the person who made the motion, that he or she publicly agrees that the proposed motion should be considered. In seconding a motion, the member is only indicating agreement that the assembly should consider the motion, not necessarily agreement with the motion.

secondary amendment A proposed change to the primary amendment. This form of amendment is not simply the second amendment made; it must *Amend* the primary amendment.

secondary motion A motion that may be made while another motion is pending. It includes subsidiary motions, privileged motions, and incidental motions.

seconder The member who seconds the motion.

secret ballot A form of voting in which the vote of a member is not disclosed. It usually involves slips of paper on which the voter marks his vote.

secretary The recording officer whose duty it is to maintain the records of the organization.

select committee *See* special committee.

sergeant-at-arms A position in some organizations whose job it is to help preserve order at the meeting, following the direction of the presiding officer.

seriatim *See Consideration by Paragraph or Seriatim.*

session A meeting or a series of connected meetings as in a convention.

show of hands vote A method of voting in which the members express their vote by raising their hand. "All those in favor of the motion, please raise your hand. [pause] Please lower your hand. Those opposed to the motion, please raise your hand. [pause] Please lower your hand."

signed ballot A form of roll call vote that is used in large assemblies to save time. The member writes "yes" or "no" on the paper and signs it. The votes are then recorded in the minutes just as they would be if there had been a roll call vote.

silent A term used to describe the absence of an issue in a document. For example, if there is nothing in the bylaws on a particular issue, one might say the bylaws are silent on that issue.

silent assent A slang term that is interchangeable with general consent and unanimous consent, it is a method of avoiding the formality of a vote by getting agreement of everyone in the meeting.

simple majority A majority—more than half.

sine die Pronounced *SIGN-ee DYE-ee.* Literally means "without day." To *Adjourn* sine die means it's the final adjournment of an assembly. The last meeting of the convention is said to A*djourn* sine die.

single slate A list of candidates for office or positions that has the name of only one candidate for each office or position.

skeletal minutes A tool to assist in the minutes-writing process. These are minutes prepared in advance of a meeting or convention that include all that will be occurring and the order in which it will occur. They contain many blank spaces that are filled in during the meeting by the person(s) in charge of the minutes. They are prepared using the agenda and/or the script for the meeting.

slate A list of candidates for office. The report of the nominating committee is usually referred to as the slate of candidates.

speaker Usually refers to the person who has the floor. In some organizations it refers to the presiding officer of the assembly, as in the Speaker of the House.

special committee A committee that is formed to perform a particular function. After it gives its final report, it ceases to exist. Also referred to as a select committee or an ad hoc committee.

special meeting A meeting called at a special time for a specific purpose. Notice of the time, place, and purpose of the meeting must be included in the information sent to all of the members regarding the meeting—referred to as the call of the meeting. Only business that was specified in the call of the meeting can be transacted at the meeting. A group cannot hold a special meeting unless special meetings are authorized in the bylaws. Special meetings are usually held for emergency purposes—things that were not, nor could be, planned for in advance.

special orders This category of the agenda is for matters that have previously been assigned a special priority, including matters the bylaws require to be considered at a particular meeting.

special rules of order The rules contained in the parliamentary authority are called the rules of order. Sometimes organizations feel a need to have additional rules of order, called special rules of order, that differ from the parliamentary authority.

staggered terms Terms of office of a board or committee arranged in such a way that only a percentage of the terms end at the same time.

stand at ease A brief pause, without a *Recess*, that is called by the presiding officer without objection.

standing committee A committee appointed for a definitive time (frequently a year), usually listed in the bylaws, that performs ongoing functions.

standing rules Rules adopted by an organization that are administrative in nature rather than procedural. Convention standing rules are rules adopted by the convention's delegates and are procedural in nature.

state statutes Incorporated organizations are governed by the state statutes of the state in which they are incorporated. These statutes are usually available through the secretary of state's office or the state attorney general's office and are available on the Internet.

state the question This refers to the third step in the processing of a motion. During this step, the presiding officer restates the motion, thus formally placing it before the body.

straw poll A method of informally determining where the assembly stands on an issue. It is not allowed because it does not take an action and is therefore considered dilatory.

Sturgis Another parliamentary authority whose original book *Sturgis Standard Code of Parliamentary Procedure* has been updated by the American Institute of Parliamentarians.

subcommittee A committee of a committee, usually formed for the purpose of study and investigation of certain matters, that reports its findings to the committee that formed it.

subsidiary motions Motions that aid the assembly in treating or disposing of a motion. They are in order only from the time the motion has been stated by the chair until the chair begins to take a vote on that motion. Motions in this classification include *Lay on the Table*, *Previous Question*, *Limit* or *Extend Limits of Debate*, *Postpone to a Certain Time (Postpone Definitely)*, *Commit* or *Refer*, *Amend*, and *Postpone Indefinitely*.

substitute amendment An *Amendment* that proposes to strike out a paragraph or more and to insert another in its place.

Suspend the Rules This motion is used when the assembly wants to do something that violates its own rules. This motion does not apply to the organization's bylaws; local, state, or national law; or fundamental principles of parliamentary law. An appropriate suspension of the rules would be a motion to change the agenda, or the prescribed meeting time. An inappropriate suspension of the rules would be to allow nonmembers the same voting rights as members.

sustain To support and uphold a ruling.

sustain the decision of the chair To support and uphold a ruling made by the chair in an *Appeal from the Decision of the Chair* motion. When the *Appeal* motion is put to a vote, the wording used is: "Those in favor of sustaining the decision of the chair …."

synchronous meetings Electronic meetings that occur when participants are in different places at the same time. Venues of the synchronous meetings include, but are definitely not limited to, telephone conferencing, video and web conferencing, chat room, instant messaging, and in-person meetings where some members attend electronically.

table A shortcut term for the motion *Lay on the Table.*

Take from the Table The effect of this motion is to resume consideration of a motion that was *Laid on the Table* earlier in the present session or in the previous session of the organization. When a motion is *Taken from the Table*, it has everything adhering to it exactly as it was when it was *Laid on the Table.*

teleconference A meeting in which the participants are connected by telephone technology or other technology that allows someone from a distance to participate.

tellers People elected or appointed to count votes.

term of office The duration of the period for which a person is elected or appointed to an office or position.

tie vote An equal number of affirmative and negative votes. It is not required that tie votes be broken since, if a majority vote is needed, the motion fails because it lacks a majority vote.

treasurer The officer entrusted with the custody of the organization's funds and the maintenance of the financial records of the organization.

two-thirds vote Having at least twice as many votes in favor of a motion as there were against the motion.

unanimous Without dissent; no votes were cast on the losing side.

unanimous ballot A ballot cast by the secretary, or other member, to elect an uncontested candidate to an office. If the bylaws require a ballot vote, it is out of order since it prevents a member from casting a write-in ballot. After an election by ballot in which the ballot was not unanimous, a motion to make the ballot unanimous would only be in order if that vote was taken by ballot and was unanimous. This requirement protects the member from revealing his vote.

unanimous consent *See* general consent.

unanimous vote A vote in which everyone present and voting voted on the prevailing side. No one voted on the losing side of the question.

undebatable No debate is allowed. Certain motions are undebatable. In essence, Step 4 in the processing of a motion is skipped.

unfinished business A portion of the agenda that includes motions that have been carried over from the previous meeting as a result of that meeting having adjourned without completing its order of business. It also includes motions postponed from the previous meeting.

unqualified A motion or vote that does not have any limitations placed on it. For example, if the vote needed is a majority vote of the entire membership, that is a qualified vote, but if the vote needed is only a majority vote, that is an unqualified vote.

vacancy An office or position that is unfilled or unoccupied.

vacate the chair To temporarily relinquish the chair so that the presiding officer can participate in debate.

vice chairman A member of the committee who is next in authority to the chairman.

vice president A member of the organization who is next in authority to the president, unless the organization has a president-elect. The bylaws should list the duties and responsibilities of this position.

videoconference A meeting in which the members participate using videoconferencing technology.

viva voce A vote by voice.

voice vote A method of voting in which the members express their vote vocally. "All those in favor, say aye. [pause] All those opposed, say no." (If the chair is in doubt of the results of a voice vote, the chair should state, "The chair is in doubt, and therefore a rising [or counted] vote will be taken." Then proceed with a rising or counted vote.)

vote A formal expression of will, opinion, or choice by members of an assembly in regard to a matter submitted to it.

vote by acclimation An election by unanimous consent.

vote immediately The result of the adoption of the *Previous Question* motion. The members will immediately vote on the motion.

voting by mail Only when specifically authorized in the bylaws can an organization conduct a vote by mail. If there is a vote requirement or a quorum requirement, the ballot serves as the member being "present." As electronic communication is becoming more and more popular, organizations are relying on e-mail as a method of casting mail ballots. Although there are some problems associated with ballots by e-mail, they are clearly a money- and time-saving approach, especially for large national and international organizations.

with power A term used to describe a committee that is authorized to take action on the matter that is referred to it.

Withdraw a Motion A request by the mover of a motion to remove the motion from consideration. After the motion has been stated by the presiding officer, it belongs to the assembly and the assembly's permission (majority vote) is needed to *Withdraw* the motion.

write-in vote A vote cast, on a written ballot vote, for a person who was not nominated for the position.

yield Give way to. A pending motion yields to one of higher rank on the precedence of motions list.

yielding the floor A speaker giving part of his or her speaking time to another speaker. While this practice is allowed in some legislative bodies, it is not allowed in deliberative assemblies, unless specifically authorized in the rules.

Appendix B

Basic Information on Motions

Here's a handy table covering the basic characteristics of motions. Feel free to copy it and refer to it during meetings. The motions in bold constitute the ladder of motions.

Motion	Purpose	Interrupt Speaker?	Second Needed?	Debatable?	Amendable?	Vote Needed
1. Fix the Time to Which to Adjourn	Sets the time for a continued meeting	No	Yes	No[1]	Yes	Majority
2. Adjourn	Closes the meeting	No	Yes	No	No	Majority
3. Recess	Establishes a brief break	No	Yes	No[2]	Yes	Majority
4. Raise a Question of Privilege	Asks an urgent question regarding rights	Yes	No	No	No	Ruled by chair
5. Call for Orders of the Day	Requires that the meeting follow the agenda	Yes	No	No	No	One member
6. Lay on the Table	Puts the motion aside for later consideration	No	Yes	No	No	Majority
7. Previous Question	Ends debate and moves directly to the vote	No	Yes	No	No	Two-thirds
8. Limit* or *Extend Limits of Debate	Changes the debate limits	No	Yes	No	Yes	Two-thirds
9. Postpone to a Certain Time	Puts off the motion to a specific time	No	Yes	Yes	Yes	Majority[3]
10. Commit or Refer	Refers the motion to a committee	No	Yes	Yes	Yes	Majority
***11. Amend* an amendment (secondary amendment)**	Proposes a change to an amendment	No	Yes	Yes[4]	No	Majority

Motion	Purpose	Interrupt Speaker?	Second Needed?	Debatable?	Amendable?	Vote Needed
12. *Amend* a motion or resolution (primary amendment)	Proposes a change to a main motion	No	Yes	Yes[4]	Yes	Majority
13. Postpone Indefinitely	Kills the motion	No	Yes	Yes	No	Majority
14. MAIN MOTION	Brings business before the assembly	No	Yes	Yes	Yes	Majority

1 Is debatable when another meeting is scheduled for the same or next day or if the motion is made while no question is pending

2 Unless no question is pending

3 Majority, unless it makes the question a special order

4 If the motion it is being applied to is debatable

Note: Motions above are in the order of precedence of motions

Motion	Purpose	Interrupt Speaker?	Second Needed?	Debatable?	Amendable?	Vote Needed
Point of Order	Requests that the rules be followed	Yes	No	No	No	Ruled by chair
Appeal from the Decision of the Chair	Challenges a ruling of the chair	Yes	Yes	Depends[4]	No	Majority[5]
Suspend the Rules	Allows the group to violate the rules (not bylaws)	No	Yes	No	No	Two-thirds
Objection to Consideration	Keeps the motion from being considered	Yes[6]	No	No	No	Two-thirds[7]
Division of the Question	Separates consideration of the motion	No	Yes	No	Yes	Majority
Division of the Assembly	Requires a standing vote	Yes	No	No	No	One member
Parliamentary Inquiry or *Point of Information*	Allows a member to ask a question about the business at hand	Yes	No	No	No	Responded to by chair
Withdraw a Motion (after stated by the chair)	Removes a motion from consideration	Yes	Depends[8]	No	No	Majority

Motion	Purpose	Interrupt Speaker?	Second Needed?	Debatable?	Amendable?	Vote Needed
Take from the Table	Resumes consideration of a motion that was *Laid on the Table*	No	Yes	No	No	Majority
Reconsider	Considers a motion again	Yes[9]	Yes	Depends[10]	No	Majority
Rescind or *Amend Something Previously Adopted*	Repeals a previously adopted motion or amends it after it has been adopted	No	Yes	Yes	Yes	Depends[11]

4 If the motion it is being applied to is debatable

5 Majority in negative required to reverse chair's decision

6 When another member has been assigned the floor, until debate has begun or a subsidiary motion has been stated by the chair

7 Two thirds against consideration sustains objection

8 Yes, if the motion is made by the person requesting permission; no, if made by another member

9 When another member has been assigned the floor, but not after he or she has begun to speak

10 Only if the motion to be reconsidered is debatable

11 Requires a) a majority with notice, b) two thirds, or c) majority of entire membership

Appendix C

What Do I Say? Scripts for the Chair and Members

Ever wonder how in the world presiding officers remember every step in the motion-making process? While it's certainly the case that many presiding officers have a complete understanding of parliamentary procedure and know exactly what to say in almost every circumstance, a lot of presiding officers rely on what some might call "cheat sheets" but in the parliamentary world are called "scripts." That's right—they read from a prepared document that tells them exactly what they need to say and do for any particular motion.

A script is written directions of what is to be said, when, and by whom during the meeting. The script is knowledge that can give you not only the correct words to say but the confidence to say them. When you use the correct words, people are more likely to listen and believe you. Scripts can help you use the correct words whether you are the presiding officer or a member in attendance at the meeting.

Main Motion Script

What follows is the script for a main motion. It provides the presiding officer and the members with the words to say when processing a main motion.

Script: Main Motion

Member:	I move that ….
Chair:	Is there a second to the motion? [This statement is eliminated if a member calls out "second" or if the motion is made on behalf of a committee.]
Second Member:	I second the motion.
Chair:	It is moved and seconded that [state the motion]. Is there any discussion? [Because the maker of the motion has first right to speak on the motion, the chair should call on the maker of the motion first.]
	[It is during this time that a motion is considered pending, and secondary motions may be applied to it.]
	[After discussion] Is there any further discussion? Are you ready for the question? [Pause] The question is on the adoption of the motion to [clearly restate the motion].
	Voice vote:
	Those in favor, say *aye*. [Pause for response]
	Those opposed, say *no*.

[If the chair is in doubt of the results of a voice vote, the chair should state, "The chair is in doubt. Therefore, a rising (or counted) vote will be taken." Then proceed with a rising or counted vote.]

Show of hands vote:

Those in favor of the motion, please raise your hand. [Pause] Please lower your hand. Those opposed to the motion, please raise your hand. [Pause] Please lower your hand.

Rising vote:

Those in favor of the motion, please stand. [Pause] Please be seated. Those opposed to the motion, please stand. [Pause] Please be seated.

Ballot vote:

Please mark your ballots clearly, fold them one time, and hand them directly to a teller.

Roll call vote:

The clerk will now call the roll.

Chair: [Announces the voting results]

Uncounted voice, rising, or show of hands vote:

The affirmative has it, and the motion is adopted. We will [state the effect of the vote]. The next business in order is ….

or

continues

continued

The negative has it, and the motion is lost [state the effect of the vote]. The next business in order is ….

Counted majority vote:

There are _____ votes in the affirmative and _____ votes in the negative. There is a majority in the affirmative, and the motion is adopted. We will [state the effect of the vote]. The next business in order is ….

or

There are _____ votes in the affirmative and _____ votes in the negative. There is less than a majority in the affirmative, and the motion is lost [state the effect of the vote]. The next business in order is ….

Counted two-thirds vote:

There are _____ votes in the affirmative and _____ votes in the negative. There are two thirds in the affirmative, and the motion is adopted. We will [state the effect of the vote]. The next business in order is ….

or

There are _____ votes in the affirmative and _____ votes in the negative. There are less than two thirds in the affirmative, and the motion is lost [state the effect of the vote]. The next business in order is ….

On my website, www.nancysylvester.com, you will find scripts for the most commonly used motions. I encourage you to print them out and have them with you during all meetings. That way, you will be prepared for almost anything that may come your way.

On my website, you will find a script for each of the following motions:

- *Fix the Time to Which to Adjourn*
- *Adjourn*
- *Recess*
- *Question of Privilege*
- *Question of Privilege Motion*
- *Call for the Orders of the Day*
- *Lay on the Table*
- *Previous Question*
- *Limit* or *Extend the Limit of Debate*
- *Postpone Definitely* or *Postpone to a Certain Time*
- *Commit* or *Refer*
- *Amend*
- *Postpone Indefinitely*
- *Point of Order*
- *Appeal from the Decision of the Chair*
- *Suspend the Rules*
- *Objection to the Consideration of a Question*
- *Division of the Question*
- *Division of the Assembly*
- *Rescind*
- *Amend Something Previously Adopted*
- *Take from the Table*
- *Reconsider*

Also on my website, you will find the beginning of a convention script. I hope you find it helpful as the building block for any convention script you might need.

Board Meeting Agenda and Script

What follows is an agenda for a postconvention board meeting and the script that corresponds with that agenda. When preparing a script, it is best to use the agenda as a guide. A script for a board meeting can be very helpful for the presiding officer because it allows him or her to pay attention to what is going on in the moment at the meeting instead of thinking about what has to be done next.

One method of formatting the script that works well is to put it in a two-column table format. The first column lists the agenda item and any voting results (**bolded** in the example given here). The second column is for words said by the presiding officer. In scripts, put in brackets all instructions that are not actually said during the meeting.

ASSOCIATION OF COMPLETE IDIOTS

Postconvention Board of Directors Meeting Agenda
Date, Time, and Place

1. Pledge of allegiance and inspiration .... Member A
2. Introductions and welcome—timekeeper plan .... President
3. Meeting appointments .... President

    Minutes Approval Committee: Member B, Chairman; Member C; and Member D

    Tellers: Member E, Chairman; Member F; Member G

    Timekeeper: Member H

4. Report of president .... President
    a) Appointments:
        1. Parliamentarian
        2. Standing and special committees (approved by the Executive Committee)
    b) Board meeting dates (board book)
    c) Committee reporting to president process (board book)
5. Report of the Executive Committee ...... Member I, Secretary
6. Report of ACI Fundraiser Committee .... Member J
7. Special Orders .... President
    a) Election of two members to Nominating Committee
    b) Approval of 20XX budget
    c) Appointment to ACI Policies Committee
8. New Business .... President
9. Announcements .... President
10. Adjournment .... President

ASSOCIATION OF COMPLETE IDIOTS

Postconvention Board of Directors Meeting Script
Date, Time, and Place

Call to Order	The 20XX postconvention board meeting of the Association of Complete Idiots will come to order. [Rap Gavel]
1. Pledge of allegiance and inspiration	The assembly will please stand and join in the pledge of allegiance to the flag of the United States. [Pledge to U.S. flag] The inspiration will be given by Member A. [Inspiration] Thank you, Member A, for those most appropriate words of inspiration to begin our first board meeting.
2. Introductions and welcome—timekeeper plan	[Welcome comments] Please go around the room and each briefly introduce yourself, telling your name, where you are from, and how long you have been a member of ACI. [Each board member introduces him- or herself] During this meeting and all of our meetings we will have a timekeeper. The timekeeper will time each agenda item, keeping the chair aware of the time spent on each item. The time-keeper will also time each speaker at the call of the president, if determined helpful. If so, there will be a three-minute time limit.

3. Meeting appointments	At this time, the Chair wishes to announce the appointment of meeting committees. The Chair appoints the following to the Minutes Approval Committee: Member B, Chairman; Member C; and Member D. The Chair appoints the following to the Tellers Committee: Member E, Chairman; Member F; and Member G.
VOTE: No vote required	The Chair appoints Member H as the timekeeper.
4. Report of president	The Chair makes the following appointment: Nonmember A as parliamentarian. In that position, she will also be serving as an advisor to the Executive Committee, the Bylaws Committee, and the ACI Policies Committee. The Chair has made numerous Standing and Special Committee appointments that, according to our bylaws, have been approved by the Executive Committee. Those appointments can be found in your board book. The board meeting dates and other important dates can be found in the board book. The process for the committee chairman and appointed positions to report to the president can be found in your board book. Please turn to that page and let's review that process together.

continues

continued

	[Review process]
5. Report of the Executive Committee	The Chair calls on Member I, ACI Secretary, to present the report of the Executive Committee.
	[Secretary gives report]
	Thank you, Member I, for your report.
6. Report of ACI Fundraiser Committee	The Chair calls on Member J to give the report of the ACI Fundraiser Committee.
	[Member J gives report]
	Thank you, Member J, for your report.
7. Special Orders	The next business in order is Special Orders.
Election of two members to Nominating Committee	The first business in order under Special Orders is the election of two members to the Nominating Committee. Article 11, Section 1, A, 1, a, of the ACI Bylaws reads: "The Nominating Committee shall be composed of five members, the chairman and two members elected by the membership at the annual convention and two members elected by the Board of Directors."
	The floor is open for nominations.
	[Pause]
	[Repeat name of person nominated]
VOTE: Majority	The vote required is a majority. Tellers, please pass out the ballots.

The following members have been nominated:

____

____

____

____

____

You may vote for two candidates. Please vote now.

Tellers, please collect the ballots.

[After ballots are collected]

We will take a 15-minute recess while tellers count the ballots.

[Recess]

The meeting will come to order.

The chair calls upon Member E, Chairman of the Tellers Committee, to give the report of that committee.

[Member E reads tellers' report]

[President rereads tellers' report]

____________________________ and ____________________________ have received a majority vote and are elected to the Nominating Committee.

They will serve on that committee with the chairman and the other two members who were just elected at the annual convention.

continues

continued

Approval of 20XX budget	The next business in order is the approval of the 20XX budget. Article VI, Section 2 of the ACI Bylaws reads that the board of directors shall "adopt an annual budget at its first meeting." You will find the proposed budget in your board book behind the financial tab. The Chair calls upon Member K, chair of the Finance Committee. [Member K: On behalf of the finance committee, I move that we adopt the 20XX budget as presented in the board book.] Since this motion comes from a committee, it does not need a second. The motion before you is that we adopt the 20XX budget as presented in the board book. Is there any discussion? [After discussion] Is there any further discussion? Are you ready for the question? [Pause] The question is on the adoption of the motion that we adopt the 20XX budget as presented in the board book.
VOTE: Majority Vote	Those in favor of adopting the 20XX budget, please raise your hand. [Pause] Please lower your hand.

	Those opposed to adopting the 20XX budget, please raise your hand. [Pause] Please lower your hand.
	There being a majority vote in the affirmative, the motion is adopted. We have approved the 20XX budget as presented [or as amended], and the next item of business is the appointment to the Policies Committee.
	or
	There being less than a majority vote in the affirmative, the motion fails. We have not approved the 20XX budget as presented [or as amended], and the next item of business is the appointment to the Policies Committee.
Appointment to ACI Policies Committee	The members of the Policies Committee will be Member L, Chairman; Member M; and Member N; with Nonmember A, our parliamentarian, serving as advisor to the committee.
VOTE: No Vote Required	
8. New Business	The next business in order is New Business.
	Is there any new business to come before the board at this time?
9. Announcements	[Make any necessary announcements]
	Are there any further announcements?

continues

continued

10. Adjournment	If there is no further business to come before this board, this meeting is adjourned, and we will meet again on [date] in [location].

Appendix D

What Do I Record? More Guidance on Minutes and Forms

While minutes of a meeting are crucial in documenting the decisions made by the organization, they are seen as daunting. In Chapter 18, I tried to dispel the idea that they should be long and involved. Here, I give you examples and guidance that will help you dread minutes no more—okay, maybe dread them less than you currently do!

What to Put in the Minutes (and What to Leave Out)

As we learned in Chapter 18, minutes are the written record of the proceedings of a deliberative assembly. They are a record of what was *done* at the meeting, not what was *said* at the meeting. In Chapter 18, you will find *Robert's* recommendation of the content of the minutes. A minutes template is available in Chapter 18, and a downloadable template is also available on my website at www.nancysylvester.com. In this appendix you will find various examples of different kinds of minutes as well as information and forms for the content of minutes, including committee reports and reports by the tellers committee. I hope you find them helpful and useful.

Sample Board Meeting Minutes

In Appendix C under the heading "Board Meeting Agenda and Script," you will find a sample agenda and script for a board meeting. Here is an example of what the minutes from that board meeting might look like.

Minutes of the Association of Complete Idiots

Postconvention Board of Directors Meeting

November 13, 20xx

Call to Order: A regular meeting of the Association of Complete Idiots Board of Directors was held in Convention City, Texas, on November 13, 20XX. The meeting convened at 8:03 A.M. with President P presiding and Member I as secretary.

Members in Attendance: Member A, Member B, Member C, Member D, Member E, Member F, Member G, Member H, Member I, Member J, Member K, Member L, Member M, Member N, and Member P.

***Members Not in Attendance*:** None, all members were in attendance.

1. ***Pledge of Allegiance and Inspiration.*** President P led the board in the Pledge of Allegiance to the flag of the United States and then called on Member A for the inspiration.
2. ***Introductions and Welcome—Timekeeper Plan.*** President P welcomed the members of the Board of Directors and had each member introduce him- or herself. She then explained that there will be a timekeeper for this and all board meetings. The timekeeper will time each agenda item and each speaker at the call of the president. The individual time limit is three minutes.

3. *Meeting Appointments.* The President made the following appointments: **Minutes Approval Committee: Member B, Chairman; Member C; and Member D. Tellers Committee: Member E, Chairman; Member F; and Member G. Timekeeper: Member H.**

4. *Report of President.* The President made the following appointment: Nonmember A as Parliamentarian, indicating that in this position she will also be serving as an advisor to the Executive Committee, the Bylaws Committee, and the ACI Policies Committee.

The President directed members to the board book where they will find the appointments made by the President to the standing and special committees. Those appointments have been approved by the Executive Committee. She also called attention to the board meeting dates and other important dates in the board book.

President P also reviewed the process for the committee chairmen and appointed positions to report to the President, which is also contained in the board book.

5. *Report of the Executive Committee.* Member I, ACI Secretary, gave the report of the Executive Committee.

6. *Report of ACI Fundraiser Committee.* Member J gave the report of the ACI Fundraiser Committee.

7. *Special Orders.* The President called for nominations for the two open positions on the Nominating Committee. The following members were nominated: Member A, Member C, Member D, and Member H.

   The election was conducted by ballot vote. Member E, Chairman of the Tellers Committee, gave the report of that committee. There were 15 votes cast. The number necessary for election was 8. Member A received 6 votes, Member C received 10 votes, Member D received 9 votes, and Member H received 5 votes. President P declared Member C and Member D elected to the Nominating Committee. They will

continues

continued

serve on that committee with the chairman and the other two members who were just elected at the annual convention.

Member K, Finance Committee Chairman, presented the 20XX budget and, on behalf of the Finance Committee, moved that the Board adopt the 20XX budget as presented in the board book. **MOTION PASSED.**

The President announced that the members of the Policies Committee will be Member L, Chairman; Member M; and Member N; with Nonmember A, our Parliamentarian, serving as advisor to the committee.

8. ***New Business.*** There was no new business.
9. ***Announcements.*** President P reminded the members of the dates of the next board meeting.
10. ***Adjournment.*** There was no further business to come before the Board, so President P adjourned the meeting at 4:32 P.M.

____________________ ____________________

Secretary Date of Approval

What Do Those Skeletal Minutes Look Like?

In Chapter 18, I covered the concept of skeletal minutes and promised to give you examples. Here they are! The first sample is the first few paragraphs of skeletal minutes of the third meeting of a convention. These will be used by the minutes approval committee to assist in preparing the minutes. The second is the first few paragraphs of the minutes for that meeting.

Sample Skeletal Minutes

The third meeting of the Seventeenth Annual Session of the American Association of Fun-Loving People was convened on August 9, 20XX, at _______ A.M. President Joyful presided and Harry Happy, secretary, was present.

The report of the Credentials Committee was presented by Geri Glad, Chairman.

Geri Glad submitted the list of delegates and alternates who had registered up until _______ A.M. The number of delegates registered was _________. On behalf of the Credentials Committee, Geri Glad moved that the revised roll of delegates submitted be the official roll of the voting members of the delegate body. **The motion PASSED or FAILED** [circle one]

or

Geri Glad reported there were no changes since the last report of the Credentials Committee, and the voting strength remained at ______.

President Joyful declared a quorum present.

Sample Minutes Prepared from Skeletal Minutes

The third meeting of the Seventeenth Annual Session of the American Association of Fun-Loving People was convened on August 9, 20XX, at 10:05 A.M. President Joyful presided and Harry Happy, secretary, was present.

The report of the Credentials Committee was presented by Geri Glad, Chairman. Geri Glad reported there were no changes since the last report of the Credentials Committee, and the voting strength remained at 555.

President Joyful declared a quorum present.

More Samples Please!

Here you will find a set of sample minutes of an organization that meets monthly.

Minutes of the Association of Fun-Loving People

Ain't-It-Fun Chapter

Meeting Date: April 1, 20XX

Call to Order: A regular meeting of the American Association of Fun-Loving People, Ain't-It-Fun Chapter, was held at the Fun-Fun-Fun Hotel in Ain't-It-Fun, North Dakota, on April 1, 20XX. The meeting was called to order at 6:00 P.M., by President Sally Never-Sad, and Mary Merry, secretary, was present. President Never-Sad declared a quorum present.

Approval of Minutes: Motion was made by John Jolly to approve the minutes of the March 2, 20XX, meeting. **MOTION CARRIED.**

Officers' Reports:

Reports were given by the President and the Treasurer.

The Treasurer reported the balance on hand at the beginning of the reporting period as $100, receipts of $25 from dues, current disbursements of $25, and a balance on hand of $100. The report was filed for audit.

Committee Reports:

Finance Committee Chairman Sam Smiley reported on the motion to purchase a computer that was referred to the finance committee at the last meeting. The committee recommended that the members approve the motion with the amendment "not to exceed $3,000." After discussion and further amendment, the following motion was voted on: "We will purchase a PC-compatible computer at a price not to exceed $3,000." **MOTION CARRIED.**

Program Committee Chairman Gail Glee reported the plans for the program for the remainder of the calendar year.

Unfinished Business:

Paint Headquarters Building

Motion postponed from last month's meeting: "I move that we paint the headquarters building green." After discussion and amendment, the following motion was voted on: "I move that we paint the headquarters building white." **MOTION CARRIED.**

New Business:

August Fundraiser

Motion: Moved by John Grin that "we sponsor a fundraiser in August. The details are to be worked out by a committee of three appointed by the president." **MOTION CARRIED.**

President Never-Sad appointed the following members to the August Fundraiser Committee: Mike Money, Cathy Cash, and Charlie Currency.

Adjournment: The meeting adjourned at 8:45 P.M.

____________________ ____________________

Secretary Date of Approval

American Association of Fun-Loving People

Ain't-It-Fun Chapter

How to Record That Heavily Amended Motion

Keeping in mind the principle that minutes are a record of what was done at a meeting instead of what was said at a meeting makes the recording in the minutes of a heavily amended motion a rather easy task. In Chapter 7, I gave an example of a main motion that had many secondary motions applied to it. Let's use it as an example.

The motions used in the example were:

- "I move that we purchase a computer."
- "I move to *Amend* the motion by adding the words 'not to exceed $2,000.'"

- "I move to *Amend* the amendment by striking '$2,000' and inserting '$4,000.'"
- "I move to *Postpone Definitely* this motion until our meeting next month."

If the motion to *Postpone Definitely* passed, the minutes would read as follows: "Judy Never-Ending moved that we purchase a computer. It was then moved to *Amend* the motion by adding the words 'not to exceed $2,000.' It was then moved to *Amend* the amendment by striking '$2,000' and inserting '$4,000.' It was then moved to *Postpone Definitely* this motion until our meeting next month. **MOTION TO POSTPONE CARRIED**"

If the motion to *Postpone Definitely* did not pass but the motion was completely processed at that meeting, the minutes would read as follows: "Judy Never-Ending moved and the motion was amended to read that 'we will purchase a computer, not to exceed $4,000.' **MOTION CARRIED.**"

Minutes as an Attendance Tracking Device

Frequently, the bylaws require members to attend a certain number of meetings or a certain percentage of meetings. This is particularly true of boards of directors. The minutes can provide a very easy method to track that attendance. Or if you want to deter poor attendance by keeping everyone informed of how many meetings each of the members has attended, this attendance tracking system is for you. Simply include the number of meetings that have occurred this year in the heading, and then after each board member or committee member's name include the number of meetings he or she has attended. It serves as a great tracking device. And you thought peer pressure only worked for teenagers!

The following example is from a board that has had seven meetings thus far this calendar year.

Minutes of the Association of Complete Idiots

Board of Directors Meeting [7]

DATE

Members in Attendance: Member A [7], Member B [7], Member D [6], Member E [7], Member F [6], Member G [7], Member I [5], Member J [7], Member L [7], Member M [7], Member N [3], and Member P [7].

Members Not in Attendance: Member C [4], Member H [6], Member K [5].

Format for Committee Report

Minutes also include committee reports, usually as an attachment to the official copy of the minutes. Here is a format for committee reports. If all of the committees in an organization follow the same format for their reports, it makes the meeting clearer and definitely adds to the clarity of the minutes.

COMMITTEE REPORT

COMMITTEE ______________________________

MEETING DATES ___________________________

ISSUES ADDRESSED BY COMMITTEE

DESCRIPTION OF THE WAY THE COMMITTEE PERFORMED TASK

INFORMATION AND FACTS OBTAINED

CONCLUSIONS DRAWN FROM OBTAINED INFORMATION

RECOMMENDATIONS

1.
2.
3.
4.

Format for Tellers' Report

In a ballot vote, whether for an election or for a motion that has multiple choices, the chair appoints a tellers committee whose job is to distribute, collect, and count the ballots and report the results. The report of the vote is referred to as the tellers' report. Since the tellers' report is entered in full in the minutes, I thought some guidance here might be helpful.

Procedures for Tellers

Let's begin by making sure that the tellers' report is accurate. That means that everyone involved in counting the votes knows how to count them—and I am not talking about knowing his or her numbers but the rules involved.

- TOTAL BALLOTS: All ballots are included in the total number of ballots cast, with the exception of blank ballots. Blank ballots are treated as scrap paper.
- LEGAL BALLOTS are votes on an official ballot, cast by a legal voter, and that clearly indicate the choice of the voter in the election.

  Where the voter's choice is not clear, the teller should consult with the Chairman of the Tellers and other members of the tellers' team in an effort to determine what the voter intended. If the tellers can agree unanimously on the evident intent of the voter, then the ballot must be counted as a legal vote.

  If there is no agreement and it is possible that the vote—or votes—could affect the result of the election, the Chairman of the Tellers must report that fact to the meeting Presiding Officer, and the assembly then determines what is to be done.

  A ballot may be marked with *up to* the allowed number of votes. If fewer votes are marked, or if one section on a multiple-section ballot is not valid, the rest of the ballot is still counted.

  A ballot is legal even if the name (or title) is misspelled or the directions are not exactly followed (for example, an X is used instead of a check mark).

If a blank ballot is folded with a marked ballot, the marked ballot is counted, and the blank ballot is disregarded.

- ILLEGAL BALLOTS are always counted in the total number of ballots cast. Illegal ballots include …

  Two or more marked ballots folded together.

  Votes for more candidates (or issues) than allowed.

  Unintelligible marked ballot.

- TALLYING: For tallying votes, the Chairman and the tellers have different duties:

  CHAIRMAN:

  1. The Chairman will unlock and open the ballot boxes in the presence of the tellers.
  2. The Chairman will provide each team with two tally sheets and at least three red/blue pencils/pens.
  3. The Chairman will monitor the counting process and be available to assist with questions.
  4. The Chairman will prepare the Tally Summary Sheet and the tellers' report, with committee signatures.
  5. The Chairman will return to the meeting room and, at the direction of the presiding officer, will read the report, not indicating who was elected. The presiding officer will reread the report and declare who was elected and/or if another election is needed.

  TELLERS:

  1. Ballots will be removed from the ballot boxes and counted in stacks of 25 with the members checking for illegal ballots.
  2. TEAMS of three will count the ballots at each table. One will call out the name (or issue number) and two will act as recorders each on separate tally sheets.
  3. Place the names of candidates (or issues) on each tally sheet—allowing lines between to provide ample space for tally marks.

4. MARKING: Each member of the team will start the tally with the same (red or blue) color across the tally sheet. The caller will mark each ballot by number as they are read, and each teller will mark after each candidate (or issue number) with the corresponding color. After the stack of 25 votes has been recorded, the team will change color (for example, from red to blue) for the next stack. If there is an error in the tally between the recorders, the last "color" will provide a limit on the number of ballots that must be recounted.
5. TALLY: After each five votes (11111) in any one category (candidate or issue), those tallying quietly say "Tally." If one teller fails to agree, stop and retrace ballots within the same color section of the ballot count. Once the error is discovered, correct the record and continue the ballot count.
6. Once the team has completed the ballots, count the tally marks across the sheet and place the number of votes in the "Total" column. Each recorder should do this individually and then check his or her addition with the other recorder. They MUST match. Total the number at the bottom of the form. Once the number has been reconciled, give the form to the Chairman.
7. The tellers should remain together until the Chairman has completed the tally. All members will sign the appropriate papers before leaving the room.

Tally Format

An official format to tally the votes is helpful in increasing the accuracy of the votes for each candidate. Here is a sample tally format.

TALLY FORMAT FOR ____________ POSITION

Name	Votes for ________ Position	Total

Tellers' Report Form

To ensure that the tellers' report includes all of the information that is needed for the minutes, a form can be helpful. Here is an example.

TELLERS' REPORT—ASSOCIATION OF COMPLETE IDIOTS

20XX ANNUAL MEETING ELECTION OF [OFFICE]

Number of votes cast __________

Necessary for election __________

_________________________ received ________ votes

_________________________ received ________ votes

_________________________ received ________ votes

_________________________ received ________ votes

_________________________ received ________ votes

_________________________ received ________ votes

_________________________ received ________ votes

Illegal Votes ________

Form for Tracking Motions in the Meeting and for the Minutes

When a meeting is well planned, a great number of the motions are known in advance of the meeting. Printing them on a form and distributing them to the members can make the making and processing of motions much clearer during the meeting. It is important to understand that the wording of the motions on this form is not binding. These are simply presented as possible wording examples. Use of this form can make the preparation of minutes much easier and far more accurate.

Here is a sample form for tracking motions:

ASSOCIATION OF COMPLETE IDIOTS

BOARD OF DIRECTORS MEETING

DATE

#	MOTION	MAKER	ACTION TAKEN
1	I move that we approve the minutes of the August 15, 20xx, board meeting as printed and distributed to the board members.		
1	I move that we approve the Executive Session minutes of the August 15, 20xx, board meeting as printed and distributed to the board members.		
5	I move that we recommend to the membership that they amend the Bylaws, Article X, Section 1 as printed and distributed to the board members.		
6	I move that we approve the proposal for website design as presented to the board members.		

#	MOTION	MAKER	ACTION TAKEN
8	I move that we approve the Health Benefit Plan for employees and direct the executive director to implement this new plan as printed and distributed.		
11	I move that we approve the XYZ Policy as printed and distributed to the board members.		

Index

A

B

C

D

E

F

G–H

I–J–K

L

M

Q

R

S

T

U

V

W-X-Y-Z